THE EDUCATION OF
JOHN RANDOLPH

The
Education
of
John Randolph

ROBERT DAWIDOFF

W · W · NORTON & COMPANY
NEW YORK

Copyright © 1979 by W. W. Norton & Company, Inc.
Published simultaneously in Canada by George J. McLeod Limited,
Toronto. Printed in the United States of America.

First Edition

Library of Congress Cataloging in Publication Data

Dawidoff, Robert.
The education of John Randolph.

Bibliography: p.
Includes index.
1. Randolph, John, 1773–1833. 2. United States—
Politics and government—1783–1865. 3. United States.
Congress. House—Biography. 4. Legislators—United
States—Biography. I. Title.
E302.6.R2D28 1979   973.4′092′4 [B]   79–16178
ISBN 0-393-01242-5

Book designed by Jacques Chazaud
Typeset in Baskerville
Manufactured by the Maple-Vail Book Manufacturing Group

1 2 3 4 5 6 7 8 9 0

For my parents:

Ted, Rebecca, and Charlie

CONTENTS

THE EDUCATION OF
JOHN RANDOLPH

INTRODUCTION

This volume concerns that remarkable and eccentric character John Randolph of Roanoke (1773–1833), the Virginia congressman and advocate of the rights of the slaveholding states. The scrutiny of Randolph's education, I believe, yields a sound version of his methods and his motives. He was raised according to the lights of Virginia's golden age and spent his life trying to square the lessons he had absorbed with the contrary facts of the democratic America in which he found himself. The sustained conflict Randolph experienced between his expectations and the circumstances of his adult life gave his politics energy and a theme which we would do well to understand if we wish to understand him. Randolph had a very literal mind. He never learned how to compromise. He preserved the codes and attitudes of his Anglo-Virginian upbringing intact and reacted to the world in terms of those old-fashioned home truths. Both his political ideas and his memorably dramatic advocacy of them developed from his peculiar refusal to change with the times. What commenced as a promising and brilliant career in governing stumbled over this refusal. Randolph abandoned ambition, as commonly understood, for a stance of lonely opposition. We remember him as a critic of his day. This book is about his happening to become a critic rather than a paragon of American democracy.

Randolph's career offers a rare opportunity to judge the first several decades of national history by the standards of pre-national, pre-Founding America, as he absorbed and expressed them. Randolph took refuge in an insistent and bitter retreat to an imagined and remembered world, founded on the expectations and lessons of his youth; as a result, his reactions to the democratic world around him have considerable interest independent of the part he played in conventional politics or the rightness of his opinions. Randolph's education proved misleading because he understood it literally. The heavily English culture and politics of the eighteenth-century Virginian gentlefolk could prepare such a student as Randolph to regard early-nineteenth-century Washington and the goings on there with nothing but horror and disdain. Of course, the acceptance at face value of *any* social and moral code would lead to some of the problems Randolph had with the messy realities of politics. But it is not just because Randolph took his education literally that it was misleading. Our recognition of his literal-mindedness makes it possible for us to see the more interesting aspect of his education: the ways in which the teachings themselves were problematic. The lessons of his upbringing described and ordered and gave aspirations for a kind of life that began to disappear with the American Revolution. Enough of the old ways remained in force to keep Randolph solvent and in Congress, but the golden age had gone and the strictures appropriate to it wanted revision. The teachings of class, literature, and politics hampered Randolph's adjustment to the great world in which he wanted to play a leading part.

A striking consistency of ill fortune marked Randolph's life, and what was accidental seemed to him (and often to the world) eerily coincidental. He thought his life argued some intentional design, and that belief too kept him loyal to his first precepts. Randolph persisted stubbornly in the practice of what he had been taught at the cost of his conventional success and hopes and expectations. This stubborn persistence in time gave his maladjustment the dignity of a prophecy and rescued his criticisms from the obscurity of the disappointment which had generated them. Randolph's story remains sad, however, because we have to confront what was at stake when the world turned upside down in 1781 and what some able and interesting people suffered as a result.

The first chapter of the book presents a sketch of Randolph's life, character, opinions, and achievements, to acquaint the reader with the individual whose education the remainder of the book details. The next three chapters concern Randolph's first twenty-five years. According to Henry Adams, a man's education ought to describe his experience. This view makes especial sense with Randolph, whose life was a testing of lessons early learned, which he did not abandon even though he found them wanting. Randolph's education in these first years, which came to an end with his entry into the public arena in 1799, involved much more than books read and schools attended; it encompassed a complete preparation for life. Modern concepts of childhood and adolescence have limited relevance to an understanding of his upbringing; the temporal period of growing up was differently defined in the late eighteenth century. The death of parents and siblings, the early assumption of some adult responsibilities and the delayed assumption of others, and above all the unpredictability of life, which made all plans and precautions subject to fortune, these differences from modern America argue a flexible temporal period of education. John Randolph spent his first twenty-five years at home under a series of influences, so to speak. By the end of this period, he had assumed the adult roles of parent, master, citizen, and legislator which marked a serious change in the circumstances of his life. For this reason, these twenty-five years will be treated together as his years of education.

The categories "upbringing," "cultural education," and "political education" reflect the three distinct but related kinds of education to which Randolph was exposed. His upbringing emphasized the lessons of family life. The eighteenth-century family provided a more complete context for its dependent members than is usual today; it was the primary agent of socialization. Randolph's family offered him an unusually intense and self-conscious preparation which included special lessons concerning class duties and clan traditions. Social pressures and family tragedy heightened their force, and the resulting impression on Randolph was extraordinarily lasting. Randolph's experience during his upbringing involved equally the nature of the lessons and the peculiar way in which he learned them. It accounts for his character.

Despite the suggestiveness of Randolph's unusually self-conscious recollections, I disclaim psychoanalytic intentions. He does present a tempting and obvious subject for psychoanalytic hypotheses. However, the use of these concepts removes the subject at least partially from his immediate context to a timeless context of universal nature. While psychoanalytic metaphors may help moderns to identify with historical subjects, in this case they would compound the distorting tendency of previous historiography to provide contexts for Randolph which reflect the writer's sense of him regardless of the claims of his actual lifetime. The analytic encounter, if it can in fact do justice to a dead subject, would only prolong the historiographical existence of "Randolph of Roanoke" at the continued expense of John Randolph. The explanations such a method can reasonably suggest cannot restore Randolph to his culture and locate him there. One would not want to write about Randolph, however, without offering some account of his truly remarkable personality. Randolph's ideas resist separation from his personation of them. His vaunted displays of eccentricity turn out to have been much more than sideshows; his personality became the medium and context of his serious objectives. I have not resisted psychologizing. I have not hesitated to offer explanations, drawn from the story of his life, for the peculiar kind of man he grew up to be. What I have not done is to separate these explanations systematically from the language and thinking of his time. In one passage, I have speculated about the probable significance of an absent father in the life of a boy like Randolph. This speculation makes sense in view of the explicit concerns of his later years, but it is speculation and is so labeled. The ruling themes in the discussion of Randolph's upbringing, then, will be those which he himself understood it to have involved.

Randolph's cultural education—his reading and schooling—was an idiosyncratic and irregular process. The particular interest is in determining how he read books, the satisfactions of style he experienced, as a guide to what he learned from them. Randolph's early reading, especially of eighteenth-century English literature, was the formative intellectual experience of his life. In many ways he acted out in his mature career the assumptions gained through this reading; its lessons were for him a consistent if not a reliable or entirely conscious point of reference. The third chapter will spell out these assumptions.

Similarly, Randolph's political education was the source of his later political views. The excitement of the Revolution, the Confederation, and the beginnings of the federal government, in Randolph's own privileged and skewed experience of them, combining with his class consciousness, the effects of his reading, and his particular personality, resulted in a full-blown and inflexible vision of politics which he consistently imposed on the events of his public life. The strands traceable to upbringing, culture, and politics are of course only artificially separate, and the discussion of Randolph's first quarter century of education will culminate, at the end of the fourth chapter, with a description of his "graduation" into public life in 1799, a dramatic instance of their nascent union in him.

The subsequent chapters trace the legacy of Randolph's education through his career in Congress and in American politics. They concern what might be called his education in and by the world, and attempt to show how he suffered from and finally adjusted to his own uncompromising attachment to the uncompromising tenets of his first years. A concluding essay suggests the grander significance of Randolph's experience.

In spite of his considerable reading and his showy cultivation, I have not treated Randolph as an "intellectual," for he had no real notion of that term or of the role in the world it has come to describe. He was a gentleman planter, a citizen, a public man who was also well educated and devoted to reading. His reading, the life of his mind, was important in shaping his career, and he was a self-conscious audience for artistic creation. However, he did not customarily address himself to intellectual issues, except in passing judgment on books or public matters. He wrote only letters, and these, fascinating and intelligent as they are, contain little sustained critical thinking or analysis, little serious play of ideas. He would not have recognized himself in the role of an intellectual; indeed, he did not even think of himself as a "man of letters" or as anything more or less than a cultivated gentleman with an intense interest in and appreciation for art and the productions of the mind. He built up a good library, and was primarily a reader, a viewer—someone who responded to other people's creations with other people's judgments. Reading was like riding and politics, one of the distinguishing marks of a gentleman. And it was as a gentleman that he wished to be known.

The question of his uniqueness plagues the biographer. Randolph was original in style and in self-presentation. He was one of the most vivid and striking characters of his day, and his moments of trenchant and outrageous wit and perception make a lasting impression upon those who encounter him in the histories. I have yet to meet an American historian who can be surprised with the best Randolph stories. Everyone remembers them; he was an unforgettable and unique personage. His eccentricity has troubled historical and biographical studies of him, however, obstructing his absorption into conventional historical accounts. I have tried not to palliate or exaggerate that eccentricity, but to make it and him more intelligible by understanding it. I think I have shown it to be a deliberate and pointed reaction to a world Randolph loathed. To be sure, Randolph was not the last American to express his dissent by making a pointed spectacle of himself, but the fact remains that he was unlike most other people—he called himself an "idiosyncracy"—and for this reason he is not representative in the traditional sense. But neither is he irrelevant. Precisely because his madness and exaggeration took the form of a consistent adherence to the forms of the old, outmoded world of his youth, Randolph tells us about the assumptions of the society in which he grew up. He also tells us about the ways in which protest against American democratic traditions may go beyond the conventional realm of votes and compromise and instead involve the vivid colors of self-presentation. Randolph went his own way, for reasons that were largely personal. Others of his generation read the same books and held the same opinions as he did, but they did not express these opinions in the same manner. Randolph's relevance thus lies not simply in his ideas, which others shared, but in the methods by which he attempted to dramatize those ideas, to make an impression. The lengths to which Randolph went, then, result from the combination of what was special to him as a human being and what was conveyed to him by his education. Others with the same kind of temperament and in the same circumstances may have acted differently because they did not have the particular burden of his principles;

similarly, those with like principles may not have shared the impulses of character that made his advocacy so theatrical and exaggerated. The character and the ideas were suited to each other—he did a marvelous job of dramatizing the assumptions of his education—but the combination was no doubt a peculiar one. The peculiarity should not deter us from trying to understand or trying to make cultural sense out of Randolph.

His contemporaries did not always know what to make of him. He had intense relationships with almost all the great public figures of his time. He dined with them, attacked them, and except for John Quincy Adams, had moments of fellow feeling and respect for them. He provoked most of them to some comment, and what is odd is how unanimous they are on some subjects—his outrageousness and eccentricity, his considerable natural powers—and, ultimately, how dismissive they are of him. He seems to have had few adherents, outside the loyal band of Quids. Randolph's political peer group, those whose service to the Republic was as long-standing and distinguished as his, were loath to offend him unnecessarily, but equally reluctant to pay attention to him in the conduct of public business. His biographer wishes that the great of his day had paid him more mind. Perhaps this absence of sustained and significant attention to Randolph—except as a curiosity, a wonder, a nuisance, or sometimes, when his sentiments were for the moment appropriate (in agreement with Calhoun's on states' rights, Jackson's on the Bank), as an effective if unpredictable ally—is the most telling evidence of Randolph's real isolation in American politics, which forced him into the ever more extravagant antipolitics which he practiced.

Randolph's career documents the persistence of traditional Anglo-American values and culture in some quarters of the newly independent American nation. Correspondingly, the difficulties he encountered in trying to make good on the expectations and education he drew from that culture are equally good evidence of the increasing inappropriateness of some of those values to autonomous Americans. His life points the way to some interesting conclusions about the nature of the cultural transformation that accompanied independence. It also throws into relief the plain fact that American Revolutionary ideology, whatever its origins, transcended its particularist sources and indigenous grievances and instituted a society with different aspirations, not at all comprehended by the conventional wisdom of eighteenth-century Virginia. Randolph compellingly represents several cultural roles: reader, interpreter, audience; his responses, though perhaps uniquely literal-minded, intense, and exaggerated, are certainly reflective of what in other Americans were milder tastes and habits.

Randolph died in considerable despair over the present and the future of Virginia and America. He has never been much good as a national hero because he set his face against the nation as it has turned out to be. That attitude in itself makes him an interesting and worthy subject of study. He may not have been as consistent and serious a dissenter as some of his biographers have claimed. But he expressed his disagreement with the American future at a time when it was still being decided, and his vivid discontents have not dimmed with the years. The disarming embrace of American culture has not absorbed and co-opted his vision: Randolph can still be seen and heard.

❧ 1 ❧

John Randolph of Roanoke

On July 4, 1826, on the fiftieth anniversary of the adoption of the Declaration of Independence, the stretching people of the American Republic received a sign. For on that day, as nearly everyone knows, John Adams and Thomas Jefferson, the surviving titans of the Founding, died. Each, in his ancestral country, flushed with achievement—his political differences with the other magnificently reconciled—breathed his last in hope for this great and glorious land. The president of the United States was John Quincy Adams, in whom the ideas and patriotic concern of both men mingled. Their joint passing was the occasion for nearly universal observance and remark in the young country, a moment of some reflection and of surging confidence, the emblem of the destiny of this people, this republic, this nation, this empire, a time for rejoicing in a moment of mourning. This last act of patriotic partnership, these dramatically linked deaths, affirmed the coming together of past and present in a happy vision of the national future. In all the marveling, self-regarding, boastful, and wondering clamor, one might, had one sharp ears and a taste for the perverse, have heard a dissenting strain. From England, John Randolph of Roanoke, the Virginia congressman who had entered politics as the companion of Jefferson in the fight against Adams, wrote a friend, upon receiving the news: "And so old Mr. Adams is dead; on the 4th of July, too; just a half a century after our Declaration of Independence; and leaving his son on the throne. This is Euthanasia indeed. They have killed Mr. Jefferson too on the same day, but I don't believe it." Had this mordant expression of disbelief been noticed, it would have been put down to Randolph's vaunted bitterness, his eccentricity, his hostile views of the great and rising North American empire of liberty. Many of his countrymen might have enjoyed his way of putting his suspicions, even as they prepared to ignore them. The meaning of his gall, however, the point of his dissent from the collective celebrations, would have escaped all but a few—those embittered like him by the past, or those, in scattered places in the slaveholding South, apprehensive in his train about the prospect for their peculiar interest and institution in this amalgamating future. Randolph's skepticism about the new gods of his nation, his pessimism and his mistrust of what the celebrated portent in fact foretold, were not generally noticed and were not commonly shared. His were older gods than these, the ancestral shades of Virginia and English North America—Pocahontas, her father Powhatan, John Rolfe, and William Randolph of Turkey Island. Their mixed blood flowed proudly in his attenuated veins and he worshiped still at their shrines. What most Americans accepted as a promise of grandeur, Randolph knew to be a Götterdämmerung, a violation. He had no hopes, refused to share in the clamor, and resigned himself to however many more years of endurance were left him: "Indeed, in the abject state of the public mind, there is nothing worth living for. It is a merciful dispensation of providence, that death can release the captive from the clutches of the tyrant. . . . I could not have believed that the people would so soon have shown themselves unfit for free government. I leave to General Jackson, and the Hartford men, and the ultra-federalists and tories, and the officeholders and office-seekers, their triumph over the liberties of the country. They will stand damned to everlasting fame."[1]

Who was John Randolph, this man who bayed so sepulchral at his country's rising star? John Randolph was born in 1773 into one of the great clans of the Virginia slaveholding gentry. Descended from and connected to almost all of the great Tidewater families, Randolph grew up smack-dab in the middle of the concentric circles that described that colonial elite whose power in the commonwealth went without saying. The further one got from Randolph, the further one traveled from the centers of political, economic, and social power in the Old Dominion. Born at Cawsons, his grandfather's home, Randolph lived his life on a series of extensive slaveholding plantations, tobacco-growing, horse-breeding centers of gentry life surrounded by country places, large and small. He grew up in the enjoyment of country matters and country pleasures and was also exposed to the imported manners and matters of such cities as there were in America at that time. From birth, Randolph associated daily with a variety of people, all of whom stood in some formal relation to him, with prescribed and necessary kinds of behavior attaching to each relation. His parents—mother, father, and later stepfather—and his brothers and more removed kin, formed the core of his world. They in turn set the tone for his relations with those equally circumstanced, older and younger, whom he might be expected to meet in society and civil life. Next, and at times even closer to him, were those of his black family—slaves, some very close indeed, who watched him and were his boon companions while he was a boy; their relation to him copied the familial but had no trace of equality. There were also the others, poorer farmers and tradespeople and the altogether unlanded whites in the neighborhood, seas of common men between the ports of Virginian aristocratic life, the plantations. From early childhood, Randolph expected from these folk attention and respect, and they from him a certain habit of command which colored his attention to and respect for them. Duties and obligations and habits of intercourse inhabited the plainest details of his life, for in a society structured as Virginia's was in those old-fashioned days, the power of the elites, their privileges, to which Randolph was born, encompassed a variety of relations to fellow human beings which had to be mastered young lest the social regime on which they depended falter.

History first intervened in Randolph's life in January 1781, when his family had to flee before the approaching British troops under the apostate Benedict Arnold. This event symbolized the intertwining of American events and those more private in Randolph's life, a connection that was in the nature of things to one of his class, and that never ceased. Randolph was educated at home and then at Walker Maury's secondary academy. He attended Princeton, Columbia, and William and Mary haphazardly, earning no degree, learning all told a great deal about the liberal arts and even more about politics and the world from his sojourns in New York and Williamsburg. In 1790–91, Randolph pursued desultory studies in the law under Edmund Randolph in Philadelphia. Thus, having witnessed the birth of the Federal Republic in New York, he was in Philadelphia for its earliest struggles. Connected as he was, the young man could hardly escape some acquaintance with the major public business of his time. He was bright and precocious and noticed many more of the events to which he was exposed than a less attentive young man might have done. His experience confirmed in Randolph the expectation that his private acquaintance and those who ran the world might substantially coincide, and perhaps that he could conduct himself the same way in both public and private matters. Although he did not admit political ambitions, there grew in him during his young manhood an understanding that politics was an adjunct of his home world and ought to be responsive to the demands and interests of the Virginia he loved and was bred to lead. Between his bouts at schooling and his adventures in the serious worlds of political foundings and lawmaking, Randolph explored the informal settings of his life. He traveled throughout Virginia and to South Carolina and Georgia, became acquainted with the idle and dissipated life of the young gentry, sowed some wild oats, tested himself on the fields of honor. He was a superb horseman who cared much for the turf and for breeding. He absorbed the habits of consequence and the moral lessons of his society and, wasting his time as best he could, made many friendships and generally acquainted himself with the world of his connections.

In 1792, Randolph suffered a mysterious illness that left him beardless, with a soprano voice and, it is generally presumed, without sexual capability. In 1795, he assumed the management of his estates and those of his two dead brothers; he devoted himself especially to the family cares of the eldest brother, Richard, looking after Richard's widow and two young sons. From his encumbered and encumbering estates, Randolph began to figure centrally in the grown-up life of Virginia. He assumed the duties of father, of slaveholder, of businessman, and in almost inevitable sequence, of political leader as well. In 1799, he stood for Congress, after making his political debut in a debate with Patrick Henry, and in December of that year, he entered Congress.

He was a striking and compelling young man. His high voice and smooth complexion, still-delicate coloring, and easy aristocratic manners heightened the impression made by his youth. When it was time for Randolph to be sworn in, the Speaker, Theodore Sedgwick, is reported to have asked whether he was old enough to serve. "Ask my constituents" was the characteristic reply. Tall and lean, even boyish of figure until he became prematurely gaunt and skeletal with sickness, Randolph was a man of many charms and beauties, already tending toward the unusual

25

fellow he would become. The burning, fixing look in his hazel eye, and the excitableness of his disposition, yet passed for high-spiritedness. He was, to use the old-fashioned word, a *stripling*. The Gilbert Stuart portrait, painted when he was thirty, shows Randolph with a mild, even sweet, expression, the very image of a child of the Founding, aristocratic and high-minded, beautiful and at his ease. He always dressed to please himself, and his clothes reflected his sense of himself as Virginian, patriot, horseman—gentleman. He wore his brown hair long and loosely gathered behind him, in a modification of the more formal eighteenth-century style, ready for a wig he never donned. His boots, breeches, thick gloves, and always handy crop lent his dress the utility in riding he valued. For Randolph was always riding, always ready to tear off on horseback, to visit, to hunt, to exercise or exorcise. He favored Revolutionary buff and blue as almost the only colors to relieve the black and natural tones of his dress and accouterments. He walked like an Indian and swaggered like a swell. Randolph's appearance was midway between the elegance and dignity of the Founding and the florid and obvious style of the silver age. His was the dandyism of a young man who wanted to be taken for nothing other than he was but thought to accomplish this without the most elaborate formalities. His ease was not western or democratic as Henry Clay's was to be, or distant and disarming like Jefferson's. His youthful appearance in the portrait catches the moment after the Founding and before the democracy, a fleeting expression of sweetness and youthful charm across the national countenance, privileged and happy and without apprehension. The young Randolph was perhaps coltish, but his lines suggested that he would grow majestic. That he was already grown and would only age into the old-young man of his eccentricity could no more be guessed than that he would not grow out of his youthful opinions or that those opinions would require growing out of. He entered Congress looking and acting like what he was, a talented scion of the Old Dominion come to represent her among the assorted representatives of the other sovereign states of the United States.

Until 1801, Randolph apprenticed himself in the Jeffersonian opposition to the Federalist administration. He was one of many men of promise in what was at once an embattled and a rising cause. He took the Jeffersonian Republican line as his creed and fought harrying actions against the entrenched Federalists. In December 1801, Randolph became the floor leader of the Republican majority in the House of Representatives, assuming the chair of the Ways and Means Committee. He was considered a chief heir in Congress to the Jeffersonian mantle of republican politics and Republican power. During those years, he proved a generally effective legislator, at once bold and co-operative. With his especial friends, Speaker of the House Nathaniel Macon and Maryland Representative Joseph Nicholson, he represented the administration policies and the "country" politics of the southern landed gentry which were a major source for those policies. He lorded it over the House, keeping the members in line, speaking often, and developing the brilliant, aphoristic, and sarcastic style that was to be his trademark.

There were strains. As Jefferson tempered the pronouncements of his years in opposition with a compromising realism about the necessities of governing, as he abandoned the strict statements of principle that had characterized the Republican position in the 1790's for a more flexible policy of application, Randolph grew restive. Although he supported the Louisiana Purchase, Randolph by temperament and conviction was a purist in politics. He perhaps resented Jefferson's sway and surely resented James Madison's playing a greater role than his own in the president's counsel. In 1805, attacking the administration compromise of the Yazoo fraud claims, Randolph saw in the attempt to compromise with the perpetrators of a public land fraud in Georgia in 1795 an outright violation of the principles of their party and of right politics. On January 29, Randolph openly dissociated himself from that policy and successfully blocked the compromise. In February he managed the administration-instigated prosecution of Judge Samuel Chase, a Federalist jurist who had denounced Jefferson and the Republicans from the bench. The trial was a disaster for Randolph, who was unprepared to match wits and law with the defense counsel, Luther Martin. His failure to impeach Chase, and the ignominy of it, speeded his discontent with the administration and theirs with him. In December 1805, he refused to cooperate with Jefferson and Madison in the attempt to buy Florida secretly from France, and openly abandoned his role as administration leader. By March 1806, Randolph had commenced a career of opposition to the Jefferson administration in company with a few southern allies equally strict in their adherence to doctrines enunciated in the 1790's and subverted, in their view, by the corrupting effects of power on the Republican party; these were called the Tertium Quids (shortened to Quids). Until 1813, when Randolph lost his seat in Congress over the war with England, which he opposed, he led what Republican opposition there was to the Jefferson and then the Madison administrations in Congress, becoming a figure of lonely and idiosyncratic independence.

Randolph's political views crystallized during this first congressional tenure. They were profoundly personal and old-fashioned, grounded in the inherited experience of colonial English America with especial reference to the social circumstances of Virginia. Like English tradition and theory, Randolph maintained that the proper basis of a stable and republican government was always the independent unit of the landed gentleman and the smaller agricultural independencies and dependencies that surrounded and clustered about him. Manufacturers, hewing to no place or time, depending on cities and the corruption of governments to their profitable purpose, while perhaps necessary, were unwholesome elements in a regime. Randolph's politics reflected unremitting hostility to the rising tide of American manufacturing:

The Agriculturalists bear the whole brunt of the war and taxation and remain poor while the others run in the ring of pleasure and fatten upon them. The agriculturalists not only pay all but fight all while the others run. The manufacturer is the citizen of no place or any place. The agriculturalist has his property, his land, his all, his household gods to defend; and is like that meek drudge, the Ox, who does the labor and plows the ground, and then, for his reward, takes the refuse of the farmyard, the blighted blades and the mouldy straw and the mildewed shocks of corn for his support; while the commercial speculators live in opulence, whirling in coaches and indulging in palaces; to use the words of Dr. Johnson, coaches which fly like meteors and palaces which rise like exhalations. Even without your aid the agriculturalists are no match for them. Alert, vigilant, enterprising and active, the manufacturing interests are collected in masses and ready to associate at a moment's warning for many purposes of general interest to their body. Do but ring the firebell, and you can assemble all the manufacturing interests of Philadelphia in fifteen minutes. Nay, for matter of that, they are always assembled; they are always on the Rialto, and Shylock and Antonio meet there every day as friends, and compare notes, and lay plans and possess in trick and intelligence what, in the goodness of God to them, the others can never possess. It is the choicest bounty to the ox that he cannot play the fox or the tiger; so it is to one of the body of agriculturalists that he cannot skip into a coffeehouse and shave a note with one hand while with the other he signs a petition to Congress portraying the wrongs and grievances and sufferings he endures, and begging them to relieve him; yes to relieve him out of the pockets of those whose labors have fed and enriched, and whose valor has defended them.

Based on the old dichotomies of court and country and city and country, Randolph's picturesque understanding of the division of society is as old-fashioned as it is expressive. Randolph did not begin with agrarian assumptions and proceed from there. Beginning with agrarian and republican assumptions, those of the Old Dominion and of England, he spent his public career trying to realize the properly ordered regime they pictured. The striking density of his images in this talk about farmers and manufacturers reflects the concentration of a long career and many talents upon a comparatively restricted world view, distilled through memory and loss, a vision of the past meant to guide the future from what Randolph perceived was its inevitable tendency to corruption. That perception of the dangers to which corruption of political principle might lead and had led gave Randolph's political descant its urgency. Having formed his views in his young manhood according to the teachings of a world—the old Anglo-Virginian world of the first years of independence—which Randolph increasingly understood to be disappearing, he developed the habit of declension, of seeing in every change a degeneration. He regarded himself as the last of the old school, a militant Cassandra of a noble and embattled tradition. Thus did the personal enter the political.

I am the holder of no stock whatever, except livestock, and had determined never to own any; but if this bill [for the National Bank] passes, I would not only be a stockholder to the utmost of my power, but would advise every man, over whom I had any influence, to do the same, because it is the creation of a great privileged order of the most hateful kind to my feelings, and because I would rather be the master than the slave. If I must have a master let him be one with epaulettes, something that I could fear and respect, something I could look up to—but not a master with a quill behind his ear.[2]

Randolph held fast to the Old Republican doctrines, which, he insisted, were clear and simple: "Love of peace, hatred of offensive war, jealousy of the State Governments toward the General Government; a dread of standing armies; a loathing of public debt, taxes, and excises; tenderness for the liberty of the citizen; jealousy, Argus-eyed jealousy, of the patronage of the President." Within the context of American politics, these views involved Randolph in crusades against the nationalist movements, foreign and domestic, which characterized most federal administrations during his career. No matter how happily he greeted a new president, as in the cases of Thomas Jefferson and Andrew Jackson, or with how much hostility, as in the cases of James Madison and John Quincy Adams, no matter what the temptations of cohesion and collegiality, these determined attitudes of Randolph's soon caused him to spiral off into opposition. It was the centralizing, organizing direction of the federal establishment that he detected and opposed. He had witnessed the birth of the new constitution, remembered it in its "chrysallis state," and early on allied himself with those who saw what Washington did not see "but two other men in Virginia saw it— George Mason and Patrick Henry—*the poison under its wings.*" He entertained an abiding suspiciousness toward the powers and ambitions of the national government and fashioned a rule from this attitude: "Ours is not a Government of confidence. It is a Government of diffidence and of suspicion, and it is only by being suspicious that it can remain a free Government." Randolph never allowed that a constituted people had collectively accorded sovereignty to the Federal Union. Rather he insisted that it was a compact of free and independent states that had granted under strict and enumerated conditions certain powers to a common federal government for certain specific and enumerated purposes. He was never surprised to detect an aggrandizing impulse in that organization, and resisted what he perceived as its tendency to grow beyond its charter:

This Government cannot go on one day without a mutual understanding and deference between the State and General Governments. *This Government is the breath of the nostrils of the States.* Gentlemen may say what they please of the preamble to the Constitution; but this Constitution is not the work of the amalgamated population of the then existing confederacy, but the offspring of the States; and, however high we may carry our heads and strut and fret our hour, "dressed in a little brief authority," it is in the power of the States to extinguish this Government at a blow. They have only to refuse to send members to the other branch of the Legislature, or to appoint Electors of President and Vice-President, and the thing is done.

Well, it was not really in the power of the states, even several at a time as it turned out, to dissolve the federal compact. Randolph knew that perfectly well, and yet fought the conditions which brought the superior claims of the nation into being with an unceasing campaign of political guerilla warfare.[3]

Randolph hated governments on principle; the larger their size and the greater their activity the more he hated them. His own career can be understood well in that light. Historians have deprecated him for failing to sponsor and support positive legislation. He is cited as a man with but a negative, delaying effect. It was, perhaps, the grand purpose of his congressional career over three decades to be just that: to cause as little as possible to be done by others. He talked on and on, about every kind of issue, every species of the public business, generally to the amusement of his colleagues and the public but often merely exasperating them in the course of their public business. Perhaps his point was made by every deliberation he confounded, every piece of legislation he delayed, and every orderly procedure he scotched. Since he felt that the evils he opposed were rampant and likely to triumph, his obvious pleasure in keeping things at some bay makes sense; believing as he did, what else could he have done? To co-operate was out of the question, to compromise in order to win was inherently self-defeating because the requisite concessions always necessitated small evils he would not stomach; the very process of political compromise he scorned. There was too much legislation, Randolph thought. Busy governments inevitably enlarged themselves and their corrupted fellow travelers, what we would call special interests, at the expense of liberty, by which he did not mean democracy. "I love liberty, I hate equality." In one speech, he declared:

... we see about November, about the time the fog sets in, men enough assembled in the various Legislatures, General and State, to make a regiment; then the legislative maggot begins to bite; then exists the rage to make new and repeal old laws. I do not think we would find ourselves at all worse off if no laws of a general nature had been passed by either General or State Governments for 10 or 12 years last past. Like Mr. Jefferson, I am averse to too much regulation—averse to making the extreme medicine of the Constitution our daily food.

Randolph counted himself the political tribune of "the rights of the States against Federal encroachment; it is the liberty of the citizen (subject, if you please) against all encroachment, State or Federal, that is and ever has been my creed." Randolph's independence of party and place enabled—indeed required—him, according to his own lights, to champion the cause of liberty as he understood it. The abiding enemy of a free and stable order of things, in his old-fashioned view, was the corruption of independence (representing virtue) by the effects of power, which always could be expected to menace liberty with the temptations of office and party. His own magnificent material independence, as well as his cast of mind, fixed him in these notions and protected him from flexibility on this matter. Randolph increased his landholdings during his lifetime, laboring to free himself from inherited debt and then to keep himself free. In his home country, by which he increasingly meant his native counties in Virginia, especially as the rest of the country grew and changed in directions of which he disapproved, his stature and proud predominance encouraged him to continue thinking that his own circumstances provided a rule for the correct ordering of the rest of the nation. This perception was strengthened by his equally powerful conviction that the conditions of his life were those mandated by the old English-American ideas of independence, and that he was the proper champion of those notions in his person and in his advocacy of them to others. His fortunate material position always authenticated his political principles.[4]

33

Randolph was patriotic but Virginian. Support of the principle of state sovereignty proceeded in his instance from a persistent and felt attachment, as his metaphors for the rights of his state attest: "Asking a State to surrender a part of her sovereignty is like asking a lady to surrender a part of her chastity." The poet Whittier understood his man when in his poem about Randolph he wrote:

> *Too honest or too proud to feign*
> *A love he never cherished,*
> *Beyond Virginia's border line*
> *His patriotism perished.*

This Virginia Randolph loved so well was both a real place and a country of his imagination. The real Virginia was more rough than smooth—Buckingham, Charlotte, Cumberland, and Prince Edward counties, which comprised Randolph's district, were in his day, as they remain to a surprising degree still, backwaters, for good or ill old-fashioned places, attached to the old ways of doing things. Southside Virginia was part of the slaveholding interest of the Tidewater, its lands belonged to many fine old families and its standards and rhetoric were Old Dominion through and through. The facts of life there, however, were ruder, the land lay less pleasantly, and the frontier was closer. Fewer roads and worse connected fewer grand establishments and smaller. The social life was less polished and less independent, subordinate to that of the older, bigger houses from which the leading planters had come, and to which they might only sometimes return. It was everywhere less settled, more dominated by the facts of weather and agriculture, newer and yet not new in its ideas. The transmontane counties, with their freer customs and greater equality, had liberated themselves somewhat from the old customs of deference and slavery. Southside had not. Randolph's country, like Randolph, lived under the sway of the antique society of the eastern portion of the state but never attained its stature and attraction; it was a planting place, an outpost, rugged and traditional, a moon of the faded sun of the golden age of Virginian greatness. Southside Virginia has its beauties, hills and trees and blue skies over red soil; it was in some parts very lovely. But just as it lacked the man-made grandeur that even in the early nineteenth century could be traced in the Tidewater, it lacked the superb beauty that made Jefferson's country to the north, in the wake of the Blue Ridge, spectacular and inspiring. The move from Williamsburg up to Albemarle might compensate for rural isolation and difficulty with sublimity. Across the mountains in the valley of the Shenandoah lay the promise of a fine new land, green with the hope of a new kind of life opening out beyond the hills. Southside was not so beautiful and not so promising. Lacking even the ruins of past glory which the romantic imagination might find intriguing, it was plain, a rural retreat. It provided little more than the independence of provincial isolation, sustaining little cultural and collective life and without much in the way of splendor, old or new.[5]

Southside in Randolph's day was largely forest and hills, hinting at the Alleghenies. The country is well watered by rivers on their way from greater heights to other places. The climate is generally mild, although Randolph found it harsh: "Such a climate may suit red men but not white ones. Even for blacks, it is too cold in winter"; at times he compared it to Milton's conception of Hell, or described it as the vengeance wreaked upon the whites for "the cruel wrongs done upon the red men." The mosquito ruled the summer. Others have found that country more enchanting and pleasant than did Randolph, who had little taste for the whippoorwill, the wild flowers, and the quiet unprepossessing country scenes. It was a good place to farm, well suited to plain country living. Randolph had his moments of pleasure in its beauties and was in any event accustomed to its companion sounds: ". . . and as for noises, I hear none but the warbling of the birds and the barking of the squirrels around my windows." The white population of the district, roughly 21,000, didn't grow much in Randolph's time. The number of slaves grew from 24,000 to 46,000, and of free blacks from 600 to 1,300, between 1800 and 1830. The leading families of Randolph's time and place were equestrian, land-poor, religious, tobacco-poor, Tidewater-bred, slave-poor, litigious, political, and countrified. Their houses, typically on the banks of the Appomattox, Staunton, or James river, were unpretending—concessions to conditions. Randolph's own place, Roanoke, was even rougher than most, consisting of two buildings. One of these, a log house with two rooms which he had inherited with the lands, was like the poor whites' dwellings that littered the countryside. This "Winter House" had a sitting room and a bedroom. The "Summer House" which Randolph had built—a small framed house about twenty yards away—had glazed windows and a more prepossessing appearance, though on a small scale and plain. Inside, the buildings were amply and elegantly furnished. In general, Randolph's household goods were simple but of high quality, and wherever possible English. Equipment reflecting his interests decorated the rooms—guns, boots, books and more books, and some pictures and plate. Randolph's library included over a thousand volumes, as well as many engravings, maps, and prints. The unadorned Roanoke grounds boasted no gardens or ornamental shrubberies. Randolph's apparent concern was to keep the scrub at bay and the grounds as clean and free of flies and infection as possible. His horses and dogs and slaves served as company in his solitude, but company at a distance. He might well call himself isolated, a hundred miles from Richmond, the nearest city of consequence. Randolph generally got his supplies from Roanoke city, maintaining almost a regular delivery line. The nearest post office was thirteen miles away at Charlotte Courthouse. Randolph was a planter on a large scale, owning over nine thousand acres of land, as many as 383 slaves at a given time, and a stud of thoroughbreds said to be worth up to $30,000.

William Cabell Bruce estimated his worth at no less than $400,000, a considerable fortune, though of course little of it was in hard cash. He was the predominant man materially as well as politically in his district.[6]

Randolph was of two minds about his native country. He loved it with an abiding love. It was what remained of Virginia; it was where he lived. Southside was more than a political borough to him; it was that one place where he might be sure of affection and respect and support on his own terms, those terms which continued to inform his vision of politics. The people of his district in their turn loved Randolph. Except in 1813, in the understandable grip of war fever, they returned him to Congress whenever he stood. He provided their greatest attraction in a culture which still regarded politics and speechifying as the ritual of collectivity and, along with church, as the major public entertainment. Wherever he stopped, his constituents crowded about him, eager for the sting and spectacle of his oratory. He had no rivals for the public's attention. Randolph complained at times that he was "neither a lion nor a tiger" when the faithful, expectant crowds closed in about his carriage at Charlotte Courthouse or Farmville, but he was, in effect, the "wild beast" on show; that was his repayment to his countrymen. He riveted their attention and kept them absorbed as he talked about politics and other matters of public concern. Randolph inherited the mantle of Patrick Henry in the country where the oral tradition was still strong, where deference and *viva voce* balloting continued long after their decline elsewhere. He spoke long and often, with great variety and resource. The melodrama and ferocity of his speeches, which rendered him idiosyncratic in Congress, fed the appetite for spectacle of his constituents, whose largely Presbyterian religion deprived them of such excess even in church. They absorbed all his wit and eccentricity, their appreciation fueling his performance. By all accounts, Randolph was a memorable stump speaker, by turns elegant and allusive, then rough

THE EDUCATION OF JOHN RANDOLPH

and colloquial, now high-minded and distant, now personal and vituperative. Fifty years after his death, the old
men of his district would talk about Randolph, quote his
sayings, remember his antics, imitate his inimitable manner. He barred no holds, restrained himself from no excess
of provocation or revenge. He would ridicule any who opposed him, driving some clear out of the district, it was
said. He boasted that he came from a race which never
forgave an offense. The stories of his carryings-on abound:

"How do you do, Mr. L? I am a candidate for Congress, and
should be pleased to have your vote."
"Unfortunately, I have no vote, Mr. Randolph."
"Good-morning, Mr. L."

He approached a small farmer who had delivered his pre-
cinct against Randolph in 1813, asking him in seeming innocence about a rather sophisticated political issue: "Passing from one puzzling and confusing inquiry to another,
raising his voice, attracting a crowd by every artifice in his
power, he drew the unfortunate man farther and farther
into the most awkward embarrassment, continually repeating his expressions of astonishment at the ignorance to
which his victim confessed." It must also be remembered
that Randolph represented the interests of his constituency
faithfully; reserving to himself an independence of judgment on many questions, he looked out for their shared
political and material concerns pretty consistently throughout his career. He bullied and delighted and represented
his people, and they apparently enjoyed his mastery of
them; it was surely in the grand style. They bragged on
him. He knew that in many ways he was one of them. They
gave him what scant sense of belonging he, "an idiosyn-
crasy all of my life," felt.[7]

There was another side to Randolph's feeling for his
people. In them, as in everything else, he saw the passing
of the old ways and the degeneracy of the age. He contrasted the rudeness of his surroundings with the magnifi-

cence of his father's world. The inside of his home might be elegantly appointed, but the plain exterior barely rose about the commonplace. The customs and manners of the district, its economic backwardness, the relative absence of good society, the isolation from cosmopolitan influences, all reminded him of a great change in the times, a change for the worse. The traveling he did, the badly gutted roads, dusty and muddy by turn, reinforced this side of his feelings. Primitive lodgings and unappetizing meals, noise and dirt and low company, attended his commutings around his district and to and from Richmond and Washington and on to England. Randolph was always on the move, regretful at returning to Roanoke, mournful and depressed in his isolation there—lonely, and subject, as he saw it, to cultural and sense deprivation. He once wrote to his protégé Theodore Dudley at Roanoke that he "would be glad to hear something of my affairs at home; although I left it without a desire ever to see it again." He was a "prisoner" there, he wrote another time: "Use reconciles me to it a little; but the first few days after I get home are almost intolerable." He likened himself to Robinson Crusoe, called Roanoke his "lair," himself a "wild man of the woods." "Here then must I live, and here I must die, a lone and banished man." He took melancholy pleasure in solitary riding, and under the stress of illness and loneliness, took to drink. This letter to his niece (by his half brother), written in October 1828, gives the picture of the unhappy life Randolph thought Roanoke enforced on him:

I write not only because you request it, but because it seems to fill up a half hour in my tedious day. No life can be more cheerless than mine. Shall I give you a specimen? One day serves for all. At daybreak, I take a large tumbler of milk warm from the cow, after which, but not before, I get a refreshing nap. I rise as late as possible on system and walk before breakfast about half a mile. After breakfast, I ride over the same beaten track and return "too weary for my dinner," which I eat without appetite, to pass away the time. Before dark, I go to bed, after having drunk the best part of a bottle of Madeira, or the whole of a bottle of Hermitage.

Wine is my chief support. There is no variety in my life; even my morning's walk is over the same ground; weariness and lassitude are my portion. I feel deserted by the whole world, and a more dreary and desolate existence than mine was never known by man. Even our incomparably fine weather has no effect upon my spirits.

The ennui which alternated with the activity of his public life and of those interludes of socializing and cheer he experienced with friends, even at Roanoke, stood for a whole strain of depression and apprehension which gripped Randolph fiercely. He was living, after all, a version of that planter's life which he had been bred to live. He struggled to view his retreat as Horatian, Cincinnatian, Washingtonian, but failed. He might in the flow of the public orating moment fuse his nostalgia and his ambitions into a picture of himself as representing these traditions, and might convince the crowds or his legislative colleagues and even himself that he was indeed an old-time Virginia gentleman. The quiet of Roanoke and the straight look at his country which that entailed wrecked his peace of mind. He recognized just how far he and his country had drifted from the grandeur of the past. He made a good job of it, kept to the lessons of his youth and the lights of his ancestors. His was a hauteur sustained with bravado in the face of ruin. Southside Virginia, for all its loyalty to the sentiments and persons of the past, mocked Randolph's notions of what the good life should have been. It was a backwater, a fallen satellite of the Old Dominion, on the defensive economically and politically, and lacking in all but the plainest of charms. Its stubborn eccentric tribune John Randolph had to see himself compromised in all this homely ruin. No wonder he called himself "a poor, half-crazy, moonstruck Southsider."[8]

Randolph's transcriptions of Southside speech capture his understanding of his *patria* as it was and as it might have been. He himself was a careful student of English grammar and pronunciation. He wrote easily and with grace and power of expression. He talked as he wrote, with brilliance and undisciplined flow. His colloquialisms were deliberate, and the power of his speaking surely derived in part from its range, which extended from the most complicated and literary of dictions to the plain-speaking common talk of his place and time. Almost alone in his day, Randolph floated in his talking and writing the many varieties of American English that might be heard. He had a fine ear and a flexible regard for language as an instrument of his ideas, responsive to the demands of his audience. He generally stayed in control of his syntax and diction, seldom making mistakes, and venturing into the newer territory of common speech only on deliberate errands. He could not stand the sloppiness of spoken and written English which even then abounded in American usage. He was punctilious, a stickler for correctness, as his letters to his wards and nephews abundantly indicate. In his view, the lax language expressed a deeper corruption. In politics, Randolph used this connection between words and meanings to great advantage:

If I were, what I am not—an acute philologer—I should sometimes amuse myself with the manner in which words slip from their original meanings, and come to purport something very different from what anybody ever attached to them when they first came into use; the word *sophist,* (a wise man), got so much into disrepute, that *philosopher* (a lover of wisdom,) had to supply its place; the word *libertine* meant what a liberal means now; that is, a man attached to enlarged and free principles—a votary of liberty; but the libertines have made such an ill use of their principles, that the word has come, (even since the time of Shakespeare), to be taken in a bad sense; and *liberal* will share the same fate, I fear, if it contracts this black alliance. There are some other words, also, such as *principle,* conscience, which are also in great danger.

For someone with his essentially static view of politics, defending old usage against change, the metaphor of language proved especially apt, allowing him to measure change against an unyielding standard of meaning, with alteration invariably a sign of degeneration. The language of his constituents and of more than a few of his colleagues interested Randolph from that point of view. He never failed to stigmatize John Marshall's pronunciation even as he lauded his character and denounced his amalgamating decisions: "Whoever said 'wuz' but you and the Chief Justice?" [9]

Under "Virginiana" in his diary, Randolph listed the following:

I happened at Curnull Purnull's, un thah wuz a purdigeous stawm that blow'd down all the cawn; but the Curnull give us a heap o' grog, un we sot it up agin.

The gals was agwine to meetin but they war abliged to return back hoame.

Cuffy bresh my coat might clean us I'm agwine a coatin un doan tetch it with yo finguz a'ter you've get done; else you'll dutty it.

One chick'n done lawce he ma-am-y.

Cap'n Dannil mecks a famous crop.

A rapid price; i.e. high.

Cuvvawtin (Curvetting applied not to a horse but a man).

Skeerd (scared). Sheer (share). Cheer (chair).

He is in a *proper* fix (a bad situation).

He done (did) it out of ambition (i.e. malice—never used in its proper sense) ("ambition," Jul. Caesar, Shakesp.).

He is ruined by paying intruss (i.e. interest).

He attached (attacked him about it, and channelged (challenged) him. [10]

These barbarisms of course distanced Randolph from the ordinary folk—language offers a measure of the man. The slackness of expression defined a separate social world, and its existence constituted an argument against that equality which Randolph denied. He described the talk of his district in the same way that the anthropologically minded always describe the talk of some other culture, with usages different from their own. In our own culture, perception of the barbarisms of other people's speech is the stuff of snobbery, class consciousness, the attempt to distinguish me from thee in the name of some standard of judgment, of correctness. Black dialect is a common subject of that nice-minded scrutiny. The language of common folk must be scrutinized to be defended against; to defend against this talk is to take a stand against more serious influences. Of course Randolph heard the slang from a height no longer shared in democratic society, which is as concerned as he with such questions but uneasy about what line to take on language. But even today a certain sort of American conservative position involves a preciseness about language and pronunciation. One can tell a lot about where somebody comes from by listening to him talk. Randolph prefigured this traditionalist response to looseness of expression, the democratization of language. However, he was very specific in his understanding and confirmed in his opinions of what looseness this signified: it indicated the wholesomeness of that system which preferred liberty and property to majoritarian claims, to democracy. The ringing promise of equality in the Declaration of Independence was an example of foolish theoretical tampering with the meaning of words, and the kinds of Virginiana he noted merely reinforced the wisdom of having the traditional elite maintain control of political life through the deference which was their due. He loved his people, with all their faults, as children, as deserving but lesser mortals whom he was bound in duty to serve but who were equally bound in the nature of things to elect him to serve them. The language standard Randolph applied, of course, was the English spoken by Virginia's upper classes before the Revolution and mandated by such proper English authorities as dictionaries. It was already stilted and in fact anachronistic. By contrast, the speech he scorned is still familiar—reading the examples aloud, one hears the twangs and melodies of what can generally be called southern speech, the soothing talk of Dixie. In some ways lazy, surely influenced by poor-white and black-slave talk, in sound and sense this speech effects a change—and if one accepts

Randolph's standards, a decline—from proper English, the king's English. It is worth noting that Randolph, so commonly associated with the South as it stood against the nation, set himself against this aspect of southernness. Perhaps this is the real import of his patriotic feeling for his state: it was Virginia as she had been, and to some extent as she was, that he loved and served. He was as mistrustful of amalgamating Dixie as of centralizing America.

Most of Randolph's views were established by 1813, but his career was by no measure over. During his years outside of Congress, he experienced several personal shocks, which taken together appear to have had the effect of turning him once and for all away from the prospect of change within the context of democracy, from the conventional practice of politics as understood in the United States at that time, from any kind of compromise with the world as he had discovered it, much to his disappointment, to be. His return to Congress in 1815 found Randolph a weathered version of his younger self. His family had been depleted, with one nephew and his sister-in-law dead, the surviving nephew a maniac. The ravages of nature and of war had menaced his lands and the nation he still loved. His own health and sanity broke down. Upon his return to Congress, there was an insistence in his ways that was even more pronouncedly eccentric than in years past, a forgoing of hope and political ambition, a determined air of resignation to the role of a prophet, whose only reward might be confirmation. Physically, Randolph had aged into what can best be termed a phenomenon. He is difficult to recreate, though his oddness was so often described and his appearance was so universally striking. At a distance, he still appeared a youth, thin and gawky and smooth. Up close, he appeared even older than his years. His face, a parchment color, was massed with wrinkles. His eyes burned furious still, set off from his face, alive with noticing, with passion and excitement and frequently with drink or the dope he took to ease his almost unceasing ills and pains. The Indian

44

and the English gentleman seemed now to blend, now to coexist, in his elongated figure. His dress was in the main somber and positively English. To his uniform of boots and breeches he added large outercoats to warm his chilled body. The times and fashions had changed, and his dress was suddenly uncommon—strikingly so. Randolph clung to the old styles, having his books bound in England, affecting the clothing and manners of his youth, as if by surrendering a particular style he might be compromising a principle. There is an evocative silhouette of him, black against his stud paddock, lean to emaciation, lone and straight, blank and irreconcilable. He could eat little; dining out, he would take toast and brandy. During the Missouri Compromise debates he became so excited that he could eat nothing but crackers and gruel. He bewailed his uncertain health. Every speech was presented as his last, in a ritual disclaimer that seemed to frame his advocacy of the past. Randolph's always eccentric behavior, his odd and olden mien, and his radical righteous disgust had blended into a self-presentation of calculatedly personal politics. He no longer made any pretense of referring to things outside his own experience and convictions. He spoke on and on, with no noticeable restraint. His periodic episodes of madness gave his more ordinary ways a special edge. "I go for blood," he warned. And so he did. His virulence and his eccentricity seemed to grow, and with them the startling common-sense wit that cut through the grandiloquence and cant of so many of his adversaries.

After Randolph's return to the House of Representatives, he soon began to take on the nationalist proponents of internal improvements and the Bank of the United States. He assumed a central role in the Missouri Compromise debates and developed the connection between states' rights and slavery that was to characterize the southern positions until the Civil War. In 1825, Randolph was elected by the Virginia legislature to a seat in the United States Senate, where he carried on a campaign against the

Adams administration and Secretary of State Henry Clay, which culminated in a duel with Clay. Among his other antagonists during that time were Calhoun, Adams, and Webster. In 1827, he was defeated for re-election to the Senate but was almost immediately returned by his district to the House. In 1828, Randolph supported Jackson for president. He retired from Congress in 1829. Also in 1829 he served in and dominated the Virginia constitutional convention, leading the conservative eastern slaveholding forces in their objections to changing the state constitution. Between the spring and fall of 1830, Randolph served unhappily as minister to Russia, returning home to fight his last battle in furious opposition to President Jackson's proclamation against South Carolina's attempt to nullify the Tariff of Abominations. During the 1820's, he had traveled to Europe four times, visiting England at length and with the greatest pleasure. On May 24, 1833, Randolph died in Philadelphia.

It was on the question of slavery that John Randolph contributed most decisively to American history. Historians have credited him with raising the consciousness of the South to the dangers lurking in the policies of the democratic general government from the point of view of slaveowners, and to the connections between states' rights, the slaveholding interest, and the strict construction of the Constitution. Randolph did not lead the southern cause, but he perhaps understood it earlier than most others, and charted the course which, starting from a conscience troubled and divided over slavery, culminated in the kinds of aggressive positions leading to disunion that the defense of slavery involved. Randolph was a major slaveholder and what was commonly regarded as a good master. It has been often remarked that his claims to being an opponent of slavery, a friend to the blacks, were absolutely subverted by his retention of his holdings and by his violent and consistent defense of the slavery interest from all attempts, local and national, to weaken it. The facts are at once simple and confusing: Randolph was the chief slaveholder in his county, and he freed his slaves in the will finally recognized by the courts; Randolph was an architect of the defense of the slavery interest within the Union, and he never ceased to stigmatize slavery as a curse upon his country; Randolph believed the African nations inferior to the white European, and he loved and cared for particular black slaves whom he kept closer to himself than he allowed almost anybody else to be.

There are general explanations for what may seem confusing, contradictory, and even hypocritical. Randolph was born into a culture which had accommodated itself to the material comforts and discomforts of slavery. And like most societies, English Virginia had developed a rationale to absorb some of the glaring contradictions of her life. Few, if any, human communities survive without some fairly troubling sets of contradictions like these—general promises and ideals on the one hand and the actual conditions of living on the other. The measure of any society is the manner in which it deals with the inherent conflict between the things men hold high and the things they hold dear, between moral and practical circumstances. Virginia, where slavery had long been established, had attained a degree of economic and social stability which allowed, even encouraged, a large proportion of her fortunate citizens to spend serious time in pursuit of more than selfish gain; civic virtue was a dominant strain in the commonwealth. In this way, Virginia sought to absorb the differences between white men with regard to property and substance. Slavery was a tougher question to handle. A tradition of deference and generous disinterested public service did not speak to the differences between white and black, between free and slave. Virginians understood at some common level that slavery was wrong, radically contrary to their cherished notions of human liberty. But at the same time they were genuinely attached to the system, based squarely on slave labor, which afforded them not only material luxuries but

47

that luxury so dear to them—the luxury of independent disinterested public service. Their very politics depended upon the comforts, security, and leisure paid for with the blood and sweat of black slaves. The late-eighteenth-century Virginian had a way not of solving but of dissolving this problem; slavery was admitted to be wrong, but its hurts to the slaveowners were stressed. Thomas Jefferson in both the Declaration of Independence and *Notes on the State of Virginia* expressed this rhetorical solution: King George saddled us with the institution; its dangers are leveled centrally at us. To the modern ear, this argument is perverse. Our society has different contradictions to absorb. Late-eighteenth-century Virginians tended to emphasize their awareness of the dilemma of slavery, a morally repugnant institution on which the very stability and comfort of the regime and its leaders depended, in a plaintive assertion that they themselves were its victims and that it was a necessary evil which subjected them to the greatest suffering. Attention to the suffering of the slave, which would have led to a differing conclusion about what was necessary, was supplanted by the self-regarding claims of the masters. They hated slavery, and those exclamations of hatred were genuine and ring still with the eloquence of human moral suffering. But the real hardships slavery presented to the master class were not hardships which might be amended or abolished. They were hardships suffered in the very nature of things, a human condition, the hurts that even the prosperous had to endure.

Virginians tried to avoid the subject of slavery, and to consider it only in those terms which might preserve both moral authority *and* the peculiar institution. This plausible rhetorical solution to the problem rested on the competing convictions that slavery was unjust and that slavery was necessary. John Randolph learned to accept both convictions but did not, it would seem, learn the lasting rhetorical lesson. Although he lamented the evils visited upon the master by slavery, he was never blinded to the primary evils visited upon the slaves. He pursued all home truths with a literal-mindedness and single-minded intensity, and it is worth looking to his attitudes toward slavery as an example of how he reasoned from his education to the facts of the world. Richard Randolph, John's eldest brother and ever his hero, had freed his slaves in his will. He emancipated two hundred slaves and provided for their settlement upon four hundred acres of land, in a community to be called Israel Hill which failed as an experiment in the absorption of manumitted blacks into a still-hostile white society. Richard Randolph's own explanation is worth excerpting; it exemplifies the high-minded effects that Revolutionary fervor had on some Virginians, and presents views which had a lasting influence on his brother's opinions about the moral issue presented by slavery:

To make retribution, as far as I am able, to an unfortunate race of bondmen, over whom my ancestors have usurped and exercised the most lawless and monstrous tyranny, and in whom my countrymen (by inquitous laws, in contradiction of their own declaration of rights, and in violation of every sacred law of nature; of the inherent, inalienable and imprescriptable rights of man, and of every principle of moral and political honesty) have vested me with absolute property; to express my abhorrence of the theory as well as infamous practice of usurping the rights of our fellow creatures, equally entitled with ourselves to the enjoyment of liberty and happiness; to exculpate myself to those, who may perchance think or hear of me after death, from the black crime which might otherwise be imputed to me of voluntarily holding the above mentioned miserable beings in the same state of abject slavery in which I found them on receiving my patrimony at lawful age; to impress my children with just horror at a crime so enormous and indelible; to conjure them, in the last words of a fond father, never to participate in it in any the remotest degree, however sanctioned by laws (framed by the tyrants themselves who oppress them), or supported by false reasoning; used always to veil the sordid views of avarice and the lust of power; to declare to them and to the world that nothing but uncontrollable necessity, forced on me by my father (who wrongfully bound over them to satisfy the rapacious creditors of a brother who, for this purpose, which he falsely believed to be generous, mortgaged all his slaves to British harpies for money to gratify pride and pamper sensuality; by which mortgage, the said slaves being bound, I could not exercise the right of ownership necessary to their emancipation, and, being obliged to keep them on my land was driven to violate them in a great degree) (though I trust far less than others have done) in order to maintain them . . .

This passionate indictment of slavery offers, by the way, a fascinating picture of the Virginia life and the Randolph family that John always romanticized—it is worth pondering simply from that viewpoint. It contains also strong testament to the seriousness with which some propertied Americans took their Revolutionary ideals. The enabling connection of this manumission is between the stated goals of revolt in the name of natural liberty and the frustrating experience of slavery. For Richard Randolph, the fervor of the post-Revolutionary moment sustained an escape from the contradictions he inherited along with his prominent sphere of society. The bitter necessity of standing master to slaves, even for a time, frames the dilemma in which John Randolph was caught. Death, premature and under suspicious circumstances, freed Richard Randolph to free his slaves. During his lifetime he never managed to see his way clear to do it. His injunction to his sons to keep themselves absolutely free of the institution appears to make the point that once inside the customary usages of slaveholding, one could not escape. John Randolph eventually came to reject the simple assertions of human equality in the Declaration, which his brother understood to mandate manumission. He arrived at that rejection in the course of defending the particularist political order of Virginia, of which slavery was the sustaining feature.[11]

John Randolph inherited his slaves and his responsibilities about the same time. He had initially to free himself of the encumbrance of primarily English debts his father and brother had bequeathed to him, and by the time he had done so, he was habituated to the practice of mastering. There is no indication that he thought of freeing his slaves while he was still alive. In spite of the controversies over his several wills, it was established by the courts of Virginia—and the conclusion is supported by a modern reading of the evidence—that when sane, he maintained his intention to have his slaves freed after his death. His fits of insanity, as will be later shown, tended to be times in which madness provided release from the burdens and insoluble difficulties of his sane life. That when his mind was disordered he rejected his tenacious goal of freeing his slaves suggests that Randolph found it difficult to keep faithful at once to the idealistic hatred of slavery of his youth and the equally strong pressures of being a representative of a slaveholding constituency, himself a slaveholder. In the long run Randolph did sustain both positions, but without hypocrisy. Instead, he *simply* pursued the contradictory injunctions of his upbringing, at once for and against slavery, literally and in their proper spheres. As a moral man bound by those duties which applied within the realm of material necessity, he was master to his slaves and a relentless champion of the interest that role entailed. As a private moral man he continued to abhor and regret the necessity slavery represented, and in death he freed his slaves. What distinguished Randolph is the extremity with which he advocated each position. He never sorted out the question, never attempted to reconcile the lessons of his youth. His example illustrates the conflicting claims of Virginian conscience and interest; the failure to connect them accounts, perhaps, for the failure of Virginian distinterestedness after the Founding generation. What the culture of his youth had absorbed, Randolph pursued abstractly, and in so doing, he revealed what had been latent and contradictory though accepted in that culture.

Randolph lived his life with the assistance of slaves. Most of them worked his lands and were known to him only slightly, as classes of workers and as possessions. A series of overseers took charge of Roanoke, from which of course he was frequently absent for long periods of time. There were, however, a comparatively few slaves with whom Randolph had long and feeling associations. If he experienced the headaches, concerns, rewards, and profits of the system, he also lived under it and participated in its mock family life and its common moments of shared emotion and affection. His slaves apparently displayed the same wonder and interest with respect to Randolph as did the Southside whites. They crowded about him upon his returns to Roanoke and enjoyed his participation in the rituals of plantation life. Surviving testimony supports the notion that Randolph was a stern but not a cruel master, except in his occasional periods of derangement, when he could be brutal to all his intimates, white and black. He looked out for his slaves at least as well as for his horses and his dogs, which is to say, very carefully indeed. One witness reported that when Randolph returned from Washington, "men and women reached toward him, seized him by the hand with perfect familiarity, and burst into tears of delight at his presence among them. His conduct to these humble dependents was like that of most affectionate father among his children." Treating grown men and women as even an affectionate father does his children, of course, cuts both ways. It was among his house slaves that Randolph found warm attachments. Quash or Quahsee, Nancy, and Sphyax had been with him since the old days of his youth, and in Mammy Aggy, who lived with his niece Mrs. Coalter, Randolph found a friend who shared memories of his mother and of those bygone days he recalled with such heaving sentiment; he sent regards to her in his letters, and answered in detail her reported inquiries after her kinfolk in his quarter. On one occasion, he sent his niece detailed instructions about the family names and connections with which she might remind Mammy Aggy about some information that the old woman had forgotten and that Mrs. Coalter wished to know. Essex, Juba, and especially John were Randolph's body servants. He sang their praises or damned them, according to his mood. Apparently John and Marse John had a long and rewarding relationship. John came to Randolph as a boy and, showing himself an apt pupil, soon played an important role in Randolph's life. Of John, Randolph wrote, "I have not a truer friend." He acquired a standing and a repute of his own: "I wish you could have seen Johnny, when Charles L. Bonaparte asked me at dinner the other day if the servant behind my chair was my famous man, John; so well known in Europe for his fidelity and attachment to me." Such is the stuff of which epics are fashioned. But it had not been an easy apprenticeship. At first, in town, apparently, John had become "a sot." Randolph then sent him home, where he quarreled with the overseer and "went away," in Randolph's phrase—perhaps, again in Randolph's judgment, in search of his master and those pleasant ways of living to which he had become accustomed. He was found, and Randolph let him rot in jail for three months, refusing him all communication and all but jail rations. Then John was sent home, coming part way by himself, on his own recognizance, and was reduced to working in the fields for three years, during which he proved himself trustworthy again. Only after all this did he become Randolph's "famous man, John; so well known in Europe for his fidelity and attachment to me." These relationships are as hard to reconstruct fully as they are impossible to doubt. The reformed John was, in Randolph's description, a paragon indeed: "He is a man of strict truth, he no longer drinks or games; I need not say, after the first attribute (truth), that he is scrupulously honest. His attention and attachment to me resemble more those of a mother to a child, or rather a lover to his mistress, than a servant's to a master." With his best slaves, Randolph thought himself to have achieved a parenting far beyond that which most Virginians could claim with their own children. He found in his relationships with some slaves an absorbing domestic concern. He employed conscious system in these relationships: "I have never known very bad servants unless to bad masters and mistresses, who either were perpetually scolding and correcting, or fell into the other extreme of leaving them to themselves, and spoiling them by false indulgence. . . . Finding fault never yet did good. Neither have I for years corrected them in any way, and then only boys. I am satisfied that, if I had habitually found fault, they would have got used to it in a fortnight. Now they watch my countenance like my faithful Newfoundland dog." Field hand, servant, friend, mother, child—slave was slave; Randolph knew that, and so, we can gather, did his slaves.[12]

Randolph's most critical biographer, Henry Adams, thought that the Virginian's role as tribune of the slave interest constituted his best claim to historical attention: that role

partially rehabilitated his reputation, and made him again, to no small extent, an important historical character. John Randolph stands in history as the legitimate and natural precursor of Calhoun. Randolph sketched out and partly filled in the outlines of that political scheme over which Calhoun labored so long, and against which Clay strove successfully while he lived,—the identification of slavery with states' rights. All that was ablest and most masterly, all except what was mere metaphysical rubbish, in Calhoun's statesmanship had been suggested by Randolph years before Calhoun began his states' rights career.

As Adams pointed out, states' rights and slavery were not always allied. The Louisiana Purchase and the Mexican War, the Fugitive Slave Act and the Dred Scott decision, were all instances of interested co-operation between slavery's supporters and the centralizing power. What Randolph saw clearly and early was that however the central government might protect the human property of the southern states, its tendency was in the other direction. He saw that the control of the federal government must always rest with King Numbers, with the democratically determined majority and its representatives. He saw too the economic and demographic indications of the rise of precisely those parts of the nation most likely to undermine the security of the slave portion. Randolph was prepared to recognize these signs by his lasting disposition—suspicious of federal encroachment, hostile to the Yankee influence, and tending through his declension-shrouded lenses to see Virginia, and by extension the South, as weak and beleaguered. His perceptive understanding, prophetic even, of the division within the Union, owed as much to the coincidence of his private vision with public events as to the kind of systematic reasoning from sectional interest which characterized Calhoun's later position and the views of the fire-eaters and seceders. Randolph's understanding of the southern position was both angry and tragic. There was never a need for him to systematize and argue his position; unlike Calhoun, he had almost no nationalist past to live down. He was saying in later years pretty much the same things he had always said. What had perhaps changed was the readiness of some of his brethren to hear him out; also, a shift in political circumstances gave his old-fashioned views new credence. Randolph had no rabid hopes. He thought slavery doomed, like the rest of his world. He advised energetic resistance less on the grounds of hope than as a point of principle and honor. He thought a fight against all odds the due portion of those in political life who cherished right and righteous views. Randolph openly regretted his own important role in bringing about the Louisiana Purchase. He called it "the greatest curse that ever befel us" and recalled the warnings, which he and the majority had not heeded, to "pause before we signed the treaty, admitting vast regions into the Confederacy. We were forewarned but not forearmed. . . ." If he had known then what consequences would follow upon the fateful precedent of that act, he "would have said to the imperial Dejanira of modern times—take back your fatal present!" Randolph's subsequent opposition to the course of empire was determined. The notion, so dear to American historians, that the frontier transformed America into a democratic nation was evident to Randolph, evident and terrible: "We are the first people that ever acquired provinces, whether by conquest or purchase (Mr. Blackstone says they are the same), not for us to govern but that they might *govern* us—that we might be ruled to our ruin by people bound to us by no common tie of interest or sentiment." He urged Congress to act to slow its rising empire in the West, proposing a resolution "that the waves of the Mississippi shall not seek the ocean. . ." [13]

Randolph's argument against western expansion reveals how much of the Founding he had forfeited in his struggle to preserve what he understood as the cause of American republicanism. From his point of view the United States of America represented a compact that had been instituted to carry on the goals of the War of Independence. That is to say, the Revolution, the Confederation, and the adoption of the Constitution were events in the attempts of Virginia and her sister Anglo-American colonies to free themselves from tyranny in order to preserve those freedoms and bounties which had been their portion during the eighteenth century. Thus economic and social decline confirmed Randolph's measure of political history. The Declaration of Independence, with its ridiculous promise of equality, and the operations of the general government under the limited intentions of the Constitution were equally to blame for present misery and future danger. He rejected Madison's notion that a republic, founded on self-interest, might span the continent and yet preserve liberty. Randolph defended the small commonwealth as the only realm within which republican liberty might flourish. He rejected the dream of American empire so dear to the Founding generation and their successors, and tried to refute the political theory which informed and animated the American national republic. He took his stand against manifest destiny. "No Government, extending from the Atlantic to the Pacific, can be fit to govern me or those whom I represent." He opposed the admission of new states "before they had acquired a sufficient population" that might entitle them to equality with the old states "and before that population had settled down into that degree of consistency and assimilation which is necessary to the formation of a body politic. . . ." The body politic, the real republic, remained the state. Randolph in effect and in the name of pre-Founding America repudiated the enabling theory of the Union.[14]

Randolph reserved for the issue of slavery his most sweeping dissent. He understood that by focusing on this issue, which figured so centrally in so many states, he might organize his general strictures on the American situation in a way that would make them palatable and accessible to many who might not otherwise take his meaning. Randolph understood from his own experience how volatile the question of slavery was. He knew that the reluctance to broach it indicated that it was a touchy subject, not a settled one. He knew that the conscience of the South was unlikely to prevail over the circumstances of its power. He was aware of the masters' fear of retribution and their inability to envision a way out from under slavery at once safe and profitable. He recognized that the South did not really intend to free its slaves, not yet anyhow, and that made to feel defensive, the South might turn fierce. Understanding all this, and with motives clouded by the kaleidoscopic volatility of his own nature, Randolph said things that were almost never said. Knowing the slaveowners' hearts and fears, he argued in a way that might be counted on to move them. He must have felt satisfaction at times in the confirming attention he received. Even the most austere of prophets can do with a little honor now and then in his own country. In the rights of the slave states Randolph had found the issue which expressed his range of dissent in a manner that compelled others to join him or at least pay him mind. Boldly and without restraint he spoke out. Essentially, his argument was simple. If the general government could make internal improvements and empower banks and cross the mountains, by construing the Constitution in such a way as to legitimate actions not specifically enumerated therein, it might free the slaves. And if it might do that, it would, because the slave interest was soon to be outnumbered by a mass of plain people hostile to the kind of society slavery alone could support in North America. The manufacturing interest, allied with the leveling democracy, would reduce the slave states to such a condition of economic dependency that "in case the slave shall not elope from his master, . . . his master will run away from him." In his famous speech on internal improvements, on January 31, 1824, Randolph clearly established the connection. He attacked the abuse of the federal authority proposed and restated the states' rights/limited-construction arguments. The extent of political community was not national: ". . . this Government, if put to the test—a test it is by no means calculated to endure—as a Government for the management of the internal concerns of this country, is one of the worst that can be conceived—which is determined by the fact, that it is a government not having a common feeling and common interest with the governed." To talk about the collected people of the states as a nation, bound by common ties and properly defended against tyranny by their representation in Washington, was a "mockery—a greater mockery than to talk to these colonies about their virtual representation in the British Parliament. I have no hesitation in saying that the liberties of the Colonies were safer in the custody of the British Parliament than they will be in any portion of this country, if all the powers of the States, as well as those of the General Government are devolved on this House." Having stated his case, Randolph proceeded to make it stick:

There is one other power which may be exercised in case the power now contended for be conceded, to which I ask the attention of every gentleman who happens to stand in the same unfortunate predicament with myself,—of every man who has the misfortune to be and to have been born a slaveholder. If Congress possess the power to do what is proposed by this bill, they may not only enact a sedition law,—for there is precedent,—but *they may emancipate every slave in the United States*, and with stronger color of reason than they can exercise the power now contended for. . . . I ask gentlemen who stand in the same predicament as I do to look well to what they are now doing, to the colossal power with which they are now arming this government. The power to do what I allude to is, I aver, more honestly inferable from the war-making power than the power we are now about to exercise. Let them look forward to the time when such a question shall arise, and tremble with me at the thought that that question is to be decided by a majority of the votes in this House, of whom not one possesses the slightest tie of common interest or of common feeling with us.

Are you willing to surrender to the nonslaveholding majority the power to emancipate the slaves? Randolph asked his fellow southerners. How powerfully do you accept the common ties of union with those who do not share this especial interest? What *are* your common ties and feelings and with whom do you properly share them? And how will you act to defend them?[15]

Randolph did not let the issue alone, although the prevailing counsel of the day preferred prudent compromise and a care not to excite precisely those emotions he hoped to inflame. He dismissed such caution with relish: "We are the eel that is being flayed," he cried. He did not fear the consequences of his interest, be they what they might:

If from the language I have used, any gentleman shall believe I am not as much attached to his Union as any one on this floor, he will labor under great mistake. But there is no magic in this word *union*. I value it as a means of preserving the liberty and happiness of the people. Marriage itself is a good thing, but the marriages of Mezentius were not so esteemed. The marriage of Sinbad the Sailor with the corpse of his deceased wife was a *union;* and just such a union will this be, if, by a bare majority in both Houses this bill shall become a law.

Time was wasting, and to delay the issue was to decide it against the southern interest.

I know that there are gentlemen not only from the northern but from the southern states who think that this unhappy question—for such it is—of negro slavery, which the Constitution has vainly attempted to blink by not using the term, should never be brought into public notice, especially that of Congress, and most especially not here. Sir, with every due respect for the gentlemen who say so, I differ from them *toto caelo*. Sir, it is a thing which cannot be hid; it is not a dry rot, which you can cover with the carpet until the house tumbles about your ears; you might as well try to hide a volcano in full eruption; it cannot be hid; it is a cancer in your face.

Randolph said earlier than most that the divided house could not stand. He spared no tactic in his consciousness-raising forays. He played upon the economic interest, the pride, and the moral defensiveness of his fellows. He harped upon their private fears:

I do not put this question to you, sir; I know what your answer will be. I know what will be the answer of every husband, son, and brother throughout the southern States. I know that on this depends the honor of every matron and maiden,—of every matron, maiden, wife or widow, between the Ohio and the Gulf of Mexico. I know that upon it depends the life's blood of the little ones who are lying in their cradles in happy ignorance of what is passing around them; and not the white ones only,—for shall not we, too, kill?

Revolt, the pornography of retribution, and a race war, such were Randolph's unrelenting prophecies. Unlike Calhoun, he did not have to think hard about alternatives. The federal compact could be replaced with a regional confederation. He needed no theories to advocate that transfer. If one sort of union failed in its purposes, there was ample reason to try another sort. Since the real political community was the unchanging state, general governments might come and go, being judged by their fidelity to the interest of the common partners rather than by foolishness about nationality.[16]

Randolph also showed the way to the strategies of the

slave interest. The country was growing. The domineering manufacturing and commercial interest was impoverishing the planting South. One might buy one's goods in England, as Randolph did when he could, and refuse American connections in little ways. The politics of blindness had to be reformed, and the leaders who advanced compromise had to be repudiated:

Sir, the blindness, as it appears to me,—I hope gentlemen will pardon the expression,—with which a certain portion of this country—I allude particularly to the seaboard of South Carolina and Georgia—has lent its aid to increase the powers of the general government on points, to say the least, of doubtful construction, fills me with astonishment and dismay. And I look forward almost without a ray of hope to the time when the next census, or that which succeeds it, will assuredly bring forth [i.e., the numerical superiority of the nonslaveholding interests], when this work of destruction and devastation is to commence in the abused name of humanity and religion, and when the imploring eyes of some will be, as now, turned towards another body, in the vain hope that it may arrest the evil and stay the plague.

If the South could see at last how desperate the situation was, Randolph could also teach southerners how to respond. To his prescience of destruction, he added a promise of saving action. He threatened the North as he tormented the South: "We know what we are doing. We of the South are united from the Ohio to Florida, and we can always unite; but you of the North are beginning to divide and you will divide. We have conquered you once, and we can and will conquer you again. Ay, sir, we will drive you to the wall, and when we have you there once more we mean to keep you there, and will nail you down like base money." In his own eccentric behavior might be traced the politics of sectional redress. Randolph, after all, forced the great compromiser Henry Clay onto the dueling field of honor; in the same way he urged the South to abandon compromise for assertion, violent if necessary.[17]

Randolph finally overbore the contradictions in his own

opinions about slavery by pursuing literally and to its logical conclusion, each tenet of the confusing position Virginia had bequeathed to him. Virginia taught that slavery was morally wrong and should be abolished. Randolph emancipated his slaves. Virginia hoped that slavery, while in existence, might be conducted humanely and with an eye toward profit. Randolph was a successful and not unkind master who experienced the complex relations between slave and slaveholder, playing his part and eliciting from his slaves theirs. Virginia also taught that slavery could be abolished only in the individual instance, that it was too central to the prevailing way of life for interference with it to be brooked. Randolph pursued these principles to their logical extremes, which were classic states' rights dogmas and their inevitable consequence of ultimate disunion. In his literal-minded adherence to these tenets, Randolph violated the spirit with which they were advanced by such men as Jefferson. Without the absorbing force of a regime like that of late-eighteenth-century Virginia, they were bald indeed, bald and inconsistent. Randolph found himself forcing the letter of a traditional agreement into a new doctrine, radical and extreme. It had always been there, muffled by the earlier Virginian capacity to sustain at once the institution of slavery and a certain level of doubt about its legitimacy. When the institution was decisively threatened, the tolerance for doubt diminished. He broke the silence and would have precipitated the issue if he could. He supported South Carolina in her intransigence over the tariff, although he had no patience with the doctrine of nullification. He clashed with Jackson over these questions and claimed to be ready to fight. At the end, of course, Randolph knew that he would not live to see the fight. This was not really a cause he had preparation or youth enough to forge. He served rather as its Cassandra, the prophet of resistance and also of destruction. In him might be seen the several levels on which slavery might threaten the American union. In him too were indications of how limited the vision and hopes of a republic founded on slavery might be.

If Randolph's sectional trail blazing makes him important today, his eccentricity made him memorable in his own time. He was a show all in himself, the very person of his old-fashioned ideas, alive with wit and menace, tense and brilliant, old and young, erratic and consistent, among the most fascinating Americans of his day. Although he separated himself from America's notions and fashions, he shared her habit of exaggeration. His was an exaggerated impersonation, theatrical and canny. Randolph insisted on his own peculiarities. When taunted about his lack of beard and his unchanged voice, he replied, "You pride yourself on your animal faculty, in which the negro is your equal and the jackass infinitely your superior." He turned his disadvantages into advantages, his oddness into a higher correctness. He did say many wonderful things, and is credited with a hundred more: "All the bastard wit of the country is fathered upon me." He described Robert Livingston as "brilliant but utterly corrupt. He shines and stinks like rotten mackerel by moonlight." Or did he say this about Clay, and was he paraphrasing Raleigh? He surely said that Edmund Randolph was "the chameleon on the aspen, always trembling, always changing." But was he the first to notice that Martin Van Buren "rowed to his object was muffled oars"? He called a rough Kentucky orator "a carving knife whetted on a brickbat" and said of a Virginia governor that like some fine blooded horses, he was "too weak for the plow, and too slow for the turf." Was he the first to talk of Jackson's "kitchen cabinet"? Witty observations, aphorism, and scathing characterizations were attributed to him because these constituted his trademark. The situations in which he found himself called forth his comments, and the more we know about the situations, the more loaded we recognize his wit to be. He turned away from a southern lady who was vocal in her sympathies with the oppressed Greeks and pointed to some black children outside her home: "Madam, the Greeks are at your door!" Whether or not he was the man who coined "doughface" for northern men of southern principles, it was the kind of thing he might have said and the kind of thing he thought more people ought to say. Characterization was like dueling, a weapon Randolph used in his fight against the evils of his day. He cannot be summoned up by the list of his remarks. As James K. Paulding observed, he was like an Indian partisan warrior: "He is the last man in the world into whose hands I would wish to fall in a debate, for he cuts with a two-edged sword, and makes war like his Indian ancestors." Like the Indian warrior, he made his stand where he could, using the obsolete weapons at his command. The tomahawk of his wit might not be an up-to-date weapon, but it still scalped. His tactics made all ground his own; he lured the enemy soldiers singly into the woods he knew best and massacred them one by one. There were always more soldiers and they kept on coming, but the Indian Randolph forced them into his kind of fight, fought them well, and made them cry out in pain. He looked around him haughtily, knowing that his native grounds were more treacherous and higher than the plains onto which his opponents wished to tempt him. He had had experience enough of modern combat and preferred the high ground of his youth; he retreated early to that place and fought from there until he breathed his last. Randolph's behavior was often eccentric, usually—though not always—deliberately so. He lived according to his own rules, a home blend of antique and idiosyncratic customs. He knew that he was an object of suspicion and only sneaking admiration, that his tactics were outmoded and his purposes effectively blunted. He knew that serious men discounted him and that others, though fearing to encounter him face to face, were not inspired by his savagery to respect his principles and follow him. He replied to his critics this way:

A caterpillar comes to a fence; he crawls to the bottom of the ditch and over the fence, some of his hundred feet always in contact with the subject upon which he moves. A gallant horseman at a flying leap clears both ditch and fence. "Stop," says the caterpillar, "you are too flighty, you want connection and continuity. It took me an hour to get over, you can't be as sure as I am, who have never quitted the subject, that you have overcome the difficulty and are fairly over the fence." "Thou miserable reptile," replies our fox-hunter, "if, like you, I crawled over the earth slowly and painfully should I ever catch a fox or be anything more than a wretched caterpillar?"[18]

In this introduction to the education of John Randolph certain evident facts bear remark. Although what follows places deliberate emphasis on the several central ways in which Randolph's world may be said to have changed during his lifetime, and on his unusual and suggestive responses to those changes and, really, to what he saw as the big encompassing change in the state of his country, it must be recognized that from our modern standpoint, those changes may appear, if not imperceptible, at least inconsequential. In themselves, reconstructed historically, the events pale before the kinds of alterations that the middle years of the nineteenth century witnessed. Randolph might well be regarded as fancying more than there was, in truth, to be seen. When, in addition, we take into our view the transformation of his land into ours, with its unimaginable particulars of inventions, materials, and peoples, the complexity of what has replaced what was still a small and simple society may unavoidably overwhelm any attempt to make Randolph's apprehensions and observations carry their proper weight. This general caveat cuts two ways. Randolph saw one big change, the establishment of that regime which subsumed and ordered all the other changes we have come to recognize. But his observations about democracy and its centralizing and leveling dangers may be taken to include too much—more, at least, than he intended. In his worst moods of pessimism and despair about his country, Randolph never conceived of the kinds of abuses we take his rhetoric to signify. The sheer number of people and vast extent of modern America make any application of his views to the twentieth century theoretical at best. Remembering that he hated theory, we must also remember that to deprive an insight of its historically determined substance and to apply it to utterly transformed conditions is a risky if intriguing exercise. Randolph's strictures on big government, for example, were meant to describe a government virtually nonexistent in our terms of reference. His warnings may elucidate contemporary worries about, say, forced social planning, overly harsh taxation, and the burdens of government bureaucracy, but there is no responsible way for the historian to interpret Randolph's perception of a tendency in our institutions as a grasp of what in fact has happened. Randolph certainly would think, were he able to join us in the enjoyment of our democracy, that his worst suspicions had been justified, but it is impossible to imagine him finding in anything important that characterizes American life in the late twentieth century ground worth standing upon, recognizably his country. Learn though we can from his reactions, we must learn with the frustrating restraint that acknowledges that what has changed has from Randolph's point of view changed utterly, beyond saving recognition. If what he feared has come true, as inescapably this book argues that it did, then the consequence is that we can learn from Randolph about the change and how it occurred but by no means how to describe or to manage what it has wrought.

At the same time, the continuity which makes John Randolph part of the history from which Americans yet expect to learn requires that the big change not blind us to the verities, big and small. Unlike Jefferson or Lincoln, Randolph cannot be said even spiritually to have founded or invented this nation. He lived in it, however, deeply and articulately. In his reaction to what he encountered may lie the contrary companion to his unfamiliarity with the conditions of modern America. The kinds of unchanging conditions that motivate men to take an angry and disappointed stand, to refuse compromise, to argue with the tendency and drift and direction of things, may in themselves be worth recovering. How Randolph took his stand, therefore, while constituting no reliable guide to the realities of our society, may offer a surer sense of where a certain sort of dissent takes its mangled stand in the cause of what has vanished. Like the Native Americans, from whom Randolph proudly claimed descent, he lived within one of the nation's historic traditions, a tradition that continues to fascinate even though it has been rooted out. The craving for what once was tells us something about our appetites—if not necessarily how to satisfy them, then perhaps how not to misunderstand our discontent with what we now gorge ourselves upon. The version of Randolph that resembles that of the noble savage, the symbolic reconstruction of a path not taken any longer, will not serve. Keeping in mind what has made Randolph irrelevant, we may discover in him some of those things lost along the way that lead to a greater understanding of our present state and future possibility.

∽ 2 ∽

Upbringing

John Randolph was born in June 1773 at Cawsons, in Prince George County, Virginia, near the joining of the Appomattox and the James rivers. Cawsons was the home of Theodorick Bland, Randolph's maternal grandfather, and its American English magnificence typified the conceits and achievements of the special social class Randolph joined at birth, the Virginia gentry. Like Randolph's other youthful homes, Matoax and Bizarre, Cawsons was subsequently destroyed by fire. The fate of these homes always symbolized to Randolph the disappearance of the social world of his fathers (and his youth) during his own lifetime. The physical destruction visited on the houses was only one early event in an external history which was unusually available for the dramatic personal symbolism he developed to explain himself. In 1814, after a visit to his birthplace, he wrote to Josiah Quincy:

The sight of the broad bay, formed by the junction of the two rivers, gave a new impulse to my being; but when the boat struck the beach, all was sad and desolate. The fires of ancient hospitality were long since extinguished, and the hearth stone-cold. Here was my mother given in marriage, and here I was born; once the seat of plenty and cheerfulness, associated with my earliest and the dearest recollections, now mute and deserted. One old gray-headed domestic seemed to render the solitude more sensible.[1]

The "scenes of my youth" were a controlling image of Randolph's imagination, gaining intensity and feeling with the passage of time. He was one of the last Virginians who did not also grow up American; his childhood was suspended between British rule and the new Continental national government, and it is not too much of an exaggeration to say that Virginia was his *patria.* Henry Adams seized upon this peculiarity of history to drive home his identification of Randolph as a symbolic embodiment of Virginia: in one dramatic moment—that of the Declaration of Independence—could be found the challenge of an independent republican America to the old Virginia regime.

The Declaration of Independence proclaimed that America was no longer to be English, but American; that is to say, democratic and popular in all its parts,—a fact equivalent to the sentence of death upon old Virginia society, and foreboding dissolution to the Randolphs with the rest, until they should learn to master the conditions of the American life. For passing through such a malestrom a century was not too short an allowance of time, yet this small Randolph boy, not a strong creature at best, was born just as the downward plunge began, and every moment made the outlook drearier and more awful.[2]

In retrospect, Randolph would have agreed with Adams that his birth was untimely, but such retrospective perceptions, whatever the motive, are untrustworthy. The Virginia Randolph grew up in was substantially the same as she had been before July 4, 1776, and he was raised according to the lights of her self-confident golden age, which might talk about decline but did not truly believe it to have come to pass. The Revolution was the emblem of Virginia's greatness, the Declaration spoke in Virginia's voice, the continental armies were Virginia-led, the war was won in Virginia by Virginians: whatever its ultimate challenge to their hegemony, the Randolphs were generally enthusiastic partisans of the American cause. This is important to remember, because the lessons Virginia taught Randolph were conceived in a period of greatness and only assumed the meaning of decline in his own perceptions over time. There is a decided difference in tone between the Virginia Randolph grew up in and the Virginia he remembered growing up in. He remembered a still life, at once perfect, realized, hoped for, and already doomed. This creation of his bitter nostalgia must not be taken for the real thing.

To say that you were a Randolph in eighteenth-century Virginia was to say a host of other things about your expectations. The descendants of William Randolph of Turkey Island, the first American Randolph, prospered and ruled; the Marquis de Chastellux was understandably "fatigued with hearing the name of Randolph in travelling in Virginia (for it is one of the most ancient families in the country); a Randolph being among the first settlers, and is likewise one of the most numerous and rich." John's family connections embraced Virginia legend and power: through his father he was a descendant of Pocahontas, and among his relatives were Blands, Bollings, Beverleys, Harrisons, Carters, Burwells, Pages, Nelsons, Carys, *ad majorem et gloriam Virginiarum.* The appellation "gentleman" had agreed-upon meanings in this society, implying landed property, slaves, known family and manners, and the expectation of deference from the public; as J. R. Pole has written, "in an agrarian commonwealth, great landed property naturally induced political power, and in view of the chronic shortage of white labor, the larger slave owner became a virtual lord of his neighborhood." The acceptance of the economic and political realities which empowered the Virginia ruling class was informed by an articulate class self-consciousness, which may have originated in self-justification and pretension but which operated independently as a standard for judging the performance of its duties to the commonwealth. According to Carl Bridenbaugh: "Above all, the leading planters were imbued with the belief that they constituted a class whose obligations to serve and govern well must be fulfilled in return for the privileges which were their birthright." This belief envisioned a society in which self-government was the political privilege and moral responsibility of the elite. The unusual degree to which the arrogance of the mighty was tempered by their principles and respected by their inferiors was the distinguishing feature of Virginia life in the eighteenth century: "Conditions of living joined with the aspirations of the people to produce in the tobacco country a ruling class more nearly approaching European aristocracies than any other America has known."[3]

Since Virginia remained an English province for most of the century, it is not surprising that the favorite models of this provincial aristocracy were drawn from the English, and more particularly from the English country gentry. The realization of English ideals by provincial Englishmen who did not live in England was not automatic upon their proclamation. The two ways of life were not interchangeable, and recent scholarship has emphasized repeatedly how differently English and Virginian Englishmen understood the principles they valued in common during the events of the 1760's and 1770's. The perception of the disparity which underlay Virginian professions of an English way of life was sharpened into consciousness in the 1770's and is therefore central to an understanding of John Randolph. Carl Bridenbaugh has shown how a misleading English model had operated throughout the eighteenth century:

This rural society, produced by the interaction of geography and economy, also was buttressed by the traditions and inclination of the yeoman stock; when some of the members prospered and moved up into the lesser gentry, they sought with determination to preserve in Virginia what they fancied and recalled of the life of the English countryside. Sprung from necessity, it came to be dignified as an ideal; but this concept of English country life was almost as unreal as the European stereotype of the Noble Savage.

The absorption of English forms, doubly compromised by bad memory and inappropriateness, was partial and haphazard, complete only in name. The planter class claimed the ways of the English gentry as a matter of form and taste, but in fact, the ostensible mores of the Virginia ruling class were a happily self-serving class ideal and a misleading clue to the actual experience, which was un-English. The aspirations of the planter elite had somewhat different sources from the established power they were intended to preserve and ennoble. Their self-consciousness assumed their position as a ruling class, a material assumption founded in the solidity of Virginia experience, and looked to England for the moral and cultural language to describe their hegemony. In discussing the role of English country ideology in the Revolution, J. G. A. Pocock has written that the country ideology did not cause the Revolution, "it characterized it. Men cannot do what they have no means of saying they have done; and what they do must in part be what they can say and conceive that it is." Although the English descriptive concepts adopted by the Virginia planter class perceptibly transformed its way of life, they were characteristically embodied in a class conscience whose English and Roman accents were supposed to judge an experience radically different from the ones which produced the lessons. The greatness of eighteenth-century Virginia, especially as a training ground for excellent public men, was perhaps due to the tension between the native experience and a class conscience so alien to it; the result was a kind of checks-and-balances system for character building, but its inherent strains were great, and the Revolution ultimately forced what had been in tension into irreconcilability.[4]

The immediate effect of the War of Independence on the ruling class was to strengthen its self-confidence and intensify its commitment to its mix of values. If Randolph's social lessons differed from those of his father's day, they did so only in the sudden relief in which Virginia might be seen. Virginia had now become the legitimate home of

English cultural values. That superior Englishness of the metropolis which must always have mortified the Virginia aristocrat was an early casualty of the war. The rebellion was fought to secure the accustomed Virginia way of life. John Randolph was born into a society that was risking itself to defend its mores. He therefore learned a version of these mores that was intensified and exaggerated by the fact that they were thought to be endangered and were being defended with blood and treasure. He was brought up according to the accustomed Virginia lights, abstracted by the pressure of the times. The values he learned were not first those of the Revolution but those of the previous generation, and their articulation of these values is the first key to Randolph's upbringing.

Jack P. Greene's essay on Landon Carter gives a clear version (the more valuable for the archaic quality it perforce conveys) of what was still expected of the planter gentleman in Randolph's youth. Landon Carter's special interest for Greene is his subordination of self to the expectations of his society; his values are a guide to the values of the eighteenth-century planter elite:

Unlike many other public men who find themselves caught in a perpetual dialectic between their own private impulses and the accepted values of society, Carter achieved a remarkable degree of unity between his interior and exterior worlds by internalizing the imperatives of his society so completely they became actual character traits. Of course, his obvious discomfort in public life and his failure to secure the kind of respect and acclaim that he thought he deserved make it clear that the values he represented were the *ideal* values of the gentry—the rules its members thought men should live by—rather than the values many of them actually did live by.

These ideal "imperatives" were conveyed to Randolph intact, although in this case their realization was complicated by having to take place in a world they did not anticipate and their internalization by having to take place in a personality radically unsuited to their spirit, if not their letter.

Randolph and Carter shared an utterly earnest attitude about these values and an ingenuously literal understanding of the seriousness with which ideals were really supposed to be taken in the world. Carter's disappointments, like Randolph's, were all in the shattering realization that society did not generally reward the man who lived by the letter of its professed ideals; and although the two men were not otherwise much alike, Randolph did struggle in his lifetime with the anachronistic imperatives of Carter's society.[5]

Above all else, eighteenth-century Virginia demanded virtue of such fortunate sons as Landon Carter and John Randolph. In all things, there was a right and a wrong, immutable and distinct, and in Greene's words, "it was inexcusable to confuse one with the other or not to adhere tenaciously to an opinion one had decided was right." Steady and sure identification of the right had to begin with the recognition of one's own "natural imperfections." To self-examination was to be added self-denial and consistent application: "Only through the kind of careful self-study recommended by this injunction could one hope to know himself well enough to subdue his baser tendencies." This dedication to "self-mastery" was the cornerstone of virtue. The concomitant risks of "introversion" and egotism were necessary in a system of values which insisted upon the individual good man as its unit of moral analogy. The chief substantive value of this society was moderation. Vice was most surely recognized in the form of extravagance, which posed a series of dangers: it subverted the material foundation of excellence—namely independence—and endangered the material foundations of the community itself; it replaced the "quest for distinction" that rightly consisted in making oneself useful to the commonwealth with the false indulgences of "good living"; the "pursuit of pleasure" was perhaps the "most pernicious" of the extravagances challenging every level of responsibility and the very perception of right from wrong. Drinking, gaming, and horses not only were wasteful of the material substance on which class membership and virtue had to be founded but enslaved a man to his wicked passions. Good purpose, usefulness, was the proper test for any human occupation; no other could serve even momentarily. It was not enough to read; reading had to be instructive. Landon Carter's "reading and writing, certainly his own greatest diversions, were always purposeful. They had to provide some 'Agreeable instruction,' and his dictum that poetry should have 'some moral truth . . . as the foundation of the Work' accurately expressed his attitude toward all forms of literature and all varieties of knowledge." The essence of virtue, however, was independence, a man's "most prized and most jealously guarded possession." Independence encompassed morality. Disinterestedness and integrity were a Virginian's visible emblems of grace: the "pursuit of distinction," the obligation of the ruling class, was founded on that independence on which, in turn, was founded the social order. "Nothing was any more destructive to virtue nor more pervasive in many than the desire for wealth and power—what in the eighteenth-century was generally subsumed under the term ambition—and the narrow concern for selfish interests that usually attended it." No human argument could weigh against independence: "For the man in quest of honor and virtue, neither love nor friendship nor applause was worth the forfeiture of integrity." Humoring popular whims, even admitting to popular direction and its attendant popularity was, like catering to special privilege, a corruption of public virtue; popular respect might attend public virtue or might not, but self-respect was all the public man should court or trust.[6]

The loss of independence was corruption; its engine was extravagance. The fear of corruption had a particular meaning for the Virginia planter class; it raised the specter of decline in a specifically generational context. In the study *Virginia Life in Fiction*, Jay Hubbell distinguishes the Virginian as "even more than other Southerners" a "deteriorationist who believed in the inevitable superiority of the former times." Declension was a concern which united many otherwise dissimilar Anglo-American subcultures in the eighteenth century. For Carter, the agitations of the 1770's endangered order and foretold decline; the disruption of family relations which he experienced itself provided him inescapable evidence of that decadence, which the cycles of history taught was the fate of all human greatness. Greene locates Carter's felt perception of decline in the personal terms of his "realization that his own achievements, however substantial they might have been, fell far short of those of his father, that he would never make the mark upon his generation that his father had made on the previous one," and in his severe disappointment with his own sons. But these personal reactions merely directed Carter's view to the inherent worry of a second or third generation of ruling-class families which considered their social dominance the necessary correspondent of virtue but were not sure *whose* virtue was really responsible for their position. The uneasy Virginian was likely to describe what unnerved him in terms of a decline from a golden age. Virginian declension is the negative corollary of Virginian virtue, as Puritan declension is of Puritan virtue. In both cases the perception of decline is not a reliable guide to social reality, but instead a characteristic expression of dissatisfaction and lack of self-confidence among a ruling elite. It extends the moral person to a generational person and fashions a critique from overacute self-examination.[7]

Carter's fears of decline in Virginia were not really typical, since the Revolution absorbed the force and the meaning of such fears for most of his contemporaries. But the unhappy issue of this virtue, his possession of which he could not really doubt for all his self-scrutiny, expressed itself in dissatisfaction with the society that did not recognize its values in him. His unhappy conviction that Virginia had declined in virtue caused him to view his independence as a kind of loneliness, the loneliness of the virtuous man in a corrupt world: "Uncomfortable with other men and afraid that too close a contact with a corrupt world would some-how stain his virtue, he seems to have been devoted to the ideal of his plantation as a rural retreat where he might enjoy a life of quiet meditation and uncorrupted virtue on the Horatian model. . . . Whenever politics took a turn he could not sanction, he always declared his intention to re-tire. . . ."[8]

Embedded here is the contradiction of Virginia's imper-atives. The goal of moderation is not reflected in the cen-tral virtue of independence: the process of achieving virtue is extreme. Permitting no moderate independence or self-examination or integrity or rejection of extravagance, vir-tue nevertheless condemns extremes. Distinction such as George Washington's may solve the problem. More likely, the expectations really embody conceits of the Founding generation which a son or grandson of a Founder cannot ever realize. Independence is a difficult inheritance to lay claim to, after all, without striking extreme poses. The haunting fear of decline is the companion of these virtues, which are impossible of realization after the Founding gen-eration. Self-distrust and the dissatisfaction with society it seems to have engendered in Carter ultimately found ex-pression in a bitter and lonely alienation from that society, in the name of its professed standards, which he alone es-poused, a bad-tempered retreat to Horatian solitude and the independence of disillusion. Carter took his society's imperatives too seriously, *immoderately*. Moderation must mean that independence and virtue are to be discounted to the market value of reality, of what is possible. Carter's ex-travagant espousal of Virginian virtue, however, is un-usually interesting not only because it delineates the social expectations John Randolph encountered, but also because it shows the inherent momentum of those imperatives in the absence of the usual restraints of worldly disingenuous-ness. John Randolph's internalizing of these imperatives was fragmented and incomplete but also extreme. His conscience alone spoke in the pure accents of Virginia's expectation for her sons, addressing other people most comfortably and himself as if he were someone else.

The circumstances of Randolph's upbringing gave a particular shape to his understanding of what was expected of him. The early death of his father (1742–1775), also named John, made him a shadowy presence in his youngest son's life. The elder Randolph seems to have been an ordinary example of the gentleman planter. His will bequeathed to his sons an obscure quarrel with a neighboring family, the land which was their title to gentility, and the following injunction of Virginia morality: "My will and desire is . . . also that my children be educated in the best manner without regard to expense as far as their fortunes may allow, *even to the last shilling* . . . and that neither of them be brought up without learning either trade or profession." In the absence of real memories, Randolph connected his father to his image of the Virginia Gentleman. He was a personified conscience. It was an impersonal imagining, conscious and mannered; and the father was most real to the son in moments of achieved conflation, when Randolph absorbed his father into himself successfully—as on his deathbed, when he had his shirt slit and his father's gold stud inserted. John Randolph's real father had to be recovered. It is hard to be precise about the effect of his father's death on Randolph, nor was his loss unique. In any event, Randolph created in his father a clear personification of what was expected of *him* by his culture and family. To be a father meant to Randolph to be better than you were, specifically to be those things you were supposed to be, expected to be. The theme of fathers and sons, which recurs throughout his life, seems to have begun with this earliest loss, and its importance must be suggested here, although its peculiar force was the product of time, best seen when Randolph was compelled to assume the father's role in his twenties. It is evident that, from his earliest experience, the encounter with a father was not natural for

Randolph, but rather involved a considerable degree of artificiality. Its meaning was not located in personal fathering but in the abstract encounter of generations. Facing the father meant facing his advice, his social world, his example or his reproach—not a man. The figure of his father easily came to stand for values and expectations; his plate, his jewelry, his land, his name, evoked not a specific presence but a generalized moral personality.[9]

It is difficult to recreate a faithful picture of the young Randolph. What little evidence there is tends to read his later exaggerations into his earliest years. He was the youngest of three sons and unusually close to his widowed mother. There is general agreement that he was an excitable and sensitive child, unusually passionate and self-dramatizing; on at least one occasion, he was reduced by his excitement to unconsciousness and only with difficulty restored to his senses. William E. Stokes, the most recent scholar of Randolph's youth, concludes that he was "precocious." Hugh Garland offers the following evidence of his dramatic disposition:

When any of the boys and girls from the neighborhood came to Matoax, he introduced the play of "Ladies and Gentlemen" in which each one personated some known or imagined character, male or female, and acted as they supposed such persons would under similar circumstances have acted. He was decidedly of a dramatic turn. And his ardent temper and oriental imagination, precociously developed, invested with an earnestness and a reality all the sports and pastimes of his childhood.

Although a probable fancy on Garland's part, this image of a very dramatic child seems true enough. The evidence of the boy's precocious reading, his decided preference for the mysterious and romantic over the sensible and useful, bears it out. The mature Randolph was always of two minds about his early and lasting taste for the dramatic. He was convinced that it was a dangerous propensity but also that it was naturally his own. In a letter of 1817 to his protégé, Theodore Dudley, he expressed this sense of himself: "Indeed, I have sometimes blamed myself for not cultivating your imagination when you were young. It is a dangerous quality, however, for the possessor. But, if from my life were to be taken the pleasure derived from that faculty, very little would remain." Dramatizing seems to have been Randolph's earliest and most characteristic emotional language, something he was encouraged to do in childhood. It is impossible to say for sure how much of his nature was fixed at birth, but it is absolutely clear that the most intense relationship of his formative years, with his mother, encouraged this dramatizing bent. Like most of his lessons, the personal ones seem to have been learned at his mother's side.[10]

Frances Bland Randolph was herself the daughter of a powerful and prominent Virginia clan, and she was well prepared to instruct her children in its intricacies. This instruction, after all, was a mother's duty in that society, as well as a widow's special responsibility. "My mother had been a faithful executrix of my father's will; a faithful steward of the effects committed to her charge in trust for her children." Her expectations for her son were lofty and effective: "My mother once expressed a wish to me that I might one day or other be as great a speaker as Jerman Baker or Edmund Randolph! That gave the bent to my disposition." Hers were stern Virginia expectations. Sentiment and loss dictated the tone but not the whole substance of Randolph's comparison of the respect and reverence she inspired to that due Washington "in the plentitude of his glory." In fulfilling a father's duties, she was always womanly, a lady "worthy to have been the mother of the Gracchi." There is more than loss and time at work in Randolph's picture of her to whom he owed "all that is valuable in his mind and character." Benjamin Watkins Leigh remarked upon her unusual charm: "The world thought her son spoke as never man spake, but she could charm a bird, out of the tree by the music of her tongue."

Randolph remembered to have learned from his mother the three tenets of his class which he cared about most—family pride, faith in the land, and religion. He was less explicit about more personal encouragement, but it is possible to discern a pattern in his closeness to his mother when he was a young child. For Randolph, his mother was his most sympathetic audience. Even through the sentimental mist of his recollections, this is quite striking: "Only one human being ever knew me. *She* only knew me." If his lost father personified the social dictates of his world, his mother was a warmer alternative, the positive response of his world to himself. She tempered her lessons and reproaches with an understanding of his sensitivity. Her religious sentiments and love of literature softened the expectations of Virginia, adding to them concern about his struggles to be good.[11]

It is revealing that Randolph connected his early lessons to this particular relation to his mother. It is not only what they were but how they were learned that matters. For example, reading: Randolph was encouraged to read, but while the usefulness of reading (which was its official purpose) was urged in his father's will and later by his stepfather's attempts to educate him properly, his love of the imaginative in literature (which he recognized as suspect in this moral world and which therefore bothered him) was made legitimate by his mother, to whom he remembered reading aloud his favorite stories. Typically the mother's version of the father's official lessons subverted their meaning in a way that fitted them to the boy's disposition. After all, she alone really *knew* him. Randolph was aware of what the purpose of reading was supposed to be, but nevertheless read to his mother the books he preferred, not the ones he was supposed to prefer. Emotion, feeling, love, the mother's ideal attributes, encouraged in Randolph a confusion between what was expected of him and what was indulged in him, a confusion complicated by his learning both kinds of lessons from one parent. Any account of his internalization of the imperatives of his class must recognize the confused and fragmented process by which this occurred.[12]

Randolph's dramatizing was not the whole of him. He was literal-minded as well. It seems that he never developed strategies to discount the meaning of what adults told him. He accepted lessons as they were given him and tried to live up to their standards. Perhaps this had something to do with his father's early death. The expectations his father personified had no human counterpart to temper their impact. They were static standards meant to be realized. However this may have been (certainly Randolph seized upon St. George Tucker, his stepfather, and put him into this formal father's role), Randolph's closeness to his mother did not affect his literal attitudes toward these lessons, but rather added the possibility of other, contradictory attitudes. Her role in each instance to be discussed appears to have been the same. She conveyed the official expectation, and in her manner altered its substance somewhat. Randolph read to his mother, repeated the Lord's Prayer, said his lessons to her, in his own dramatic, sensitive, immoderate way and received her approval, as much for his style as for their content. When it is recalled how inappropriate his excitable style might be to the morality of Virginia, the importance of attempting to reconstruct these emotional lessons becomes even more evident.

The general impression of Randolph's childhood is that his temper and sensitivities were indulged. Henry Adams came close to the confusing realities of the situation when he emphasized the contradictions inherent in eighteenth-century Virginia, although his specifics were too much controlled by his several biases: "The life of boyhood in Virginia was not well fitted for teaching self-control or mental discipline, qualities which John Randolph never gained; but in return for these the Virginian formed other advantages which made up for the loss of methodical training." Adams overlooked the stern imperative of the Virginian to develop self-control and discipline, but was right about the difficulties a plantation childhood in a self-styled aristocracy might oppose to such an injunction. In fact, the eccentricity of Randolph's character, so clear to subsequent observers, was easily taken by his family for the high-spiritedness which was an unofficial but nonetheless cultivated personal characteristic, the expression of pride in family and class. To indulge his individuality was not necessarily to subvert his soberer responsibilities. It was another form of class education, although not usually made explicit. In Randolph, the effect was to confirm him in his self-willed and arrogant emotional extravagance, which never did blend with his sense of what he ought to be.[13]

His literalness about things, whatever its emotional sources, was the obstacle to his making better sense of his youthful situation. As it was, he learned on the one hand to aspire to the expressed standards of his culture and to expect himself to be able to achieve them, and on the other to encourage in himself personal characteristics and habits which did not refer to these standards at all except negatively. His mother's impact, as he realized it, focused these contradictions in one confused belief—that to be what was expected of him, he had merely to be himself. Actually, Randolph's "self" was at odds with these expectations, and his childhood only encouraged their simultaneous and warring possession of him. The image of Randolph and his mother which constantly frames what we learn from him about his earliest experiences sharpens the impression that his preparation to live in the world was compromised initially by two implicit and unarticulated contradictions. He was not let into the adult secret that ideal standards are not really supposed to be taken literally (nor, it must be added, did he break the code on his own). And he was encouraged in all sorts of habits of thinking and acting that were contrary to the expressed standards which he was simultaneously taught to revere. He was told how he was supposed to act in the world without learning anything about what it was like to be in the world. His literal-mindedness was the crucial element in the notoriously unsteady mix which resulted, but his confusion is intelligible and so are his responses. For such a child as Randolph, life involved a series of contrary injunctions—equally, though differently legitimate—the acting out of which was education. That his mother came to stand for the understanding audience for his theatricality is not surprising. She represented the confusions he never sorted out, but instead acted out.[14]

Recent studies of the colonial American family have emphasized the increasingly acknowledged role of the mother as a softening or interpreting medium of the socializing purpose of child rearing, previously regarded as the province of paternal authority. Daniel Calhoun identifies this as the "tension between civilized paternal authority and archaic maternal indulgence," and considers it a central issue in eighteenth-century child rearing. The views of family governance which the eighteenth century inherited posited "a neat collection of ruling part and subordinate parts," modeled on a father and sons: "Actual families did not consist only of father and son. They included mother and servants, and these intervened between father and child. . . . especially during the early years of a child's life, they could surround the child with an atmosphere of maternal indulgence *and* continuing correction." It is in the last half of the eighteenth century that historians have begun to locate the relaxation of the paternal regime into a more contradictory structure fostering greater maternal indulgence: "The maternal indulgence that had always been a latent feature of the well-ordered family was coming to the fore as the regime of liberty and persuasion that fitted the temper of the revolutionary generation." The Virginian attachment to the classical tradition no doubt facilitated this change; a Roman mother, especially widowed, was an appealing figure to that imagination. J. William Frost's study of Quaker families in the eighteenth century confirms the emergence of the maternal and sentimental softening of family discipline and order. In Randolph's instance, his mother's widowhood coincided with his early childhood and perhaps threw into greater relief than must usually have been the case the abstract quality of paternal civilizing order and the warm impulses of maternal affection. What scholars, following Edmund S. Morgan, have called family "tribalism" had come by this time to stand for the importance of well-raised children to the future of the race, class, or country. This social necessity, to which child rearing in a secular society cleaved, made it a parental duty to instill whole codes of values. In Randolph's life, this tribal function was carried on in a way that skewed his lessons toward one pole of the continuing tension that existed in standard family upbringing. His mother for some years took on both roles and conveyed all lessons. His view of things, therefore, was not likely to include a differentiation between the socializing paternal injunctions and the indulgent maternal mediations. To develop this he would have had to separate his mother's voice from his father's texts. His upbringing was not necessarily unique, but it did decisively affect the way in which he came to understand and accept the official lessons of his culture, in a process perfectly consistent with what we know about the usual practices of his day.[15]

Investigation by R. D. Laing and A. Esteron of the family situations of diagnosed schizophrenics has revealed the tremendous difficulties children may have in resolving the unadmitted contraditions in "normal" adult life. However, to suggest that adult society, as represented to Randolph by his family, was a mystifying presence in his youth is not to argue in any way that Randolph was "schizophrenic" or the victim of a neurotic family. Laing and Esteron emphasize that implicit understandings are not necessarily transferable to children: "Sarah had taken seriously what she had been taught, so that when she discovered the double standards of her family she was bewildered." Elsewhere, Laing argues that "impersonation" is an intelligible and common response to a family situation where various expectations are at odds. Freed of a specifically clinical focus, these notions can illuminate the process of Randolph's education. In *The Image of Childhood* Peter Coveney has described the educational theory of the eighteenth century as "associationist," "concerning itself with the swift creation, through controlled environment, of the rational adult man. It seldom considered the nature of the child as a child. Treated as a small adult, the child was to be trained out of his childish ways into the moral and rational perfection of regulated manhood." To be a son was not necessarily to be a child. Expectations took the form of injunctions to be a good man, as defined by society.[16]

That a child like Randolph could become confused about what this in fact meant is not surprising, especially since, in addition to the explicit expectations, he was also held to other expectations, which reflected what adults knew about the world but did not necessarily say. These other expectations, which contradicted the articulated standards, were the distillation of the adult process of discounting the ideal, a process which by its nature could not be admitted explicitly to a child. The child, being regarded as a small adult, was assumed to be in on the secret; even today, actions which do not recognize this double standard are often described as "childish" behavior. In any case, the assumption is that the child will "grow up," "grow out of" this childishness, and *learn how the world is* soon enough. (Countless adult phrases which express what growing up means finally come down to this chastening by the "real world.") Randolph's response was to encompass all expectations in the way most natural to him, dramatically. Education, from his point of view, was a process of becoming each of the persons he saw specified by his lessons, in his literal construction of theory. The fact that *persons* were specified complicated but did not shake his obedient purpose, and he accommodated them in his radically shifting moods. The attitude Randolph struck was precocious and lasting. His was a concerted effort to redeem the discounted coin of expectations at full value.

Randolph reconstructed his early home lessons as stories about his mother and himself. While it is difficult to accept the stories themselves as literally true, the precepts they frame are undoubtedly authentic renderings of what John was taught to respect, most probably by his mother. However received, these lessons encapsulate the ruling-class ideology, the central concerns and duties of the Virginia gentleman planter: land, family, church. The boy Randolph and his mother were riding over the family estates at Roanoke on the Staunton River: "Johnny, all this land belongs to you and your brother Theodorick; it is your father's inheritance. When you get to be a man you must not sell your land; it is the first step to ruin for a boy to part with his father's home: be sure to keep it as long as you live. Keep your land and your land will keep you." This injunction conveys the central fact for any landed class: land is the basis of wealth and power; it must be held onto. The moral significance of this economic fact of life is underscored by the warning it incorporates. The land is only the material emblem of a greater inheritance; it symbolizes all the duties and responsibilities the proper Virginian son is equally the heir to. The land is more than property; it cannot be converted into equivalent value without the loss of all that the possession of it has meant. "Your father's inheritance" encompasses the virtues necessary to maintain its integrity: to lose the land is to betray the father and fall from the special grace of gentle folk, to prove oneself unworthy of a great name. This teaching is not physiocratic, although it may appear to be. Its political implications, as will be shown, derive from English "country" ideology and the peculiar emotional fear of decline. Nor is its point necessarily agrarian. Inherited land is the symbol of the privileges and imperatives of the gentry class. The lesson goes beyond the traditional sense that virtue is the political and social characteristic of the independent landowner to a more complicated statement which ties the fortunes of a class to the family's continued possession of its lands and to a static, backward-looking definition of that class and its appropriate characteristics. Its deepest meaning is a warning: the threat of decline haunts Virginia moralism, and this decline is explicitly presented as arising from betrayal of the father in the loss of his lands; a family without land is no longer a real family.[17]

This specification of social sin was lastingly impressed on John Randolph. The identification of his father's land with continued class virtue was complete and constant in his mind. Indeed, he seems to have taken the lesson more literally than it was meant, greedily adding to his patrimony throughout his life, sacrificing all other financial interests to the accumulation and preservation of landed property, freeing his land from an English indebtedness which had not especially troubled his father. For Randolph, land was a controlling and specific social metaphor. He did not, it must be emphasized, see land simply as a stable unit of any social order, or in a strictly physiocratic or agrarian way. Landholding signified the social system of the eighteenth-century Virginia planter aristocracy, a system which described the good American regime precisely, the absolute standard against which social progress had to be measured. The early lesson—keep the land and the land will keep you—located in the increasingly recollected Virginia of his father's time, organized Randolph's perception of society. In so far as he had a philosophy, this maxim expressed it. When Randolph tried to understand what had happened to the Virginia planter hegemony of his youth, the terms he chose were those of this first lesson; the planters had failed to keep the land: "The old families of Virginia will form connections with low people, and sink into the mass of overseers' sons and daughters; and this is the legitimate, nay, inevitable conclusion to which Mr. Jefferson and his levelling system has brought us. They know better in New York, and they feel the good effects of not disturbing the rights of property. . . ."[18]

The eclipse of Virginia was thus a moral phenomenon. Her decline was figured in the dissipation of the great inherited family lands, effected by Jefferson's reforms but located ultimately in the failure of nerve and principle of the degenerate sons of the old Virginia families. Other Virginians, John Taylor of Caroline and later Edmund Ruffin, fashioned economic and political lessons from this decline, but for Randolph the decline itself was a sufficient phenomenon. The apprehension of decline was the central teaching of his youth and the fate of the great landed estates its surest evidence. The loss or decay of one's estate was caused by a failure of virtue—scientific farming was altogether beside the point. Exhaustion of the land, however exacerbated by social reforms or sectional politics, was the objective correlative of moral exhaustion in a distinguished line. That this lesson was defective is certain, the economics and ethics were equally misleading. Virginia's degenerate sons were only sentimental causes of her economic and political decline, if "decline" is even the appropriate term for her ante-bellum history.[19]

Taken literally, the injunction to keep the land and in turn be kept by it incorporates a confusion. Questionable even as it applies to the mid-eighteenth-century situation it allegedly describes, it is advice extrapolated from one set of social assumptions and offered as a sure guide to any future situation. It is conservative wisdom, reliable, perhaps, when conditions are static. But the conditions of the soil, not to mention the commonwealth, changed dramatically during Randolph's lifetime in unanticipated ways. Not only was he unprepared to deal with these changes practically, but conceptually he was limited by the predictions of decline: there was nothing new in the world, only the degeneration of the old. The land stood for the whole of Virginia's planter aristocracy, idealized and abstracted as the people of a golden age, fixed in the virtues which were supposed to have characterized it and which theoretically could recreate it if attained once again. The realistic under-current of this lesson, the part which implicitly recognized how unattainable the ideal might be (even in the first place) was expressed indirectly in the threat of decline. Its inevitable conclusion was the conviction that things had deteriorated since the fathers' day and that the sons' morals must be to blame.

It is interesting that Randolph told this particular story about his initiation into the mystique of the land. There is no question that its moral should be understood as a con-centration of the imperatives of his class. The circumstances of his instruction reveal how seriously he took it. The lessons concerning class are specified in his father's inheritance and voiced by his mother. There were no higher authorities in Randolph's life. The self-dramatization illustrates the intensity of Randolph's feelings about the matter, an intensity for which the attitudes and actions of a lifetime consistently vouch. What is most striking is how completely this youthful lesson governed the mind of the man. It seems never to have occurred to Randolph to doubt its authority. The story epitomizes the assumptions of the society he was born into so dramatically that it is echoed almost exactly in the quintessential twentieth-century plantation romance, *Gone with the Wind*, in Scarlett O'Hara's most intensely learned southern lesson. What Randolph learned about his social world at home was skewed by the eager literalness with which he took it. At one level he observed the commandment to preserve his patrimony more zealously than did his father, adding to it, clearing it of debt, living on it despite his disinclination for the lonely life, defending its boundaries and prerogatives in numerous legal battles and neighborhood quarrels, and, in general, busying himself with the responsibilities of landholding. When this industry failed to "keep" him (except in strictly financial terms), he moved to a figurative understanding of the land, as a material index to the fortunes of the Virginia planter class—the loss or exhaustion of the land symbolizing the planters' social and hence moral decline. Again, what is striking is not that Randolph was exposed to traditional counsels but that he heeded them exactly. His own story of how these social truths were impressed upon him distills the essence of his class, sharpening shared assumptions into consciousness and making a rule of them. What is unusual about Randolph is his insistence that the events of his life conform absolutely to this rule twice removed from reality, first as an idealization and second as a foregone confusion.[20]

Randolph early learned to understand himself in the complicated terms of class. He was disposed to see his own fate mirrored in the fortunes of his family. He prided himself on being a Randolph and was notoriously sensitive about what that might mean in any situation. This family pride emerged doubled from his home lessons in lasting ways. For one thing, family pride was a consistent source of self-confidence and especially self-consequence. Randolph took his family name and his own line of descent with great seriousness. The apocryphal story of his addition of "of Roanoke" to his surname shows him trying to avoid being confused with another John Randolph, one "Possum John," a low and feisty ruffian. His own account, in a letter of 1824 to his niece Elizabeth T. Coalter, is instructive: "I did not tell you my reason for insisting on the 'of Roanoke' in your subscription. It was the designation of John Randolph my father to distinguish him from JR of Wmsburg (Edmund's father) & by it He 'did plead & was pleaded' as the lawyers say. In consequence of two signatures of J.R. jun[r] & of J.R. being passed off as mine, I adopted it & it has stood me in good stead." The reason for Randolph's father having insisted on this original distinction may have been that John Randolph of Williamsburg was "perhaps the most important Virginia loyalist." Other examples of Randolph's family pride abound. Among the most interesting are his transcriptions from the family headstones at Turkey Island, the site of the original Randolph settlement in Virginia. An example of his transcription and his notations follows (Randolph's notes in italics).

In the year 1772
This monument was raised
To the memory of the first Richard
And Jane Randolph of Curles
by their third son*   *Ryland*
To whose parental affection
Industry & economy
He was indebted
For tenderness in infance
A Good Education in youth
   and ample fortune
   at Mature age*   *which he squandered most pro-
                                       digally*

Randolph concerned himself with the family name and fate throughout his life. In describing the significance of family in the upbringing of John Quincy Adams, David Musto has posited the central importance of family myths: "Families, like individuals, function on two levels of reality. On the one hand they are in and of the world of society—the public, the outer world. But families also possess a unique, intra-familial reality—a private view of their history and destiny." Randolph imbibed and elaborated the family myth of the Randolphs, a story of greatness and misfortune and decline. In time, it described the imagined world he lived in and became more real to him than the outer world.[21]

His sense of himself as a "Randolph" was evidenced in his precocious pride of manner. One of the earliest descriptions of Randolph, as he was at twenty-three, was by a Charleston, South Carolina, bookseller who thought him "the most impudent youth I ever saw." The account illustrates how he carried himself: ". . . with him [Randolph's companion] was a tall, gawky-looking flaxen-haired stripling, apparently of the age of from sixteen to eighteen, with a complexion of a good parchment color, beardless chin, *and as much assumed self-consequence as any two-footed animal I ever saw.*" Apparently Randolph took himself very seriously, although his self-consciousness and his self-dramatizing had not yet developed the magnificently expressive poses of his later years. The young man was aware of who he was supposed to be and was obviously straining to appear in that character; his posturings revealed a self-consequence as yet rather assumed than deserved. Randolph's self-assurance and cockiness, however, was only one manifestation of his early-learned pride in family. The more interesting expression of this pride was his habitual use of his family as a metaphor to order the world. He reasoned from family outward. His thinking assumed that the Randolph family offered a dramatic rule to the race at large. In a sense this was a literal understanding of the traditional philosophical notion, prevalent in his youth, that society is the family writ large. Randolph typically combined this understanding with his sense of the importance of his clan in Virginia, and with his dramatic sense of himself into a disposition to interpret the world in terms of the lessons of his own family. This kind of thinking was most characteristic of his later life but had its origins in the family pride his youthful training instilled in him. "My whole name and race lie under a curse. I am sure I feel the curse cleaving to me." His family was the allegorical setting of the moral drama of declension. Randolph's family pride corresponded to his divided sense of its greatness and its decay. The bizarre eventfulness of his family life only confirmed and enriched this early fixation. That a child descended from Pocahontas should confuse his family history with history generally is not surprising. When Randolph's unusual imaginativeness, self-dramatizing, and literal-mindedness are also considered, it is not even surprising that he remained thus confused.[22]

Randolph was also taught to love God. His Anglican religious training survived his excursion into Francophile deism and even disciplined the enthusiastic outbursts of his bitter middle age. Religious sentiment became increasingly important to Randolph, primarily because it offered the surest road to recovery of his childhood world. Again, his recollections dramatize the connection in his mind between an early lesson and the social circumstances its memory evokes. The following reminiscences particularize his religious education and indicate something of its remembered significance:

I shared my mother's widowed bed and was the nestling of her bosom. Every night after I was undressed, and in the morning before I rose, I kneeled down in the bed, putting up my little hands, and repeated after my mother the Lord's Prayer and "the Belief." [1813]

I am now conscious that the lessons [in religion] above mentioned, taught me by my dear and revered mother, are of more value to me than all that I have learned from my preceptors and compeers. On Sunday I said my catechism, a great part of which at the distance of thirty-five years, I can yet repeat. [undated]

The meaning of religion was freighted with the old times and all they came to stand for. Of all Randolph's attempts at recovery, his effort to recover his childhood in the Anglican faith is the most explicitly personal. Randolph's enthusiastic reconversion to Christianity in 1815 gained much of its intensity and purpose from his memory of *who* and *when* the church represented as much as *what*. Salvation had the emotional meaning of recovering the past: ". . . having been born in the church of England, I do not mean to renounce it." Again, his remarkable literalness intrudes itself. Whatever our conjectures about the scenes of his religious lessons, it is clear that in Randolph's terms to assert one's Christianity is to recover the lost moral world of childhood. The wish is to have again childish innocence. It seems to deny the lessons of experience, of being in the world, in favor of the lost garden—in this case Virginian, not Edenic. The Anglican Establishment itself, so soon an anachronism in America, was but another ruin of the lost world of childhood to be joined, literally, as one had been taught.[23]

Randolph's home lessons encompassed more than his exposure to traditional wisdom. His family situation itself, as has already been suggested, amplified explicit precepts in important ways. The early death of Randolph's father, in 1775, and his mother's marriage to St. George Tucker in 1778 appear to have resulted in a heightened and anxious sensitivity on Randolph's part to the roles of fathers and sons, as well as some confusion about them. Randolph's literalness is nowhere more evident than in his relations with his "fathers." He received his stepfather eagerly, it would appear, and his few surviving letters to Tucker betray a solemn and touching concern to be a son and create for himself a father. Originally from Bermuda, St. George Tucker was an eminent Virginia jurist and, by all accounts, a distinguished and cultivated gentleman of the old school. He made it his business to take the father's place, especially in the education of his stepsons. In 1781 the eight-year-old John wrote to his stepfather, who was with the continental armies:

Sister [John's young half sister] is worth a dozen of what she was when you left her. She says anything and runs about all day. I hope you are in favor with the Marquis. I don't doubt it for I think you a very fine officer and will be able to make the militia fight, for if they do not now I don't think they ever will be collected after running away. . . . I thank you my Dr. papa for telling me in your letter to be a good boy and mind my book. I do love my book and mind it as much as I can myself, but we want a tutor very much. . . . I will try all I can to be a good boy and a favourite of Mama's and when you come home I hope I shall be one of yours.

In reading Randolph's letters, one is struck by their careful penmanship, their solemn attempts at ingratiation and even self-deprecation; in one letter the boy calls himself "your talkative Jack." His earnest hope of being a son to his "Dr. papa" is even more interestingly expressed in a letter he wrote to Tucker from college in New York at fifteen:

Be well assured, my dear sir, our expenses since our arrival have been enormous, and by far the greater than our estate, especially loaded as it is with debt, can bear, however I flatter myself, my dear papa, that upon looking over the accounts you will find that my share is by comparison trifling, and hope that by the wise admonitions of so affectionate a parent, and one who has our welfare and interest so much at heart, we may be able to shun the rock of prodigality upon which so many people continually split, and by which the unhappy victim is reduced not only to poverty but also to despair and all the horrors attending it.

Here, Randolph's confusion about roles provides a striking context for his struggles to internalize his social lessons. His elaborate construction of a traditional father/son relationship with Tucker involves him in an attempt to show how good a Virginian son he is. Thus, he must demonstrate that his college expenses are not *extravagant,* will not lead to prodigality and encumbrance, of the dangers of which, sir, he is most certainly aware. There is something unrelaxed and conscious in all this—precociousness in assuming the burdens of his class and a literalness in understanding them which betrays a double anxiety. His internalization of the lesson of prudence appears incomplete, forced—it is not so much second nature as literally *learned;* all seems exaggerated and deliberate. A parallel anxiety is evident in his addressing Tucker as his "dear papa." His letter to Tucker, in Randolph's mind, has become the son's letter to the father. There is more to it than anxiousness for approval. Its formal, almost ritual, anticipations of what a Virginian father ought to say to his son away at college, what his strictures and worries would be, are remarkably rigid. Randolph hoards all the imaginative power himself, creating both sides of the relationship, taking both parts, as if adhering to some abstract guidelines. The letter addresses the father rather than Tucker. Even allowing for the formality which characterized eighteenth-century family relations, this is an unusually set piece, more learned than simply felt. "My dear papa" is identified with injunctions to education and virtue, made to personify lessons whose true voice is not so much Tucker's as Randolph's own conscience, the location of his internalization of his society's imperatives. This is not only a rigid and self-willed imagined relationship, but also a confused one. There is more to being a father than giving moral instruction, as there is more to being a son than realizing that instruction. This personal element was something Randolph had no experience of, however. His education was terribly misleading, although his continued creation of fathers for himself belied any recognition of that on his part. This theme of fathers and sons is explicit throughout his life. In time his fathers all disappointed him, and he turned on them with a son's traditional weapons.[24]

John Randolph had two older brothers—Richard, the eldest, and Theodorick. After his mother's death in 1788, they were all his family. His stepfather and his half brothers and sisters, although loved as his mother's husband and children, were a step outside. The lessons of family were left incomplete. But the fates of his own brothers rewrote on John's mind certain of the old lessons in italics. Theodorick died unmourned in 1792, the victim of his own indulgences. He had been a distracting and corrupting influence, dissipated and self-destructive: "Of all things in the world, he detested most a book. Devoted to pleasure and fun, he not only set a bad example but (with his dissolute companions) absolutely prevented me from reading. . . . In two years he had undermined his constitution and destroyed his health forever." Theodorick's example was a caution. His vices which were those of his class, incurred a swift and merited punishment. The lesson was straightforward, a personal echo of the familiar moral injunctions.[25]

The eldest brother's example was neither so conventionally pointed nor so easily taken in stride. Richard Randolph was a hero to his youngest brother. In 1813 John remembered him in a letter to Richard's son, Tudor:

He was in his nineteenth year and the most manly youth and most elegant gentleman that I ever saw. . . . Yet he was neither debauched nor dissipated. He was regular, studious, and above low company of any sort, 'the great vulgar or the small.' His apparel, according to Lord Raleigh's advice, was 'costly not fine' and you might see in the old attendant, Syphax, whom he carried with him to New York, that his master was a gentleman.

Richard epitomized the worthy son. The prudent and admirable virtues John found it so difficult to come by were natural to him. One senses in the younger brother's idealization of the elder a feeling that Richard's excellence is the guarantee of future greatness, that the line is not degenerate. In many ways, he is the mirror-image of John, and the more beloved for it. His talents and virtues were the straightforward and solid coin Virginia prized, and they freed John to live the private and carefree life he evidently preferred: "I prefer a private life: and domestic pleasures to the dazzling (though delusive) honors of public esteem." By 1792, John had joined his brother's household, at Bizarre.[26]

It was apparently also in 1792 that Randolph suffered his most acute personal loss, when disease left him without the palpable signs of manhood. The subject of Randolph's sexuality and physical characteristics will likely remain mysterious. In the letter of 1813 to his nephew Tudor, which is the source of so much autobiographical information, Randolph writes of an illness suffered at Richmond: "In this town, on my way to Williamsburg, I was taken with scarlet fever and brought to the brink of the grave. So few charms had life for me, so strong was the disgust that I had taken to the world that I was indifferent to the issue of my disease." He never fully elucidated the matter in his writings, nor is it of especial interest here to fix the nature of his sickness. What is important is that from this time on Randolph was probably unable to father natural children. It was a common belief in his own day that his beardless chin and shrill, high-pitched voice were indications of his sexual incapacity. What evidence there is certainly points to this conclusion. It is clear that he did not contemplate marriage after the age of nineteen, and expected to have no sons of his own. One suspects that his claims of romantic attachments were a matter of form. (Indeed, the effect on Randolph's relation to women was fundamental. The available evidence suggests that he sought only the intimacies of a friend and uncle with the many ladies he knew and valued. His correspondence reflects his polite and interested friendship and sympathy for a variety of women, characteristically his nieces and the wives of his friends. Few things angered Randolph more, in the social world, than the indelicacy and forwardness of women liberated from strict standards of ladylike behavior.) The impact of the disability on a man of his temperament was understandably severe. Given his strong expectations of decline, this particular blight was hideously meaningful: what more literal evidence of degeneration could there be? It was soon after his illness that Randolph began to sharpen his self-dramatizing, his family pride, and his understanding of the morals of Virginia into a sense of himself as the victim of fate. The characteristic self-centeredness of his later years that readily transformed the accidents of his personal life into a pattern of moral judgment and special punishment emerged in part from the experiences of his nineteenth year. Randolph never addressed the question of sterility directly. The closest he came was in a letter written in 1826, in which he seems to have been talking about one thing but meaning something quite different: "There is no accounting for the thinness of skins in different animals, human or brute. Mine I believe to be more tender than many infants of a month old. Indeed I have remarked in myself, from my earliest recollection, a delicacy or effeminacy of complexion, that, but for a spice of the devil in my temper, would have consigned me to the distaff or the needle."[27]

Randolph's surface discussion of his sensitivity may stand for a deeper strain of startlingly frank self-analysis which implicitly questioned his very sexual identity; even the most obvious fact of life was cruelly uncertain in his case: by his own admission, his fiercely assertive temper was his sole evidence of masculinity. That this uncertainty should result in the quarrelsome and defensive disposition toward attack for which Randolph was notorious is not surprising. This feisty disposition is intrinsically less important, however, than the habit of egotism which was the other consequence of his situation—the habit of interpreting this and other uncertainties, the frequent accidents of bad fortune which plagued him, as specific judgments on his head. In his own mind, Randolph himself embodied family curse and class degeneracy. He discerned in the way things happened to him a pattern which was his rule for explaining everything else.

This unfortunate situation heightened Randolph's dependence on his eldest brother's steadiness and exemplary virtues. Richard had become quite literally the only hope of family survival and was the more precious for being John's surrogate. It is therefore difficult to overestimate the force with which Richard Randolph's public disgrace and unexpected death struck his admiring brother. In the fall of 1792, Richard was implicated together with his wife's sister Ann Cary (Nancy) Randolph in a grotesque scandal of incest and infanticide which culminated in a public trial in 1793. Although Richard was acquitted—in part by the efforts of a spectacular set of lawyers, Alexander Campbell, Patrick Henry, and John Marshall, and in part by laws which severely restricted admissable testimony—his good name was disgraced and his kin tainted by his misfortune. There is no record of John's immediate reaction except these curt entries in his diary for 1792–93: "Bannister gives me the first intelligence of what was alleged to have happened at Glenlyvar. . . . To Cumberland Courthouse on stand; return the same night; accompanying Judy and Nancy . . . the trial. Return. Quarrels of the women." Beyond these details of movement, he could not go. For twenty years Randolph repressed his intense outrage at his brother's shame. In 1815 his feelings were suddenly loosed in a bitter exchange of letters with Nancy Randolph, now Mrs. Gouverneur Morris. The scandal stunned Randolph. It was simply too terrible for him to assimilate. In a sense, he never recovered from the shock, compounded as it was by Richard's sudden death in 1796. It is difficult to say which he felt more deeply, the loss of Richard's reputation or the loss of Richard himself. Randolph never reconciled himself to these events, never completely accepted them. The pain was always fresh. Years later he wrote to Henry St. George Tucker, "Our poor brother, Richard, was born 1770. He would have been fifty-six years old on the 9th of the month. I can no more. J.R. of R."[28]

The lessons of Richard's fall were too numerous and too freighted with meaning for Randolph to handle directly. His immediate reaction was to avoid them by escaping their immediate scenes. The Glenlyvar incident temporarily drove him out of the family circle and into the social world of young planters and gentlemen. His experience of this world had in fact begun somewhat earlier, but the family troubles he did not want to think about gave it urgency and energy. It is a fair conjecture, although it is a conjecture, to say that Randolph first attempted to make sense of the whole business by transforming it into a dramatic rationale for dissipation and idleness: the something to forget which gives the good boy his excuse for being a little bad. In any case, he did spend the next years in dissipation, returning home upon Richard's death in 1796 only because he had to, and even then, reluctantly.

Randolph sought diversion in towns, country houses, race courses, and travel. Once he reached his majority in 1794, he was officially his own master and "lived the life of a mere lounger" in public places. His brother's home at Bizarre and his own Roanoke estates were uncomfortable stopovers. Until 1796, Randolph was officially carefree and resolutely dashing, sowing, with accustomed literalness, his wild oats. Actually, his "young manhood" had begun when he ended his collegiate sojourn in the north to attend the College of William and Mary in 1792. Williamsburg was still a capital, and it afforded many opportunities for gentlemanly dissipation. In 1793, Randolph's college ties were severed on account of a duel with a classmate occasioned— it appears—by disagreement either on politics or on pronunciation. Correctness being the order of the day, Randolph wounded his opponent, Robert Barraud Taylor, and thereupon a reconciliation took place. That the incident probably arose over a mispronounced word is an appropriate irony for this dangerous trifling by precocious sticklers. The seriousness and literalness which governed Randolph's understanding of virtue also governed his social senses. A schoolboy quarrel must issue in a challenge. His sensitivity and reckless temper directed him to the field of honor in much the same way that his college expenses raised the specter of extravagance: Randolph took any situation as he took himself, with utter seriousness, and worked it through. Typically, he tried to realize in himself the attitudes and responses which were authentic and appropriate for the circumstances in which he found himself. His were not the chameleon's gleaning gifts, however. His poses were prior determinations, letter-learned and then put into practice. The assumed self-consequence, even arrogance, with which he brazened things out was his birthright.[29]

The stripling Randolph had yet to grow comfortably into himself. His uneasy taking up of social roles was still at odds with his air of being at ease in the world. He was moving around, growing and testing himself outside the family. Williamsburg had now become a third place to avoid: a letter on the subject to St. George Tucker, written from

Philadelphia early in 1794, shows the familiar Randolph
taking his new stance:

> I will now my dear sir touch upon that part of your letter, dated
> New Year's Day, which related to my studying in Williamsburg. I
> have found my conduct and character, during my residence in
> that place, canvassed in so ungenerous and malicious a manner
> that, were it not the residence of yourself and your beloved fam-
> ily, I would never set foot in it again; but, if you wish me to re-
> turn, I will conquer my aversion to the place (I ought to have said
> its inhabitants) as far as 'tis in my power, and endeavour to avail
> myself of every advantage which it may afford.

The conscious strains of independent manhood, the bravado and condescension of the self-proclaimed adult, have
complicated if not replaced the son's simpler anxieties. The
man must now be recognized in the son. Randolph's language is stiff with self-consequence; the stifling formality,
sophomoric and innocent, imitates in good faith; the words
make the man, don't they? The attitude he strikes is letter-
perfect, but he does not inhabit his writing, its voice is not
yet his. There are echoes of Richard in his exaggerated
concern for his own reputation in Williamsburg. These
reveal how his thoughts did run on home scenes and also
something of his struggles to assimilate them, typically by
dramatizing them in himself. The gentleman he creates in
the letter is the creature of his aspirations, imaginings, and
experiences. Randolph is pretending to his voice. That he
hasn't got the hang of it yet is obvious in the misplaced impersonal politeness to his stepfather—"were it it not the
residence of yourself and your beloved family." Other passages in the letter are even more artificial: "Present my love
to all the family, particularly Mrs. Tucker and Fanny. Why
does not the latter write?" The precocious earnestness of
his charming letter of 1788 is missing in his defensive assertion of financial prudence in 1794: "You may depend
on my contracting no debts. I have known the sweets of
that situation too well again to plunge into the same gulph
of extreme misery for a long time by dint of extreme parsi-

mony, extricating myself from that most horrid of all calamities." The moral is the same in both letters; what has changed is the person who protests too much. This is a curious letter precisely because it illustrates the way in which Randolph began to assume for the occasion the role his sentiments imply. Unformed, he was forming himself in his characteristic way: his stilted prose is the analogue of his several stilted selves. The striking unifying element of these years was movement: Randolph was always mounting up and riding off somewhere. His own memorandum of travels for several weeks in 1795 records nineteen moves, three on horseback in dead winter: between December 24 and December 31 he covered 120 miles; crossing his own tracks, ceaselessly active, Randolph also took the Virginian's horsemanship to extremes. The point of all this movement may have been escape, sport, or diversion, maybe a quest. Perhaps he felt at ease with himself in his world only at a gallop. It is hard to make sense of this image of Randolph mounted and perpetually on his way somewhere without resorting to anachronistic conventional wisdom about modern adolescence, but Randolph was not a teenager. He described himself as at loose ends; we can only add, *tautly* at loose ends.[30]

Nathaniel Beverley Tucker was convinced that Randolph changed completely in the 1790's, that his mysterious illness and Richard's shame and death framed a dramatic personal crisis. It is difficult to prove that Randolph's character suffered a sea change, but Tucker's intuition that these last events of childhood made a decisive difference is very shrewd. To begin with, Randolph was forced by Richard's death to assume the responsibilities of paterfamilias. His recollections of the event in 1813 to his nephew Tudor convey a sense of the suddenness of this elevation, following his return from a spring visit to Charleston:

. . . a few weeks afterwards (whilst I lay ill of bilious fever at Petersburg), your father, who had left me convalescent, although I immediately relapsed, was in the most strange and mysterious manner snatched from me. . . . He left considerable debts of his own, produced (as I have before explained to you), and my father's whole estate was under mortgage for debt. Unpracticed in business, ignorant of the value of property, I made a compromise with the creditors and saved much of the estate that must otherwise have been sacrificed. On you and St. George my affections and hope centered, and in you I had the sweetest companions and the most dutiful children. In 1799, chance threw me into public life. The rest you probably know.

It was a difficult time; the family lands and the family itself were endangered, and it was Randolph's duty to save them, to reverse the decay.[31]

The effects on Randolph were contradictory. He took excellent care of business matters. The conservative lessons of the planter class in time served the family's material fortunes reasonably well. His literalness in these affairs, amounting as it did almost to an obsession with preserving, freeing, and profiting from his lands, accomplished what his father and brother could not. The emotional responsibilities were more of a strain. His residence at Bizarre coincided with the first reliable evidence of Randolph's waywardness: riding his fields at night with loaded pistols ready, nightly pacing whilst declaiming, "Macbeth hath murdered Sleep! Macbeth hath murdered Sleep!" As so often turns out to be the case with Randolph, this "mad" behavior is intelligible as a response to a problematic situation, which for various reasons could not be clearly articulated. The undeniable exaggeration shows how intensely he felt the strain, but does not necessarily show that the feelings were misplaced. In his nighttime rides, he was literally acting out in dramatic parody his role as protector of family and lands; the action described anxiety and self-doubt (for which there was cause enough)—his was an immense responsibility for any twenty-three-year-old to have to assume so suddenly, and the particulars in Randolph's instance intensified its magnitude. Furthermore, Randolph had no other way to express his concern; he could not worry his dependents. Above all else, proper performance of his duties was the fulfillment of the expectations of his upbringing. To own himself any kind of a failure would involve the failure of his identity; destruction of his family would be his fault. Nor was this his only source of strain. Painful memories of Richard tormented him, the more because he had not organized their meaning into some dulling explanation. This is the likely sense of his nightly declamations from *Macbeth*: although the parallel was not exact, Macbeth's torment could easily stand for his own; he too was sleepless, haunted by ghosts and perhaps by guilt.[32]

Randolph's choice of this scene to dramatize his thoughts is thus comprehensible, especially in view of its availability. His letters sometimes revealed his state of mind. To St. George Tucker he wrote:

I have nobody to unburden myself to. In silence, are all my sorrows and, in the solitude of the night, indulged. 'Twere more than childish weakness to be unable to preserve some fortitude in the presence of those whom I am bound by every tie to comfort and protect. I am stupefied. . . . with regard to myself, I am tolerably well; but find it scarcely possible to sleep. I go to bed but cannot sleep . . . nor am I at all sleepy.

Much had changed since 1794. More than attitude had shifted. In comparison with his earlier letters, there is less discrepancy here between Randolph and the person who speaks in his writing. They share experience at last. Style and content are now balanced; they have a real relation, where before they had none except where stylistic aspirations overwhelmed all meaning. The writing is mannered still and straining for effect, but on the whole it is more comfortable. The key to this change is that the writing is about Randolph, not some figure of him. Its melancholy suits him. Egotism is a pardonable fault in misfortune, as Randolph increasingly discovered. This letter explores a central element in his accustomed style, melancholy egotism. One result of his experience in the 1790's was to fit the fragmentation of tone to the several roles he assumed.

It was a dynamic process whose stirrings are evident here. Randolph might be the householder by day; at night and in letters, directly and covertly, he was something quite different, the embodiment of his contradictory, negative thinking about the defined role. Indeed, the result of Richard's death was to force Randolph into a series of permanent well-defined roles: planter, father, and the like. The nervous energy which had sustained his earlier travels now fed his intense realization of these responsible adult positions and sustained his insomnia, his waking hours of undefined being. To be what he was expected to be was still a matter of acting out literally what was expected, but it was no longer play. The melancholy brooding tone is a counterdevelopment to this proliferation of roles. Like insomnia, madness, or fear, it is an expression equally complete in the moments of acting out, of whatever in Randolph was not reconciled to his role playing.[33]

The necessity of taking Richard's place helped Randolph deal with the meaning of his own disease and his brother's fall. There was diversion: Richard's sons were now his to raise. To be a father, one had only to find sons, just as to be a son, one still had only to find fathers. Randolph found other sons and more fathers, creating an imagined family to assuage his loss. As the lone person of the Randolphs, he was fortified in his already strong self-centeredness. His sense of himself resembled a lightning rod, drawing all dangerous eventfulness to itself. He came to regard his life and himself as shaped not by his will or ambition, but by the movements of fate. Richard's ultimate lot was thus one in the series of happenings which produced Randolph. He was disposed to see Richard tragically. He admitted no flaw in his hero, and might be said to have substituted his own *hubris* for Richard's unnamed sins. Ultimately, this tragedy, like all other personal events, reflected the operation of some principle of doom. The rote fear that the Virginia ruling class was degenerate hardened in these days into a premonition. These two kinds of explanations sufficed for the time. The decline of Virginia was the abstract render-ing of Richard's story, diverting grief. It was also a safe sublimation for any anger at the brother's betrayal, fears for himself or unaccountable guilt. For these were feelings he could never express. The theme of declension first made sense to him at the lesson of his family experience. The tragedy is a personal story. In this, Richard's fate rep-resents his line's and John's own—they are under the curse of doom. It was the only available way to explain what had happened. There is much pride in all this, and Randolph clung to it increasingly, perhaps as the last sign of family grandeur.

This vice [he is speaking of satire by women, in 1824], aggravated by long habit, and seeking something poignant, that might excite jaded appetites, consigned my most amiable and unfortunate brother to a dungeon and might have dragged him to a gibbet, blasted the fair promise of his youth, and rendered an untimely death a welcome and happy release from a blighted reputation. My dear child, when I look back upon the past, the eventful his-tory of my race and name (now fast verging towards extinction) presents a tragedy that far outstrips in improbability and rivals in horror all dramatic or romantic fiction.

The events of the 1790's, which seemed so disruptive to Beverley Tucker, instead completed Randolph's earlier ini-tiations into self, class and clan. Certainly they gave him no more than illustrations of lessons already learned. By 1796, Randolph understood in his own way what it meant for him to be a Randolph in Virginia.[34]

Randolph's home lessons ought to have led him from being a son to being a father. In fact, he continued to act out both roles. His education resulted in fragmentation into the stances of father and son: each comprehended a different exploration of life, complementary but separate. It is as a son that he has largely been seen up to now, exploring in a literal and exaggerated way the character-istics and aspirations of his class. It has also been suggested that he was on occasion father to his own son, that his filial stance was self-defined in all important respects. The assumption of adult-fatherhood in 1796 only intensified this part of Randolph. His role as a father specifically incorporated his conscience, his foreboding sense of the future, his friendships and stewardships, exploring the ways of realizing what the son had learned he ought to be. It comprehended duties in relations. Randolph could not really conceive of duties abstracted from family and *patria;* he therefore created relations to frame his duties. Unlike the son's imaginings, the father's started nearly *ab initio.* It is important to look briefly at the assertion of his adulthood, which was his first autonomous setting for himself; the thrust of his personal education confirmed his natural inclination to be himself dramatically in a social, moral, and interpersonal setting. It was also much clearer about the details of this setting than about the individual within it, and hence Randolph was encouraged to see himself as acting out the role appropriate to the given setting. Events, however, had begun to make it difficult to find the setting which his early training had intended him to grace. The loss of his family specified the loss of the old world.

To be himself, therefore, Randolph was going to have to recreate the setting as well. The wonder is that to do so he chose invention over reality, and the basis for this choice can only be seen in the confrontations which compromised his early education. By 1796, he was bound by expectations and experience to his old-fashioned sense of himself, which only events, transformed by his imagination, could justify. This early division of his consciousness prevented self-recognition independent of his warping experience. In his remarkable *Something Else,* Jonathan Bishop has described in himself a state of mind which illuminates Randolph's: "Had I not always been too painfully somebody who lived in the awareness of what others were expecting of me? I had felt that being, but not my own; and called the omission a virtue, assuming too quickly that self-affirmation could only be selfish." Randolph the son and father "lived in the awareness" of what was demanded. This awareness had a double consisting of forebodings, melancholy, and madness, the subversive shadows of expectation. In the son the result was little more than indiscriminateness, a refusal to pick and choose among adult words. It was essentially a doubling of the father which entertained in turn "that being but not my own" and the alienation it engendered. Randolph failed to transcend his doubleness, resisting ironic or critical self-awareness. Instead, "assuming too quickly that self-affirmation could only be selfish," he preferred to indulge his melancholy second thought and then, calling himself an egotist, to leave it at that.[35]

Randolph's thinking informed his energetic performance of paternal duties and the offices of friendship. These relations of his young adulthood mirror the completion of his years at home. Randolph's youthful friendships were a testing ground of attitudes. Typical of them was his relationship with William Thompson, the brother of John, whom Randolph also valued and admired and whose premature death in 1799 sealed a devotion to the survivor. William Thompson was wellborn and talented but undisciplined and self-destructive. He studied law and medicine in Germany and Virginia but preferred wandering to application, and soon exhausted his inheritance and respectability. Repeated attempts at reform, supported in every way by Randolph, ended in marriage and emigration in 1804 to Louisiana, where he suddenly died. Randolph's friendship with Thompson, like many of his others, began in good fellowship, the sharing of the pleasures and hopes of youth. The surviving letters of Randolph's youth which recorded these friendships are curiously conscious. Perhaps this reflects the self-awareness characteristic of young men who know they are free to enjoy themselves and are always judging their good times by the idealized picture of what they are supposed to be enjoying. That Randolph's tales of dissipation and pleasure sound most convincing as recollections may be true of all such stories. Randolph's accounts of his exploits, except for those on horseback, are suspect; especially open to question are his supposed romantic exploits. His stories of youth remembered, however, began when he was still very young and are moral fables, not nostalgia. This moralizing tendency is paralleled in his friendships, which quickly moved beyond fellowship to a more serious feeling, usually expressed as a family relationship—with brother, son, father. William Thompson, who like Randolph had lost a revered brother, was soon his "dear brother," and his dissipations and disappointments suggested too keenly Randolph's other brothers and excited in him the tones of elder brother and father. In Thompson, Randolph concentrated two other figures, Richard and himself. Thompson obviously represented Richard, but more interestingly, Randolph's advice to him played out his own inner drama: Randolph identified strongly with Thompson's need for discipline, and his letters of exhortation worked through his own failings at this comfortable distance; for by this time, he was also in public life and even more unlikely than before to be direct about his inner tensions. His exhortations reflect Virginia morality: the emphasis on study, discipline, moderation. "Your destiny is in your own hands." "Self-examination, when cool and impartial, is the best of all correctives." In so far as it concerned Thompson, Randolph's stern and loving counsel was straightforward and traditional.[36]

The intensity of feeling in the letters had its source, however, in identification: "You bid me regard your foibles with a lenient eye; you anticipate the joy which I shall derive from your success. I will not permit myself to doubt of it. You shall succeed—you must. You have it in your power. Exertion only is necessary. You owe it to the memory of our departed brother, to yourself, to me, to your country, to humanity!" The collapsing of Richard Randolph and John Thompson into "our departed brother" epitomizes Randolph's twofold purpose: his advice to his friend duplicated his conscience's reproach to himself. The correspondence has many of these doubled moments which capture Randolph's uneasiness with himself, but its tone is most revealing of his resolve and his determined faith that exertion will justify the expectations of the dead. In one letter to Thompson, he expresses with absolute clarity his own methods of living right: "Make to yourself an image, and, in defiance of the decalogue, worship it." Friendship is a moral relation but also a passionate one. Randolph's letters are written in the heightened language of friendly love. His friends are brothers, lovers, and sons, vicarious livers of his life, extensions of himself; although his tone varies, its authority is constant, Randolph *knows* what his friends experience. In a letter to the broken-hearted Joseph Bryan, Randolph sounds like Dickens' Julia Mills: "The eagle-eye of friendship finds no difficulty in piercing the veil which shrouds you, which, until now, I did not dare to lift. You have related nothing, yet I know everything." His friends constitute a family and are ultimately transformed by his imagination into a band or fraternity who share talents, love, or opinions not shared by other men. Friendship is a turning away from the disappointments of the world; the implicit movement of Randolph's friendships is to a higher ground than that of "a contemptuous and contemptible world." The moral authority of friendship is superior to public respect. The deepest meanings in Randolph's friendships, however, remained reflections of himself which he could not own completely, none more revealing than the following written to Thompson: "Too well I know that readiness of apprehension and sprightliness of imagination will not make amends for application. The latter serves but to light up our ignorance."[37] In this and in "make to yourself an image and . . . worship it" he articulated the warring impulses of his inner life.

Randolph's letters to his nephews and his protégé Theodore Dudley retail an interesting refraction of his upbring-

ing. He urges upon them the virtues he had learned to admire, the old Virginian virtues. His negative strictures,
however, are sharply drawn to reflect the informal lessons
of his family and are covertly self-critical. One example of
the old injunctions will suffice: "There is one point on
which I feel for you both—want of *exertion* in the prosecution of your studies. Upon vigorous and *steady* application,
all hopes of your future advancement depend. Your hours
of study must be fixed, and not broken in upon by others,
or wasted in lassitude or indolence." Randolph's
restatement of the old virtue sharpens it. It is a more
pointed lesson than his own, and its urgency reflects his
sense of himself, and the necessity of re-establishing the
family's respect. The imminence of decline haunts his letters; replying to Dudley, who was then reading Voltaire's
Louis XIV, he talks of the Dutch and their decay: "May we,
my dear son, take warning of the fate of that once powerful
republic. Their cruel task-master is now forging chains for
us." the danger of family decline and death and reputation
surfaces in a way which suggests Richard Randolph: "We
should study that our deaths, as well as our lives, should be
innocent, if not honorable and glorious; so that our friends
should have no cause to blush for the folly or rashness of
either." The most interesting parts of his fatherly advice,
however, are the comments concerning personal disposition which explicitly warn against qualities he exemplifies.
He warns against "desponding and low spirits" because
their habit is hard to break, once fixed, but otherwise dis-
pensable: "This is more in our power than we are in general aware of: especially early in life. It is only when the opposite *or any other ill habit,* is formed and fostered upon us,
by that tyrant custom, that we see and feel, and fruitlessly
bewail our error." It is not inferring too much to see in this
statement some real recognition that habits Randolph felt
he had learned early contradicted and obstructed more
serious matters. His sense of himself, here implied, is reflected in his advice to his "sons"; the example he offers

them is his conscience, what he knows is right, and he consistently warns them off the example he sets: "There is no fault more common, or more to be avoided, than egotism." Virginia's practice becomes the counterimage of her virtue; this conflict stands for the education which produced Randolph: ". . . it is truly deplorable that both self-conceit and indifference flourish in Virginia, as if it were their native soil. A petulant arrogance, or supine listless indifference, marks the character of too many of our young men. They early assume airs of manhood; and these premature men remain children for the rest of their lives." Whether or not Randolph recognized in himself the airs of this arrogant child-man is beside the point. These serious efforts to make sense of his twenty-five years at home for the benefit of his "sons" distill the lessons which remained with him. He had the highest regard for the standards of the planter class as Landon Carter understood them. What distressed him was the failure to realize these standards, which he tellingly saw as evidence of decline. There was no tempering of the ideal in his reflections; indeed he was, if anything, more absolute in its espousal. Whatever failed the highest standards was evidence of moral decadence, not the way of an imperfect world. The father was as literal and inflexible as the son. Randolph's first twenty-five years in the world not only exposed him, as we have seen, to various lessons and reinforced his natural inclination to take them literally, they also gave him an urgency about them, the sense that the stakes were as high as could be, an almost apocalyptic sense that the world could end. Their cumulative force was to make virtue a battle cry on Randolph's lips.[38]

∽ 3 ∾

Randolph's Reading:
Cultural Education

The life of the mind had an ambiguous status in the training of Virginia gentlemen. Except for a flourishing group of minor satirists and belletrists, Virginians were not particularly distinguished for their book learning; study was supposed to have more material purposes than the pursuit of knowledge. Carl Bridenbaugh has described a practical-minded society: "The denizens of the Chesapeake country were not a reading people. . . . the planter read for practical reasons rather than for entertainment or self-improvement, such literary culture as he possessed came . . . from conversation, not from reading." Wealthy Virginians did respect intellectual cultivation. They were provincial Englishmen who prided themselves on their familiarity with English culture, which was most readily available to them in books, manners, and objects. The Virginia in which Randolph grew up was self-consciously English in cultural matters. Learning meant classical learning, and culture meant English culture—the literature and manners of the old home. Revolution did not challenge this identification; Virginian Whigs would not have given place to Englishmen in England as custodians of their common heritage in cultural matters any more gracefully than in political matters. Randolph's early training confirmed him in a lifelong attachment to what was English. His furniture and effects were always English; he was supposed to have been the last Virginian to drive an English coach and four or keep a park; he even sent his books to London to be bound. He intended to keep his tradition alive, "so long as my tobacco crop will enable me to get supplies from *old* England." And he affirmed, "When I speak of my country, I mean the Commonwealth of Virginia. I was born in allegiance to George III; the Bishop of London (*Terrick!*) was my diocesan. My ancestors threw off the oppressive yoke of the Mother country, but they never made me subject to *New* England in matters spiritual or temporal; neither do I mean to become so, voluntarily." In later life, his Anglophilia expressed his discontents with America, but the attachment was originally a normal part of being an American gentleman reared in Virginia.[1]

St. George Tucker attended to Randolph's formal education, which was designed to prepare him for a profession, as had been his father's stated wish. John attended Walker Maury's school and briefly studied at Princeton, Columbia, and William and Mary. He did not take to the discipline of formal schooling, however, and his recollections read like Dickens:

> . . . at the tender age of nine years, I was exiled from my mother's house and sent to school in Blue Run, in Orange County. . . . there I was tyrannized over and tortured by the most peevish and illtempered of pedagogues, Walker Maury. This wretch excommunicated me, body and soul. To this day I have a perfect recollection of the shock which the vulgar habiliments and boorish manners of my schoolmates, and squalid appearance of the whole establishment, and economy of the place, inflicted upon me, and, when coachman Tobey took leave to return home, my heart died within me. This cruel punishment was unattended by the slightest good. . . . you may judge what I was made to endure—the most thin-skinned, sensitive little creature in the universe.[2]

With the exception of his experiences with one tutor, he remembered all his schooling to have been torture. Randolph's bitter dislike of school was intensified in retrospect; he did receive a solid classical training, and his early letters show him to have been an earnest and submissive student who largely fulfilled his promise to his parents: "When we get into college, I shall study very hard, not only to be the best scholar in the class but to give you and Mama all the *pleasure* in my power." As this letter suggests, however, Randolph's purposes at school were quite his own; he accepted Tucker's word that formal education was necessary, "if not cheerfully, willingly, because I am sure that you know what is best for us better than we do ourselves." Randolph had a low estimation of schools altogether; he particularly resented being compared with other students and a rule generally imposed:

At Princeton College, where I spent a few months [1787] the prize of elocution was borne away by mouthers and ranters. I would never speak if I could possibly avoid it. . . . I was then as conscious of my superiority over my competitors in delivery and elocution as I am now that they are sunk in oblivion; and I despised the award and the umpires in the bottom of my heart. I believe that there is nowhere such foul play as among professors and schoolmasters.

To be worth while, education had to recognize his individuality. There was more to this attitude than pride, although plenty of that was involved. Randolph took education seriously and classically to demand a *personal* relation between teacher and student. Thus he remembered a tutor at Columbia gratefully, saying that the loss of him ranked after his mother's death, being sent to Maury, "and one other I shall not name," as "the greatest misfortune of my life. . . . We read Demosthenes together, and I used to cry for indignation at the success of Phillip's arts and arms over the liberties of Greece." True learning required a witness to the student's progress, someone sympathetic to be pleased. Randolph always protested his ignorance, by which he meant that he was un*taught* and undisciplined.

" 'Tis true that I am a very ignorant man for one who is thought to have received a learned education." Education was, like most things, a matter of expectations.[3]

Randolph knew that his schooling had been meant to lead to a profession. He did read some law and attend some lectures in medicine, but without taking up either one. He blamed himself for failing his father in this regard. Apparently minor collegiate dissipations resulted in bitter self-reproach; early in 1791 he wrote:

After having led a life of dissipation for the last three months, I soon found that ignorance and vice were the unerring attendants of what is the surest road to Infamy and Guilt. It is impossible, my dear Henry, to conceive in what manner a life of debauchery destroys the finer feelings of the mind and repels those virtuous emotions which alone, as you have observed, render us superior to the brutes of the creation.

Professional distinction did not captivate him: "I have but little thought of practicing law." He entertained no hopes of a glorious future: "You enquire after my plans. I have none, my dear Henry. I exist in an obscurity from which I shall never emerge." In so far as formal education was practically intended, it failed to interest him. He was always sensible of this, attributing it to his own moral failings or the failings of his masters.[4]

What he did value in his schooling was the limited introduction to intellectual pursuits for their own sake, given in the secure context of an immediate personal relationship and softened parental-like expectations. Randolph enjoyed one such teacher/student relationship with his tutor in Greek; it was a model of community, like friendship. Randolph always connected true intellectual seriousness with this kind of community, with his mother, his tutor, his friends, and his "sons." The utilitarian impersonal expectations of schooling were hateful to him—the reproachful antithesis of a cherished intellectual idyll.

Truth was at its loveliest as something shared among intimates.

Randolph did his real learning outside of the classroom, by reading. From childhood he devoured books with "more eagerness than gingerbread." This reading was not purposeful in a practical sense, however; he read as he pleased. Randolph's perception of reading as the pure locus of intellectual life and emotional community is apparent in the autobiographical letter to his nephew Tudor written in 1813; describing a visit to Bermuda in 1785 for his health he wrote:

> My sojourn in Bermuda was of essential service to me in many respects. . . . there was a good country gentlemen's library in old Mr. Tucker's house (where I staid), and here I read many sterling English authors. Your father [Richard Randolph] and myself were always bookworms. It was a sort of bond to the affection that united us. Our first question at meeting was generally, "What have you read?"; "Have you seen this or that book?"

True cultivation begins at home. Reading is both an individual and a social activity. Socially, it distinguishes the community of good men; the language of fraternal love is literature. Randolph learned this ideal from books, and he pursued it in relationships throughout his life: to talk seriously with a friend meant to talk books. But reading was also and even more characteristically an individual experience for Randolph. It was what he did by himself.[5]

Randolph's love of literature, like his other treasured lessons, was associated in his mind with his mother and, specifically, with her softening of the stern demands of the father. "She taught me to read and indeed all that I know that is worth knowing—from her I learned to relish Shakespeare—to aspire to be something better than a mere Country Squire." Randolph's love of literature originated differently than did his love of virtue. Although he did believe proper reading would result in moral improvement, its appeal to him was passionate and imaginative. Randolph read promiscuously and without discipline. His taste responded to his feelings and not to some idea of study. His earliest and most lasting love was the tradition of English imaginative literature. Writing in 1817 to Theodore Dudley, he recalled his first readings, which comprehended the familiar English and some continental classics: "Shakespeare and Milton and Chaucer and Spenser and Plutarch and *The Arabian Night's Entertainments* and *Don Quixote* and *Robinson Crusoe* 'and the tale of Troy divine' have made up more than half of my worldly enjoyment." Hugh Blair Grigsby's account of Randolph's library emphasized his "rich" collection of English novels, drama, and poetry.[6]

Randolph's reading habits were fixed early on in the stance of sensibility. He prided himself on his sensitivity to and his capacity to be affected by literature, especially poetry, claiming a poetic temperament: "I have been all my life the creature of impulse, the sport of chance, the victim of my own uncontrolled and uncontrollable sensations: of a poetic temperament." This was not a simple pose. Reading was his metaphor for personality, a way of expressing one's attitude toward the world. Randolph's criticisms of himself for his undiscipline and morbid, self-centered sensitiveness have an element of boasting. He laments his wasted talents, but lurking in his self-lacerations is always the pride that he is of another, higher order of beings, whose acute feelings cannot be appreciated by ordinary folks. He warns his "sons" away from his own example, but upon examination, his self-deprecation has the look of conceit. Randolph may have known that "readiness of apprehension and sprightliness of imagination will not make amends for application," but it is certain that in his own case he preferred them and that he prided himself on his unstudied brilliance.[7]

Randolph loved poetry but would not write it, because he felt too deeply the pain of bad verse. "For poetry I have had a decided taste from my childhood, yet never attempted to write one line of it. This taste I have sedulously cultivated. . . . I thought none but an inspired pen should attempt the task." His poetic temperament was all sensibility and no craft. Randolph's love of poetry intensified over time. It is difficult to explain the way in which he read books except by making reference to the work of contemporaries, such as Jane Austen, who explored the then common literary posture which Randolph exemplified. His aesthetic stance resembled that of Marianne Dashwood in *Sense and Sensibility,* and especially that of the bereaved Captain Benwick in *Persuasion,* as seen in the captain's comparison of Scott and Byron:

. . . and having talked of poetry, the richness of the present age, and gone through a brief comparison of opinion as to the first-rate poets, trying to ascertain whether *Marmion* or *The Lady of the Lake* were to be preferred, and how ranked the *Giaour* and *The Bride of Abydos;* and moreover, how the *Giaour* was to be pronounced, he shewed himself so intimately acquainted with all the tenderest songs of the one poet, and all the impassioned descriptions of hopeless agony of the other; he repeated, with such tremulous feeling, the various lines which imagined a broken heart, or a mind destroyed by wretchedness, and looked so entirely as if he meant to be understood, that she ventured to hope he did not always read only poetry; and to say, that she thought it was the misfortune of poetry, to be seldom safely enjoyed by those who enjoyed it completely; and that the strong feelings which alone could estimate it truly, were the very feelings which ought to taste it but sparingly.

Too impassioned a taste for poetry risks imprudent self-indulgence. Randolph's lifelong love of poetry was wrought up into a conscious attitude of sensibility which in turn framed the expression of his private emotions and gave them legitimacy, even in excess. Sensibility of this sort sabotages self-discipline in the name of a loftier ideal. Randolph's reading in this sense was a figure of his only rebellion against that which his class expected of him.[8]

Randolph looked for himself and his feelings in what he read; the satisfactions of style which he experienced were self-indulgent, not self-controlling or self-improving. Reading did not make him proud, but it did encourage his pride and gave form to his conceits. The self-consciousness in his literary taste resembled his response to other things. His acceptance of the stance of sensibility was exaggerated; he took the poets literally and identified too readily with their voices and imagined worlds. Randolph made a point of scorning detachment and distance as a reader. The premise of his reading was always that it would affect him. His criticism was founded in enthusiasm and affect. The cult of sensibility expressed itself in posturing and quotation. Randolph's intense commitment to this variety of appreciation may have begun in youthful conceit, but his *was* the very kind of sensitive and egocentric temperament which lay behind the conceit and authenticated it.

Two Randolph stories document his attitude. The Charleston bookseller who found young Randolph so self-consequential a stripling in 1796 also noted his reaction to a book which "struck his fancy": "I handed him from the shelves volume after volume, which he tumbled carelessly over, and handed back again. My eye happened to be fixed upon his face at the moment, and never did I witness so sudden, so perfect a change of the human countenance. That which before was dull and heavy, in a moment became animated and flushed with the brightest beams of intellect." The bookseller's otherwise harsh description of Randolph's youthful awkwardness reinforces our sense that it was in the imagined worlds of his favorite books that Randolph first enjoyed comfort and ease—that literature was home, where he could be himself as he saw himself. This is surely suggested, too, by his close association of early reading and maternal sympathy. An interesting reminiscence of Randolph by a nephew's playmate gives an account of his sensibility in action. William Elliot, in presumably unintentional parody of Parson Weems, remem-

bered Randolph's reaction to his felling of a young hickory
sapling in the dense Roanoke woods:

> I went immediately to Mr. Randolph and informed him of what I
> had ignorantly done, and expressed regret for it. . . . [Randolph
> dolefully examined the stick, and after finding out that it had not
> been cut down for any purpose, went on to say] "We can be jus-
> tified in taking animal life, only to furnish us food, or to remove
> some hurtful object out of the way. We cannot be justified in tak-
> ing even vegetable life without having some useful object in view."
> He then quoted the following lines from Cowper: "I would not
> enter on my list of friends, tho' graced with polished manners and
> fine sense, yet wanting sensibility, the man who needlessly sets
> foot upon a worm."

This was so much a stock posture as to have become in
sophisticated minds like Jane Austen's the subject of irony.
Randolph, however, having learned it from his reading, assumed the attitude with his customary literalness. Elliot
wondered that such tenderness could coexist with Randolph's notorious ferocity. That is no mystery to the man
of sensibility, to whom moderation and consistency be-
speak at best a tame insipidity. Randolph was always utterly
serious about literature; his view of its importance went far
beyond the limited utilitarian notions of his class. His self-
conscious stance as a reader reflected this seriousness, as
did his frequent identifications with the voices of his favor-
ites: "Madness, suicide or piety—(perhaps both the first!)
in some of these must Lord Byron take refuge. I think I see
passages that shadow out my own story." His reading encouraged Randolph in harsh and candid judgments of
himself as well as in self-indulgence. Literature was only
nominally an escape; it was a descent deeper into self.[9]

The best description of John Randolph's reading is one
that W. B. C. Watkins actually offers for Lawrence Sterne:
"For Sterne was of imagination all compact, and what a
man reads imaginatively is not just mental furniture; it
becomes a part of the man himself, especially if literature
has for him what it had for Sterne, dramatic immediacy."

Literature had precisely this "dramatic immediacy" for Randolph; from the first, and throughout life, what he read became "a part of the man himself." The process was elusive, impossible to recapture completely, but worth serious attention. Unlike most subjects of intellectual history, Randolph did not write (except letters); he read and he talked. So it is all the more essential to explore his reading, the foundation of his intellectual life. Randolph's inclination to the dramatic, his coddled imagination, his self-centeredness and his literalness contributed to make him a distinctive reader. His precocious reading reflected instinctive tastes for drama, romance, and fancy as well as the cultural bias of his class toward the ancient and the English. It is difficult to identify exactly the impressions made by this reading on Randolph's mind. He emphasized its cultivation of his imagination. In books he found emotions and situations which added vitality, as it were, to the still-life expectations of his childhood. The characters of novels and romance had a suggestive influence on his vision of action in the world. His behavior prompted literary allusions from his contemporaries and biographers, and much of his living of life was intended allusively. Like David Copperfield, Randolph found in "Roderick Random, Peregrine Pickle, Humphrey Clinker, Tom Jones, The Vicar of Wakefield, Don Quixote, Gil Blas . . . a glorious host, to keep me company. They kept alive my fancy, and my hope of something beyond that place and time,—they and the Arabian nights, and the tales of the Genii . . ." Penetrating life and landscape, they peopled Randolph's life as they did David's. Randolph remembered reading *Humphrey Clinker* to his mother, and his "first sea voyage thirty-four years ago when I read Sinbad and Robinson Crusoe." He found more than excitement and models in reading, however. He found himself, constantly and differently mirrored, in every way. His early fondness for literature, as has been seen, did not disappear with his formal education; it remained a distinct, even stubborn, alternative to his schooling and to other duties. If life required discipline, reading did not. Randolph could be himself in the conflations and daydreams of the imaginative, responsive reader—perhaps only then. These aimless intellectual habits in time infected all his living, but were in youth still circumscribed by his determined moral seriousness (although even then his reading was visible in his ideas about living).[10]

If Randolph read for any profession, it was the profession of the imagination, which for him meant, not writing, but the acting out of expectations. Literature was a source for living. His ideal was education as letters. Cultivation and taste authenticated education. Moreover, reading reflected that natural, true cultivation which could not be learned. At the core of Randolph's love of literature was a sense of himself which legitimated his undiscipline and subverted his surface moral strictness. Thus his claims to a poetic temperament only appeared to be laments; in fact, they were vainglorious: "I admire and pity all who possess this temperament." He prided himself on his *natural* taste: "An exquisite ear, which has never received the slightest cultivation . . . I have a taste for painting but never attempted drawing . . ."; and he declared that in England, his eye "astonished some of connoisseurs." Randolph may well have possessed the gifts he claimed, but his way of claiming them leave him open to our suspicion. If his was a poet's soul, why didn't he write? He did not content himself with a connoisseur's appreciation of culture. He insisted on his status as an artist *in posse*. Yet he refused to risk his conceit in actual responsible creation of any sort. As a legislator, he seldom bothered to write out his speeches and as a rule disclaimed all printed versions. Randolph sensed this failure of nerve, responsibility, or energy in himself—indeed, it was the constant theme of his self-reproach—but he did not overcome it. Rather, he never ceased to claim for himself the special privileges of sensibility without substantiating his right to them. Randolph's self-pity was an unacknowledged boast.[11]

To Randolph, culture represented the leisured accomplishments of a gentleman, an English gentleman. Books furnished the materials of self-knowlege and the appropriate testing ground of self-scrutiny. He warned Theodore Dudley to beware of the fanciful and to apply himself to regular study, and at the same time allowed himself a radically different kind of reading, which undermined official moralizing. The Randolph presented in his advice to others was a caution, totally at odds with the version of himself he offered to justify his own intellectual self-indulgence and imaginative excess. It is this identification of reading with his undisciplined self that made Randolph more than a bluestocking. It implicitly recognized that reading offered a haven to those elements of his character which more conventional teachings ignored or stifled, but which he would not relinquish or could not. It governed the way in which he did what he was supposed to do and, in time, translated the meaning of his duties into a language consistent with the whole of himself.

Randolph's earliest reading encouraged his self-dramatizing imagination. He did not read ironically, but literally. To be sure, he did not take fairy tales for truth, but he did assume the direct relevance to his world of what he read. In so doing, of course, he shared a prevailing assumption of his time, but his espousal of it was characteristically more extreme than most others'. The creed of humanism—that good books make good men—was something Randolph took for granted. To Dudley he wrote, "Yours is the time of life to acquire knowledge. Thereafter you must *use* it." Teachers might help, but reading informed by purpose was all-important: ". . . there is a wide diference between a boy's getting his lesson from a sense of duty, or a fear of punishment, and his applying himself with zeal, from a conviction that he is consulting his future advantage. . . . the taste for reading, which you are now forming, will be a source of pleasure to you through life." The moral usefulness of reading is the proper source of its pleasure. Randolph's letters to Dudley and his nephews reflect a faith that properly serious books will result in properly serious men. The works in his lists of suggestions differ strikingly from those comprising his own early reading. What he urged on his "sons" connects the "dramatic immediacy" of reading to morally secure content. He discouraged imaginative literature in favor of histories and translations from the Greek and Latin. The assumption operating in his advice is that early reading impresses itself lastingly and that *good*, i.e., "moral," "serious" reading will have a correspondingly "good" result. He was trying to pass on the lesson of his own experience. His letters attempted to convert his own intense, literal, and imaginative reading to surer moral purpose. When reading, he advised, imagine the presence of the speaker, but it was a particular speaker he had in mind: "Think that I speak to you in his words—accustom yourselves to act, as if in the presence of some friend, whose approbation you are solicitous to gain and preserve." Randolph spoke to his charges in the accents of his conscience—do as I say, not as I have done. Here, he extended the pressure of expectation to the one place where it had functioned incompletely for him, his reading. His reiteration of the moral purpose of study to his "sons" reflects interestingly the fragmented reader he himself was. He read seriously and literally, assuming the books made the man. At the same time, his dissatisfaction with himself as an imaginative, sensitive reader—which was also, perversely, his satisfaction—prompted his attempts to make sure that the literature they read would have a contrastingly sobering effect on them. Randolph's important recognition here, however, was that his own impression of books did in fact guide his view of the world and that its substantive emphasis was imaginative.[12]

Although he could read Latin, Greek, and French, and was well versed in classical and continental literature, Randolph especially loved English literature. His attitude toward this tradition was complicated. He always suffered from the provincial's defensiveness, something he inherited as a Virginian. This resulted in an exaggerated need to show off his cultural proficiency and in an unrealistic picture of England, drawn too exactly from her representation in all kinds of books. Randolph displayed a niceness about the language itself which had its roots in this provinciality as well as in his literalness and in the concerns of the writers he read. His letters to Dudley, his nephews, and other young friends, are full of corrections of their written and spoken English. Sloppy and incorrect English symbolized various horrors, and the significance he attached to precise English increased and intensified as he grew older.[13]

Randolph's reading was of two kinds. First, there are the books which he read to himself in his youth and which formed his mature biases, and second, there are those works which became important to him at various particular moments throughout his life. It is the first kind that created the terms of his literary experience which will be discussed here. This reading was also of two kinds. There are those works, especially Shakespeare, Milton, and the *Arabian Nights,* that struck the boy's fancy, enriching his language and his imagination. These seem to have encouraged his dramatizing inclinations and given him great pleasure but their influence is otherwise difficult to locate in his life, except in references and quotations, until after 1815. They contribute to our general knowledge of him, especially as they informed his exaggerated impersonations of his several roles in life. In the second category are works from which Randolph received substantive, specific ideas. The distinction is *ex post facto,* grounded in knowledge of his later career, but is altogether necessary. For it was from eighteenth-century English writers, especially the Augustans, that Ranolph got his clearest notions about the world, the notions upon which he based his career. This reading was of the greatest moment for his whole life. In the satire and politics of the Augustans, especially Pope and Swift, one can locate a connection with Randolph that goes deeper than quotation.

This is not surprising. It was roughly contemporaneous literature. The world of the Augustans was not far distant to Randolph. It merged in his mind with the world of his fathers. Much in these writings is didactic, and he found there impressive versions of his other lessons. Most of all, the assumptions of these writers harmonized with the pretensions of Randolph's social world: the English life the Augustans proclaimed comprehended the Virginian ideal, which Randolph took for reality. The process by which their works affected Randolph is obscure in detail. Influence cannot be specifically pinned down in each case. It is not always clear exactly which books he knew. But we do know that he read and reread the Augustans and their followers in the Age of Sensibility. Throughout his life, he drew on their writings consciously for illustrations and unconsciously as a source for ideas about the world and attitudes within it. Randolph's habits of reading left him without complete control over how he might be affected by it. Literature gained its own momentum in his mind and shaped his thinking and language in ways he could not recognize, let alone control. Precisely because he did not read—as Jefferson did—for particular, defined reasons or to draw immediate, limited, or practical lessons, his reading gathered a cumulative force within him which is evident not in notes and acknowledgment but in the very conduct of his life. The discussion that follows emphasizes selected aspects of Augustan writings which surfaced in Randolph's adult life. Here, they are treated independently, as background. The connections with Randolph will become evident in the following chapters.[14]

The temptation to present a chronological survey of the works is strong, but to do so would be misleading. Randolph's absorption and use of this literature was responsive not to its chronology but to his own. It is the cluster of assumptions and concerns that permeate this literature and that would have been conveyed to a reader like Randolph—self-conscious, literal, and self-dramatizing—which has been assembled: Augustan satire in its restatement of humanism and related themes involving nostalgia, declension, and language. Above all, the *person* this literature reveals is important. This reading was a major element of Randolph's education, confirming his other lessons and, in particular, giving him the metaphors he needed to express what he knew. Like his other teachers, the Augustans were misleading. Their assumptions were not widely shared or especially helpful in America after 1800. Randolph's insistent commitment to them under apparently inappropriate circumstances is therefore all the more interesting.

Eighteenth-century English literature reflected a particular state of English society and was heavily weighted toward a critical view of it. The Augustan writer was self-consciously political, and his writing reflected very particular notions of society and virtue as well as of the power of literature to reform society. That society was in need of reformation was abundantly clear to Bolingbroke and the gifted writers who fancied and surrounded and followed him. The development of modern financial practices and institutions and their ever-increasing legitimacy and sheer power in English politics were blamed for the great decline in virtue and for the style of political life, symbolized by Robert Walpole and his hated Robinocracy. The Augustan satirists were exercised by more than corrupt practices; to them this corruption "signified the disorder and chaos brought to the traditional political and social world by money and financial innovations." The opposition nurtured a nostalgic vision of an Elizabethan golden age by which contemporary corruption could be measured. The role of the poets in this opposition was increased by the nostalgic and aristocratic ideals invoked, and by the fact that an old-fashioned style was associated with the old-fashioned public virtues the opposition sought to restore. As Isaac Kramnick has noted, "politics for Bolingbroke's circle was supposd to be played out in an elaborate theatre where the style of the performance was almost more important than deeds done." This stylistic vision of politics in its particular nostalgic idealization was essentially literary. The class basis of their politics was realized best in literary versions. The opposition considered style to be the mark of a man's character and preferred the style of rank to that of money. Political criticism of this kind necessitated *ad hominem* attacks, and the satirical mode reflected this need.[15]

The concerns of the opposition were specific. They opposed the standing army as destructive of the values of local attachment and individual subordination to traditional loyalties. They sought a context for individualism which was not commercial or democratically impersonal. The South Sea bubble symbolized the dangerous "projecting spirit," and it became a catchword denoting the social disorder they apprehended. In such times, which were by definition the worst, opposition was a moral obligation. It had to embrace all questions. The misuse of power had to be called to order. As the Tory writers saw it, the social causes of England's decline paled before the moral lessons. It was "assumed that degeneration is caused by a decline in virtue" and that regeneration must be the work of virtue. Their positive thought was therefore to establish an image of what constituted good men in a good society. Their political program of retrenchment and reform was founded on the ideal of independence. Socially, this began with the independent country gentleman, "an owner of property who was therefore capable of exercising his own judgment on matters of state, calling upon his own wisdom, virtue, and good sense." The proper function of goverment was to protect his independence. The movement of this politics was back to first principles, toward the recovery of a virtue now lost. This recovery was typically seen as somehow outside of the political process: "Most of the energy of these boy patriots went into romantic nostalgia and poetry." This politics unsurprisingly found its most successful embodiment in literature. The Augustan writers captured both the negative and positive sides of the opposition; in their satirical writing, opposition thinking came together into a unified vision. This vision was sustained by political concern but was not really political, in that it issued in a program idealized and unrealizable. Undertaken in the illusion of power, it assumed the force of words in the world and relied on words for its effect.[16]

It cannot be too strongly emphasized that the political world of Augustan writing was an imagined alternative to England, meant to be taken for the real world. The writers seem to have taken this metaphor literally themselves at times, but it is one thing for Pope to credit his poetry with the fall of Walpole and quite another for us to accept him at his word. Since a major assertion of Augustan writing advances the political power and legitimacy of art, it is necessary to distinguish between artistic pretensions and the truth of those claims. The political implications are clear enough; the writing was informed by opposition thinking. But the literature reflected most deeply those elements in that thinking which were unpolitical: nostalgia, declension, and idealized virtue, in fact a disgust with politics as practiced. The pretensions of the poets rationalized a despairing realization of their helplessness and the desperate straits of their cause. Their politics were metaphorical alternatives to actual politics. The poets intended their politics to supplant current corrupt practices, but typically expressed helpless outrage. Their movement paralleled and mirrored but did not join the actual struggles of power. Their desire to credit literature with great deeds confuses the issue, which concerns the implications of a serious, literal reading of literature. To reconstruct Randolph's reading of the Augustans, one must restore them to their "real" world. They did not have much success as politicians. Although they embarrassed Walpole and perhaps speeded his fall, their interest was equally unattended by the ministries which succeeded the Robinocracy. The literary opposition was objecting to history, to the state of the world. Their politics were the politics of the imagination, interested in the regeneration through style of a better world. Their satire began with reference to actual political issues and personalities and could always be taken on that level, but the surface of contemporary allusion could not contain its moral energy, and its real momentum was antipolitical.[17]

The Augustan satirists did have decided views on political questions. Their sympathies were Tory. What this meant in a specific case might vary, but Samuel Holt Monk's catalogue of Swift's opinions can represent also those of his fellows:

In economics he was an agrarian; in politics a royalist; in religion a high churchman. He disapproved the founding of the National Bank; could make no sense of a national debt, a gadget invented in his time: he distrusted the new moneyed wealth, the ancestor of modern capitalism which increased the political power and importance of the merchant class, and he found his distrust justified in 1720 by the disastrous collapse of South Sea stocks. Innovation and experimentation in politics he detested and fought. And were he alive, he would fight the abstract state of this century with every weapon within reach.

In Swift was accomplished the transformation of these political views into imaginative literature. Swift's pen had been at the service of the Oxford ministry, but it sharpened in opposition. There were certain limitations on what one could say, of course; a cover for *ad hominem* attack, at once decent and transparent, was needed: "I have therefore since thought of another expedient, frequently practised with great safety and success by satirical writers; which is, that of looking into history for some character bearing a resemblance to the person we would describe and with it the absolute power of altering, adding or suppressing what circumstances we please." This was the central technique of Augustan satire. It was better not to name names if one's meaning was clear enough. The sacrifice involved in this essentially political caution signifies the emergence in pamphleteering of imaginative fiction. The crucial event in Swift's satirical career was the failure of the Tory ministry he supported. Political disappointments expressed a deeper disgust with human nature. His 1714 pamphlet *Some Free Thoughts upon the Present State of Affairs* was "a castigating sermon to his friends, the Tory ministers, who had been measured by the moral test and found wanting." The pamphlet blasts the ministry in which Swift had placed his hopes, emphasizing failures of moral and common sense. It is not satire. Swift's subsequent retirement from politics expressed his disillusion; he was "weary to death of courts and ministers and business and politics. . . . I shall say no more but that I care not to live in storms when I can no longer do service in the ship and am able to get out of it." The importance of this retirement is that it liberated Swift from a contending position within the political struggles and facilitated a satiric stance which consulted something other than political advantage in its political attacks. It was the necessary condition of satire. Swift's reunion with Bolingbroke was on a new plane of politics, "a prolonged satirical crusade against the degeneracy of the times." Prerequisite to this satiric stance, then, was the disappointment of conventional political hopes and the redefinition of politics to exclude the ordinary party channels and issues of interest. Instead, the greatest moral issues of human nature and morality were to be raised. The failure of conventional expectations feeds the ambition of satire.[18]

When the Augustans resorted to satire, they made use of established literary conventions. They assumed that right and wrong, good and evil, could be distinguished and acted upon, and that men were responsible and therefore culpable. Unlike the world of tragedy, which is ordered without reference to human action, the world of satire revolves around the good and bad acts of men and women. Thus, satire requires distinct and contending representative speakers. What Maynard Mack has called the *ethos* of the satire, "the weight of authority that comes from the hearer's estimate of the speaker's character, his *ethos*," locates the good man in the satire. Satire originates in an ironic vision of the world, but is not identical with it. The disparity between how the world seems and what it is initially informs satire, but does not contain it. The central fiction of the satire is the speaker, and it is the reader's response to the speaker's stance that governs his general acceptance of the satire and authenticates its point of view. Maynard Mack has isolated in Pope's satiric verse three speakers, who represent the three general satiric voices: the *vir bonus*, "the man of plain living, high thinking, lasting friendships," whose strictures are reluctantly articulated; the naïf, the *ingenu*, "the simple heart," whose innocence is the unconscious mirror of corruption; and the "public defender" or "hero," whose response is to crisis. The object of a satire may also be variously pictured: openly or covertly, derisively or hysterically, grossly or subtly. The resolution of a satire is a fiction pretending to be the world. Martin Price has written, "A man may write satire because he is indignant, but he may also cultivate his indignation in order to write satire. The talent for irony and ridicule may rise from temperament, but the talent is fostered by a vision of man and the world that gives satire depth and resonance." The satiric stance involves an imaginative act not easily disowned or abandoned without consequence.[19]

The social and political circumstances which encouraged Augustan writers in their characteristic ironic view combined with the satiric form itself to produce in England a remarkable body of writings characterized by a central speaker whose vision of the world is crucial to the proper reading of the work. Swift, Pope, Fielding, and Sterne all wrote literature "that demands that we take account of a voice, of a point of view, of a state of the soul that may also imply a world view and a religion." The reflection of a point of view in the self-conscious posturings of a character/narrator/subject is an innovation of the eighteenth century and a crucial one, especially to the reader who apes the style of his reading. In *To the Place of Wisdom*, Martin Price emphasizes that the world views implicit in this fiction are coherent orders forged in the service of opposition, that identity is a function of distinction. The effect of satiric writing, he argues, is the confrontation of total pictures, founded in particular objections: "Men are not simply limited and partial in their vision; they confront each other with more than different perspectives of a common world." The Augustans habitually perceived what was corrupt as a species of disorder and in reaction developed a fictive, alternative order. Their literature reflects this process: "The internalizing of order makes of each of the limited orders a peculiar pathologic state which, like paranoia, imposes its special vision upon all that confront it. Men are locked up in private worlds, and the more order they achieve within them, the greater the disorder in the larger world of which they are members." These private worlds, imaginatively engendered, are represented in the fictions of the Augustans. They are the response of the imagination to a hateful world. They are also the supposed creations of the satiric speakers who notice what is wrong. The methods of satire are all directed at exposing the chaos that underlies mock order, "a confrontation in which the satirist can engage his subjects in dialogue and pursue the dialectic of their exposure. . . . The dialectic will reveal that their pretended order is a chaos of inconsistency or that the elaborate attempt to sustain the appearance of one order can be explained away in terms of another." Failure clues the satirist in, and failure guides his quest.[20]

The satirist is driven to demand of men that their actions be consistent with their natures in all matters, grave or silly. His own vision only seems to proceed out of the sophisticated recognition of deception and corruption. The drama of satire is ultimately the setting vice gives to a vision of virtue. Thus in Pope's "Epistle to Dr. Arbuthnot" the apocalyptic din of denunciation ceases with the introduction of the good man, the father, whose quiet virtues are thus enhanced by furious contrast:

> *Born to no Pride, inheriting no Strife,*
> *Nor marrying Discord in a Noble Wife,*
> *Stranger to Civil and Religious Rage,*
> *The good Man walk'd innoxious thro' his Age.*

False order dramatically frames imagined true order, and the satirist's rage authenticates his alternative:

> *Oh grant me thus to live, and thus to die!*
> *Who sprung from Kings shall know less joy than I.*

The speaker is father, son, madman, or fool, through each of these attitudes managing differently to uncover the same corruption. Pope's favorite personification of virtue is a father, but virtue is ultimately his own, the son's, to define and identify.[21]

The real community of satire is the one envisioned as the community of the few good men battling wickedness. The satirist recognizes that maturity is in knowing that the world is good without childishly and egotistically insisting that its goodness be proven in one's own case. But this maturity is infrequent, and the dominant satiric mode is outrage expressed in precisely the egocentric way—the world as "I" see it is how the world is; as it treats *me,* so it treats man. In his *Lives* of the poets, Dr. Johnson was critical of Swift and Pope for just this reason: "From the letters that pass between him and Pope it might be inferred that they, with Arbuthnot and Gay, had engrossed all the understanding and virtue of mankind, that their merits filled the world; or that there was no hope of more. They show the age involved in darkness and shade the picture with sullen emulation." Dr. Johnson has been criticized for misunderstanding his subjects, but in fact he understands them quite rightly—as they saw it, theirs was the community of hope; virtue was alone sustained by their advocacy. The satirist's community is built on his independent pride. His friends are those, equally independent, who have proven themselves worthy in the same effort. That they are outnumbered and beleaguered is their mutual reassurance and glory. Friendship coincides with the community of embattled virtue, and one's circle of friends defined in this way comprises the community of good men:

> *Names, which I long have lov'd, nor lov'd in vain,*
> *Rank'd with their Friends, not number'd with their Train;*
> *And if yet higher the proud List should end,*
> *Still let me say! No Follower, but a Friend.*

And:

> *To Virtue only and Her Friends, a Friend.*

It is the wickedness and corruption all around which justifies, even demands, the satirist's excesses. The pride of the satirist is as much that he is lonely as that he is good. His public self is a conscious response to corruption and degeneracy. The speaker denounces evil and is himself an opposing human possibility. The sustaining energy in all this is rage—righteous rage at an unrighteous world. Frustration and resentment all too often inform moral feeling with their demonic energy.

> *Ask you what Provocation I have had?*
> *The strong Antipathy of Good to Bad.*
> *When Truth or Virtue an Affront endures,*
> *Th' Affront is mine, my friend and should be yours.*

There is an imaginative hoarding of power to oneself; a moral role is played out to the logical end. For Pope in these poems, and more generally for the Augustan writers and their most literal readers, virtue ran truest in the moment of testing. Virtue and friendship formed a reinforcing circle, a revolution away from the real world. Virtue became a partisan notion.[22]

In the service of virtue, vicious and angry methods may appear justified, thus the satirist's resort to naming names. The Augustan convention is that books do matter, that satire can topple empires. The naming of names is an unconscious admission that moral sentiments alone will not do, that poetry must enter the political world of reputations and power directly. Under the disinterested, disdainful cover of literature, the poet uses his effective weapons to make his moral felt in the rough and tumble of the real world. Name calling and innuendo are employed to advance grand themes. The nobler claims are informed by, and in turn legitimate, the name calling. What is argued in these works is a different justification from politics for politics. The poet's anger originates in humanist claims for the meaning of books. Corruption's particular affront is to his art. Thus the Augustans' concern for the breakdown of language focuses their political perceptions: "They saw it as symptom of a decline of culture, and the greatest satires of the age have this as their central themes." The very meaning of words is not safe in such chaotic times. This preoccupation particularized the threat of degenerate times as Augustan satirists responded to it. Pope's outrage is as much the result of wounded humanist pretensions as anything else. The weapons he uses consciously and unconsciously furiously reassert the sacredness and power of words. In this way, he can continue to believe that good books will make good men, that the writer of good books is among the best men, and above all, that the reading of good books is not empty cultivation but the most serious business of life. This sustaining faith is especially important, since it offers to the reader signposts for a degenerate age, and the justification for the descent into *ad hominem* attacks. Whatever else satire may come to mean, its lasting impression connects a citizen's outrage at a corrupt social world, his laments for a shattered past, with a remedy; not resignation, but full-voiced indignation is the dominant tone:

Time was, a sober Englishman wou'd knock
His servants up, and rise by five a'clock,
Instruct his Family in ev'ry rule,
And send his Wife to church, his Son to school.
To worship like his Fathers, was his care;
To teach their frugal Virtues to his Heir;
To prove, that Luxury could never hold;
And place, on good Security, his Gold.

And:

Yes, I am proud; I must be proud to see
Men not afraid of God, afraid of me.

And:

Who'er offends, at some unlucky Time
Slides into Verse, and hitches in a Rhyme.[23]

In a discussion of the possible effect of Augustan satire on its reader John Randolph, one final aspect remains to be examined: the outer limits of human perception to which it might lead. Jonathan Swift is especially useful here, not only because his fate was the one Randolph feared for himself but also because he most pointedly raised and exemplified the problem. The focus of Swift's satire is not *them* but *us*. The corruption he describes is so overwhelming that the satiric speaker himself cannot withstand it. Swift's concern is with the hurts incurred by the righteous. This concern is shrewd and difficult. By refusing to exempt the satiric speaker from the corruption of the world, he sharpens his indictment but makes it harder to perceive reliably. *Gulliver's Travels* presents at one level the story of what happens to a man whose perception of corruption is sure but limited by his unreal expectations. If, as W. B. C. Watkins has written, "disillusioned idealism is, of course, the state of mind which usually generates the satiric spirit," and "the satirist lashes his fellows from the vantage point of at least implied superiority," Swift's satire is equally turned against the false idealism which engenders a suspect superiority. Gulliver's voyages expose him to a hideous world too often taken to be Swift's. His disgust with mankind upon his return has also been seen as Swift's. In fact, to Swift this response is the proof of Gulliver's weakness of mind in the first place. Gulliver's misanthropy parodies the partial vision of a morally incomplete man: "Swift argues that the man really in danger of becoming a misanthrope is he who holds an unrealistic view of the potentialities of human nature and who expects that men can somehow transcend their limitations and become, shall we say, angels." The figure of Gulliver, railing against his fellow men because they are human, is the necessary corollary of self-consciousness in the satiric writing of the Augustans. For Swift, the moral risks of satire were as serious as its moral purposes.[24]

The figure of Gulliver and what he represents deserve attention here because they help to explain the themes to which the Augustan satiric stance might lead. It is significant that Swift and Gulliver have been so often confused, because the ironic meaning of the figure has been all too easy to miss. Gulliver is, after all, as Thomas Edwards has written, a logical response to his voyages: "The point is that both Gulliver and Pope's P. [Pope's poetic persona] find virtue achievable only in utter rejection of worldly subtleties and sophisms, that both are theoretically right to do so (the world being what it is), but that both end up seeming obsessed and mad to an eye that views them from any part of that rejected world." The eye which sees corruption in England can, in the absence of some restraining principle, move to Gulliver's outer limits. For nothing can stand against the standard of ideal virtue. Moral idealism does not contain within itself the proper restraints to make it apply to the world. These must come from the moral idealist himself. Some common sense must temper the satirist's rage to keep him humane, or his honesty will drive him mad. Swift and Pope were usually controlled in their satires. They were, after all, writing.[25]

The satiric stance, unchecked, seeks to judge the world by its highest professed standards. It does not take the limits of an imperfect world into account, because it does not understand that principles are usually goals. The necessary isolation of the lone, just man ends in solitude and bitterness. Dr. Johnson understood that solitude undermines the compromise of balance necessary to living in the world, and for this reason considered solitude a dangerous state; he was not alone in fearing its effects. The satiric stance, taken up in opposition to a corrupt community and pursued immoderately, leads to solitude and courts its dangers:

> When politics, with all the misimaginations of self it implies, is no longer a strong enough figure of antagonism, the old dialectic can only be transformed into a confrontation between the solitary self and *death*. The solitary man considers not other men, or their collective embodiment in social and political institutions, but tokens of mortality, churchyards or deserted villages (both monuments to ruined, lost lives), some ruined form of a past whose human purposes and feelings have been forgotten, whose meaning can only be validated by the death of the solitary contemplating mind itself, as it *enters* the oblivion it has pondered and found inscrutable but wholly compelling.

This describes, of course, the literary movement away from Augustan satire toward the Age of Sensibility and ultimately Romanticism; it is important here because it illustrates an inherent direction of the satiric attitude. One is led by the disgust with human vice to a disdain for the human community, for humanity, and, at least rhetorically, for life itself. This mistake—and it is a mistake—is made by Gulliver, as by King Lear and Timon of Athens: "Like King Lear, he begins in simplicity, grows into sophistication, and ends in madness. Unlike King Lear he is never cured." The disparity between the ideal of virtue and the human failure to realize it unbalances Guilliver. Pursuing the satirist's course without a firm grasp of the possible or a viable self-consciousness, he finds himself unable to live with other men. He lacks a realistic notion of his own limitations and is betrayed by himself. Gulliver takes the Augustan satirist's claims too literally. His is the human problem of moral outrage. Speaking of Gulliver, Samuel Holt Monk declares:

> The grim joke is that Gulliver himself is the supreme instance of a creature smitten with pride. His education has somehow failed. . . . the countries he visited, like the Kingdom of Heaven, are all within us. The ultimate danger of these travels was precisely the one that destroyed Gulliver's humanity—the danger that in his explorations he would discover something that he was not strong enough to face. This befell him and he took refuge in a sick and morbid pride that alienated him from his species and taught him the gratitude of the Pharisee—"Lord, I thank Thee that I am not as other men."

These observations implicate any incautious imitator of the Augustan stance—for example, and under the appropriate conditions, John Randolph.[26]

The intention of the foregoing has been to establish the kind of reader Randolph was and to emphasize certain themes in some of the books that he read. He was not alone in reading these books; his selections seem to have been reasonably typical for his time and culture. Randolph's literal-minded and dramatic nature were, however, exaggerated and atypical if not unique, and the interaction between his nature and his reading produced some peculiar exaggerations of commonly accepted intellectual and political conventions. Nor did Randolph's reading focus exclusively on the Augustans. He read widely in continental literature, loved Milton and Shakespeare as much or more than he did Pope and Swift, and was at times a budding classicist. What is worth singling out about his reading of the Augustan satirists, and what makes it important to examine them separately, is the subsequent and central role their assumptions and methods were to play in his career of opposition. It was in their works, in the stances analyzed and detailed in the preceding discussion, that Randolph found the models for his own speeches and positions. This discussion, despite its apparent lack of focus on Randolph, has shown the central connection between the figure of opposition and the source of his stance. The disillusioned idealism, the exaggerated belief in the power of the word, the uncompromising, nostalgic conception of political honor, the rude resort to name calling, the entire imagining of an alternative to a corrupt political world, itself the reflection of a changing and alien social world, and of the satiric speaker who opposes himself to this conventional degraded world—these were to become Randolph's stock in trade, to form what little political method he had. His historian cannot overlook the correspondence between his career and the import of this particular aspect of his early reading. It is lurking and implicit in much of Randolph, rising out of his convictions and character. His assumptions and those of the satirists just examined are connected by his reading of them. An open and candid juxtaposition argues, I believe, that the connection was intense and learning and lasting. That Randolph read these authors most carefully and was informed by them is certain. The evidence, however, remains circumstantial, and the case can only be completed by the public use that he subsequently made of this humanist education. That will be a central concern of the concluding chapters.[27]

❧ 4 ❧

Political Education

The sources of Randolph's politics cannot be distinguished from the traditions in which he was reared or the books he read. His expectations of political life were decisively shaped by his class, his *patria,* and his experience of the tumultuous events of the American Revolution. On matters of state, as on everything else, Randolph's ideas were fixed early and interpreted literally. He never got over the heady emotional triumph of the Revolution, whose enthusiastic mood he caught as a boy. Everything that succeeded it proved a disappointment and a degeneration. Henry Adams placed Randolph's birth at the untimely moment "just as the downward plunge began, and every moment made the outlook drearier and more awful" for those of his kind, and this comment is appropriate to Randolph's political education as well. It seemed as if it could not have been better; it turned out very badly indeed. Virginia's version of English republican thinking in the immediate context of the "spirit of '76" created in Randolph a political expectation which America was bound to disillusion.[1]

Randolph's political traditions were English and "country," aristocratic as well as republican. Hugh Blair Grigsby's description of Randolph's library shows it to have contained not only the great historical works in English "but the tracts and essays which the contest about Whig and Tory for a century had called forth." Recent scholarship has emphasized how very dependent colonial political ideas were upon the English tradition of opposition, the commonwealth radicals, and, especially, the "country party." J. G. A. Pocock has characterized its conclusions this way:

It is now apparent that the Revolution employed—and in some measure was occasioned by—an oppositional ideology that had been nurtured in British politics for nearly a century. Late in the reign of Charles II the idea developed that the main threat to parliamentary liberty lay in the crown's effective employment of an enlarged patronage power. During the reigns of William III and Anne, England–Great Britain had emerged as a major European and Atlantic war-making power, fortified by an expanding, professional army and a system of public credit and national debt. Both of these phenomena were seen by their adversaries as not only increasing the crown's patronage powers, but also multiplying the incidence in society of individuals whose modes of social and political existence entailed a dependence upon government that made them a menace to their neighbors.

Consequently, an ideology opposing all of these things arose, variously known to historians as "Old Whig," "Commonwealth," or . . . "Country." It stressed the independence of the organs of mixed government (Kings, Lords, and Commons; executive, judiciary, and legislative) from one another, as against the supposed attempts of patronage manipulators to bring the second and third branches into dependence on the first; and it stressed the role of the independent proprietors (ideally the landowner, although merchants were not excluded) as against the rentier, officier, placeman, pensioner, and (lowest of all in the scale of humanity) stock-jobber or speculator in public funds.

Although historians have yet to fix precisely the limits and role of this "country" thinking in American colonial life, it certainly figured prominently in the outlook of the Virginia gentry to which Randolph belonged. The absolute connection between virtue and independence in a setting of land ownership was something Randolph learned at his mother's knee and never forgot. Extensive reading in English literature and history, and in the literature of American independence, only confirmed him in these fundamental teachings. It is therefore important to examine some of the particular emphases of country thinking to recapitulate Randolph's starting assumptions.[2]

The country way of looking at politics involved primarily a series of worries about the dangerous encroachments of *power* against *liberty*. That power *always* corrupts, that political power must always be suspect, is the indispensable attitude of the country world view. The suspicion of power was sensible for the English gentry who entertained it. If the origins of this viewpoint were thus "relative," however, its preachments were not. Good country thinking began with this suspicion and offered two kinds of advice. It identified the enemy, and it put forward a positive vision of the good state, a nostalgic mix of historical myth and self-righteous fantasy based upon the concept of the virtuous man. (The resemblance of the country party's program to the Augustan satirists' notions was, of course, not coincidental; they were about the same business.) The gentry were at their best in denouncing and identifying the enemies of liberty. J. H. Plumb has called this "the politics of resentment." The combination of fierce antagonism to the governing power with a nostalgic rhetoric invoking virtue and the saving traditional values characterized this political outlook.[3]

In the country view, the foundation of society properly consisted of landowners, the only element of society whose material independence of centralizing corrupting power could be counted upon with any certainty. All political particulars followed from this assumption: militias were good, standing armies dangerous; landed property was good, 'capital subversive of liberty; elected representatives were good, ministers dangerous; and so on. In Pocock's words, "The function of property is to guarantee the citizen his independence. The dependence from which it must save him is the political dependence upon others which constitutes corruption, and the modes of economic being which it is important to avoid are those in which property and political dependence go hand in hand." The apprehension of the increasingly powerful role of money in politics, as a force in policy-making or as a motive of policy-makers, triggered the country conscience and rage. And as Pocock also points out, this awareness grew "out of an ultimately mythical idealization of the role in politics of propertied independence. . . ." This critical view of modern times, founded on unreal memories of a golden age and an abstract notion of independent virtue, was as clear as it was fantastic in its prescriptions for reform. Denying as it did the existence of government and society separate from the moral individuals who made up Parliament and its constituencies, this country thinking always had some*one* to blame and therefore to be removed. If times were bad, there were bad men to be blamed and recourse to be had in their replacement. Retrenchment and reform were the eternal watchwords. If money was corrupting politics, the remedy was to eliminate the debt, administer necessary government frugally, reduce the number of public servants to be paid. Retrenchment and reform necessitated, above all, a *return to first principles,* the restoration of the original purity of good government. The expectation of decay, which, as Pocock has shown, was central to a world view that could not "admit of change," and the explanation of what was politically intolerable in terms of degeneration from a previous standard of excellence, culminated in insistence upon the static, restorative nature of political solutions and in a characteristic hue of moral urgency. That things now were bound to be very hard; that a return to first principles, abstracted from and located in some nostalgic golden age, was imperative; and that everyday politics involved the assertion of conflicting moral stances, with political language reflecting the apocalyptic energy of this kind of situation— all these opinions were country-party staples. There was always the possibility that a great man might appear whose appeal would unite all classes in a return to social virtue. It would be, of course, especially necessary to watch such a man carefully to keep him on the strait and narrow, lest he lead us down the primrose.[4]

The country habit of mind, therefore, was to insist on abstract principle, which is not at all the same thing as abstract theory, as a continuing operative function in everyday political life. The country party claimed to speak *for* the people, although it was not democratic. Included in its nostaligic romance was a happy yeomanry, specially and mutually bound to the independent aristocracy, which was its proper public mouthpiece. The values of country life were extolled, as opposed to the horrors of the city, the scene of corruption and moneyed politics. The cult of independence, with its Horatian overtones of retirement and distance, was the central moral myth of this thinking. There was a literary, posturing quality in the articulators of the country ideology, a quality that intensified over distance and time. They tended to expect *great things* of the rising generation, or to be excessively disappointed in the degenerate aristocratic youth. Bolingbroke turned "my eyes from the generation that is going off to the generation that is coming on the stage. I expect good from them. . . ." But the energy of his young friends "went into romantic nostalgia and poetry. Only Pitt among them would master the art of politics." And not to the entire satisfaction of his fellows.[5]

It is not accidental that this organized suspiciousness produced politicians ill at ease with practical politics; that was in large measure the point. One observes in country politics the same self-righteousness and absorption with principle as in Augustan satire. There was anger about many of the same things and for many of the same reasons. One suspects that the country position was basically not susceptible to compromise (although on specific issues compromise might be possible) because it objected to the very way of the modern world and the kinds of actions necessary to accommodate to it. Country politics was above all an expression of a world view, resentful and moralizing and apocalyptic, intermittently hysterical, a way of articulating a total protest at the passing of particular times by inventing a memory of better times than those, which were then said to be better than the times now present. It is important to present some account of the mood and expectations it engendered because it was these as much as anything specific which proved influential. In Virginia, the specific issues that kept the opposition in some working order were often unclearly perceived. The rhetoric and apprehension, however, might easily come to fit different issues. In order to place John Randolph in the proper context of political thinking, therefore, it is necessary to get to the meaning of the rhetoric and assumptions he read about and absorbed long distance.

At the core of country thinking, as in Augustan literature, one senses the assertion of a particular kind of individual man claiming for himself the virtues he believes are lost to public life in his time. Surely this belief haunted the cult of independence: principle was understood as individual honor, integrity, *character*. The character of a people and its rulers is what country politics comes down to. And it is character as virtue under attack that typically triggered the country response.

Growing up in Virginia at the end of the eighteenth century, John Randolph encountered country thinking as a matter of course. It was embedded in the traditions of his class. The self-conscious gentry, Englishmen in Virginia, were of all American colonials the most prone to country thinking, with its emphasis on independence and republican political virtue and its apprehension of decline. J. R. Pole describes Virginia's political tradition in these terms: "What really mattered here was the essential connection between independent circumstances and independent principles. Expressions such as this [George Mason on gov-

ernance by men] 'of independent circumstances and principles' stood at the centre of Whig social thought; such men
would never be swept into enthusiastic movements or allow
themselves to be corrupted by party." The control of the
gentry was relatively secure until threatened by British imperial energy after the Seven Years' War. It was the struggles with Parliament that activated the country thinking
implicit all along in the beliefs of the Virginia gentry, beliefs which became identified with the American Revolution. "The fathers of the Revolution—Dickinson, Adams,
Jefferson—feared that English rule was seeking to perpet-
uate this corruption in America; and the Revolution once
achieved, Jefferson and his heirs continued to dread that
government, great cities, banks, concentrations of finance
capital and professionalized armies and navies . . . would
corrupt. . . ." The Revolution as waged and understood in
Virginia provided Randolph's lasting political education
and was the occasion of the deepest impression of country
ways on him.[6]

Born in 1773, Randolph grew up in the great years of
the Virginian and American political founders and in an
atmosphere of intense political interest. Numbered among
his family connections and acquaintances were many distinguished patriots of the struggle for independence and
the subsequent attempts at national republican government. Although he himself lacked any early professed political ambitions, Randolph's political opinions were as precocious and literal and boldly offered as his other opinions.
His boyhood friend Littleton Waller Tazewell remembered
the "precocious proclivity of John Randolph to the investigation of political subjects." Patriotism was the special
privilege and responsibility of his class, and Randolph saw
it in this light even when he himself was disinclined to enter
active politics. In 1781 he fled with his family before the in-
vasion of Benedict Arnold. He always talked as if he had, in
fact, experienced British tryranny himself. Years later, in
describing his first encounter with his half brother Henry

St. George Tucker, who was born just days before the flight, he said, "The first time I ever saw that gentleman we were trying to get out of the way of the British." Revolutionary lore was family lore to young Randolph, and it is not surprising that he grew up equating Virginian history with American history.[7]

The fundamental fact of this political learning seems to be that *patria* to him meant English Virginia, then becoming American Virginia. He was fifteen before he saw a map of any country but Virginia, and sixteen when the new federal government was inagurated in New York. It is not surprising that there is no substantial evidence of his having any concept of an American *nation* in his early experience. His was a Virginian's outlook. But unlike the older Virginians, such as Jefferson, Washington, and Henry, who acquired a national vision in the course of forging an American cause and fighting a war of national liberation, and unlike the younger Virginians, who were born under the new constitution, Randolph grew up in that odd period of time when Virginia was in fact a large territorial republic confederated with but not joined to other American states, and he never learned, as some of his contemporaries apparently did, to supplant his first loyalty with American nationalism. John Alden sensibly reminds us of this point in *The First South:*

Above all, the War of Independence aroused an American emotion. Virginians served at Boston and Quebec, Carolinians at Brandywine and Germantown, Yankees at Trenton and Yorktown. The 'hard core' of the Revolutionary forces was the Continental Army; and 'Continental' was, or rather soon became, a synonym for 'American.' Few of the men who served in it could afterward be easily convinced that they fought only for their home state, or for a South, or for a North.

Randolph was a loyal and devoted servant of the American nation, but his loyalty proceeded from what can only be called his local attachments. "I confess that I have (and I am not at all ashamed to own it) an hereditary attachment to the State which gave me birth. I shall act upon it as long as I act on this floor or anywhere else; I shall feel it when I am no longer capable of action anywhere. . . ." William Cabell Bruce places England after Virginia in Randolph's loyalties. To the extent that he did owe England special allegiance, this was cultural and emotional; England was the country of his imagination and of better times. The United States, for Randolph, came after Virginia as the object of political allegiance, and meant "the good old thirteen United States," the partners of '76, on the self-respecting co-operative terms of '76.[8]

Indeed, Randolph's experience led him toward a particularist identification of Virginia as his nation. He came to intellectual awareness when negotiations between the states about the nature and purpose of a national union were the burden of national public business. The opinions of his family's circle were uniformly anti-Federalist. His uncle Theodorick Bland was among the leading opponents of ratification at the Virginia Convention of 1788, as were his Tucker relations. He particularly admired "that best of men" the staunch anti-Federalist Thomas Tudor Tucker. Writing to Josiah Quincy in 1813, Randolph reminded him, "You know I was an Anti-Federalist when hardly breeched."[9]

Randolph was in New York on March 4, 1789, and witnessed Washington's first inauguration. His comments reflect his early attitude of suspicion and worse toward this new national government: "I saw Washington but could not hear him take the oath to support the Federal Constitution. The Constitution was in its chrysalis state. I saw what Washington did not see; but two other men in Virginia saw it—George Mason and Patrick Henry—*the poison under its wings.*" Lacking any real understanding of why a strong national government might be a necessary good, Randolph characteristically understood it as a potential threat to state liberty and never acknowledged its primary sovereignty. (Like another institution, it was a necessary evil at best and susceptible of abolition.) Many of Randolph's generation learned to appreciate American nationality as a concern superior to state patriotism. It was typical of Randolph that he never saw the need to change his opinions, which were after all the traditional ones. To the end of his career, he called Virginia his "country" even on the floor of the Congress. "When I speak of my country, I mean the Commonwealth of Virginia."[10]

What did Randolph's commitment to Virginia mean politically? The primary political event was the Revolution, and its significance for powerful Virginians was relatively straightforward. To begin with, the Revolution was a moral drama in the old, country sense. Jack Greene has described Landon Carter's feeling that "the American Revolution was a moral drama. With his fellow Americans he was waging a war on corruption, a battle against nothing less than the imperfect nature of man." Others have shown that the American fear of corruption and tyranny was deeply, even hysterically, felt. The colonists were at a fever pitch of emotion. This high-spiritedness was the crucial triggering element for all those Whiggish anxieties that characterized the American turning on England. The moral framework of the Revolution carried with it in Virginia, as in New England, an expectation that virtue somehow held the key to victory and vindication:

In Virginia, especially, the public and private literature was filled with fears of the conspicuous consumption and high living of the aristocracy. There the attacks on luxury and extravagance represented not so much the resentful protests of the socially aspiring, as was often the case in the less structured and more egalitarian societies of the north; rather they represented the uneasy introspections of the ruling planters themselves, fearful of what some took to be social corrosion, apparently caused by the fantastic growth of pride, ostentation and debts among the would-be aristocrats.[11]

To win independence would be to reassert the old virtues and stem the corrupting tide that Virginians could not merely disclaim. Indeed, they saw it not as something external to them but as the central social problem of their society. The blaming of England offered a solution to Virginia's moral problem. Thus, while independence might—and did—mean vindication, the whole issue was posed in such a way that the meaning of the Revolution would always be related to one's perception of Virginia's gentlefolk. Their decline and degeneration would compromise the historic success of the achievement of independence, which was supposed to have preserved their regime. To the Virginian the meaning of the Revolution involved a test of the health of his society.

This interpretation of the Revolution also emphasized the abuses committed by corrupt governments. There was a heightened sensitivity to possible abuses of power, which was the legacy of the struggle with England. Thus, Norman Risjord has argued, "Nurtured on the idealism that attended the birth of the republic, Randolph received his political instruction from men whose greatest fear was arbitrary power in the hands of a single man." This sensitivity also manifested itself in a special sense of Virginian prerogatives, originally called out by the encroachments of the crown but waiting like a chip on the shoulder for any signs of American tyranny. In the war years, this attitude manifested itself in what John Alden has called "the First South," which "feared lest they [the southern states] become a minority in an American union dominated by a Northern majority, lest they suffer in consequence."[12]

The comparative absence in Revolutionary Virginia of economic and class conflicts resulted in a strong sense of state identity, in general agreement on the meaning of independence, and also in the continuation of pre-Revolutionary political ways. As Thomas Jefferson wrote in 1826, remembering the post-revolutionary period: "The abuses of monarchy had so filled our minds that we imagined everything republican that was not monarchy. We had not yet penetrated to the mother principle that governments are republican only in proportion as they embodied the will of their people, and execute it. Hence, our first constitutions had really no leading principle in them, but experience and reflection." Ringing statements of principle warned Virginians of the host of dangers to liberty, but did not necessarily offer guidelines for internal social change. The gentlemen freeholders continued to govern the commonwealth to their own satisfaction. This meant that the country party attitude persisted, for as Gordon Wood has shown, "as long as politics remained such a highly personal business, essentially involving bitter rivalry among small elite groups for the rewards of state authority, wealth, power, and prestige, the Whig distinction between country and court, legislative and executive, people and rulers, remained a meaningful conception for describing American politics." The Revolution seemed to Virginians to validate the attitude of opposition that had excited the fight for independence. The events of the 1700's confirmed country-party suspiciousness, and the events of independence marked a golden age against which future American government might be judged. And, perhaps above all, the Revolution established a standard of character, of disinterested patriotism, of the conduct of public business with integrity, by good men. This vision of public life was in all respects taken from a period of extreme crisis and was therefore a dangerous standard by which to judge ordinary times.[13]

The political culture absorbed by John Randolph was thus both particularist and traditional. The American Revolution was the source for an understanding of what was proper in politics and how to respond to what was not. He took literally the injunctions and apocalyptic moods of the "spirit of '76" and its incorporated country doctrine. The Revolution always remained the archetypal political event, the ultimate reference point. Writing in 1815 to Senator James Lloyd of Massachusetts, a Hartford Convention man, in a letter intended to dissuade New England separatists, Randolph came back again and again to the Revolution. It was not nationalism he appealed to but the shared experience of that great battle against tyranny:

What! Boston, the cradle of American independence, to whose aid Virginia stept forth unsolicited, when the whole vengeance of the British ministry was wreaked on that devoted town. Boston! now to desert us, in our utmost need, to give up her old ally to ravage, at the price of her own impunity from the common enemy—I cannot, will not believe it . . . agreeing that the foreign policy which resolved in war was a bad one. But they have reduced us to such a condition, that nothing short of the knife will now do. "We must *fight*, Mr. Speaker!" said Patrick Henry in 1775, when his sagacious mind saw there was nothing else left for us but manly resistance or slavish submission. . . .

It may be said, that in time of peace the people of every portion of our confederacy find themselves too happy to think of division; that the sufferings of a war, like this, are requisite, to rouse them to the necessary exertion: war is incident to all government; and wars I very much fear will be wickedly declared, and weakly waged, even by the New England confederacy, as they have been by every government (not even excepting the Roman republic), of which we have any knowledge; and it does appear to me no slight presumption that the evil has not yet reached the point of amputation, when peace alone will render us the happiest (as we are the freest) people under the sun; at least too happy to think of dissolving the Union, which as it carried us through the war of our revolution, will I trust, bear us triumphant through that in which we have been plunged, by the incapacity and corruption [*sic*], neither willing to maintain the relations of peace, nor able to conduct the operations of war.

The Union was not mystical, but it was useful, and grounded as it was in the sacrifices and glories of the Revolution, it had to be given the benefit of some doubts. Randolph found in the War of Independence the political lessons necessary for his own times; it is a direct and deciding reference. In the letter just quoted, the principle that tyranny may legitimately be overthrown is outweighed by the example of that Union which independence had effected. His argument is a kind of explication of the Revolutionary text; it is interesting and significant that he does not appeal to the Constitution. The Constitution, to Randolph, was the compromise on paper that formalized the principles of the Revolution. He consulted the event, not its result.[14]

Randolph's view of politics, informed by country conditions and the great moment of the colonial revolt against English tyranny as well as anti-Federalist opposition to the new constitution, was crystallized in his first political activity, in which he was an increasingly fiery partisan of the Jeffersonian opposition. Bred to be suspicious of the new government, Randolph detected dangerous signs of pomp and corruption from the start. As a student in New York and Philadelphia he was not preoccupied with politics, but he was observant and interested. In 1813, he recollected that he saw "the coronation (such in fact it was)" of General Washington in March, 1789, and heard the speeches given by Ames and Madison when they took their seats in the House of Representatives. At the time, he had had more to say in his letters about the ceremony than about its sinister impact. By 1794, however, Randolph was writing more sharply about governmental affairs, supporting Madison's challenges to Hamilton in Congress and waxing furious about delinquent and tardy southern legislators: "Thus are the interests of the Southern states basely betrayed by the indolence of some and the villainy of others of her Statesmen." Randolph was sympathetic to the Republican faction. Like many other young Jeffersonians, he was skeptical in religion and very taken with the radicalism of the French Revolution. His correspondence of the mid-nineties abounds in the term "citizen" and uses the new calendar of the Revolution: "Bizarre, 16 September/23rd of Independence." But the Francophilia was neither especially lasting nor deep. Rather, it was the badge of those Republican politics that Randolph certainly accepted when his mind was occupied with political questions.[15]

After assuming his brother's responsibilities and residence in 1796, Randolph naturally turned his attention to the civic duties that accompanied them, finally standing for

Congress in 1799. His ambition for office had surprisingly little effect on his political opinions, providing instead a series of challenges for him to meet, characteristically, head on. His political education resulted in a series of expectations and understandings about how public life was to be conducted. The questions that politics involved had already been defined: politics was the business of categorizing public issues and then taking the principled stand on them. The categories were those operative in the American Revolution and its underlying English and Virginian country tradition. One was suspicious of power. One did not temporize on principle. Character was the basic value, not compromise. The best way to resolve a difficult situation was to return to first principles. Randolph's own "first principles" were the libertarian, particularist, independent principles of the Virginian Revolution. He entered public life at twenty-five as Jefferson's associate in the crusade to return the United States to those principles that Federalist tyranny had corrupted, to do what he understood the patriots to have done in 1776 when they returned the nation to principles that English tyranny had corrupted. One of the great problems with country thinking was its reluctance to accept change and its tendency instead to answer altered realities with nostalgic reruns. The nostalgia for the old days transformed the past into something marvelous, and this false standard of comparison made the present appear far worse than it really was.

The American Revolution was to some extent grounded in this resistance to change. Randolph, the product of Virginia's provincial gentry, seems never to have understood the transcendent sense of the American struggle. Merrill Peterson has shown that Thomas Jefferson's politics had "roots in English law and government" and that then, under pressure of reading and events, they moved "from the particularism, the local patois, of English law and government to the rationalism and universalism of the natural rights philosophy." For Randolph the universals of

Thomas Jefferson never made much sense except locally, as affirmations of the rights of freeborn Virginians. Randolph's sense of Revolutionary times was not so abstract as Jefferson's; he perceived the drama and absorbed the mood of the eternal battle of the righteous and independent patriot to restore the true values of the golden age against corrupt and menacing tyranny. The Revolution was something he grew up hearing about and expecting to fight in. It involved a series of expectations. These expectations surfaced in his first encounter as a public politician.[16]

In 1799 Randolph stood as a candidate for Congress from the Southside Virginia district of Charlotte, Prince Edward, Cumberland, and Buckingham counties. His candidacy was the result of careful planning by prominent citizens, particularly Creed Taylor, a distinguished attorney and politician. From the first, Randolph protested that he had no ambition for office and no qualifications; this protestation he continued throughout his life, but he was not impelled to refrain from standing for office: "You must be equally conscious with myself that the idea of representing this district in Congress never originated with me; and I believe I may with truth assert that it is one I never should have entertained, had it not been suggested, in the first instance, by my friends. . . . interest I have none, and did I possess any, my principles would forbid my using it on such an occasion . . ." Randolph's premiere public appearance was exceptionally challenging and dramatic. He was chosen to speak opposite Patrick Henry, who had been summoned out of retirement by George Washington himself to run for the Virginia Senate. Henry had opposed the federal constitution, but he was disturbed by the reaction of Virginia's Republicans to Federalist legislation, and especially by the threats of interposition and worse posed by the Kentucky and Virginia Resolutions, which had been passed in opposition to the Alien and Sedition Acts. Henry appeared in the unfamiliar stance of reason and compromise, to argue caution and restraint. He was old and sick (he died soon after his election in 1799), and his legendary powers had certainly diminished. Still, he was Patrick Henry, and for John Randolph to face him was an unusually demanding debut.[17]

Randolph dared to answer Henry at Charlotte Courthouse, Virginia, on March county court day in 1799. The veneration in which his countrymen held the great Henry excited attention, drawing "to the court green and its environs almost every white man in Prince Edward and Charlotte Counties who was not sick, halt or blind; even emptying Hampden Sidney Collge in Prince Edward County, twelve or fifteen miles away, of its professors and students." Henry had been Virginia's popular tribune and was therefore especially beloved by the people. Randolph lacked a reputation but represented the current opinions of the people: they loved Henry still but had little use for his current cause. Since only fragmentary and unsatisfactory records of the actual confrontation survive, it has naturally been the occasion of considerable biographical invention. The popular account of the meeting, however, reveals certain themes which sound authentic enough and which present a picture of John Randolph as he entered national politics after twenty-five years at home. Randolph's biographers, especially Garland, have sought to establish that his debut was spectacular and successful, and that he was Patrick Henry's anointed and deserving successor in oratory and principle and popularity. The evidence concerning this first encounter simply does not support these conclusions, or the contrary ones. Henry spoke. Then Randolph spoke. And they were both elected.[18]

Henry's argument seems to have been one of prudence and caution, dwelling on the dangers of division and civil war inherent in any rash contradiction by one state of duly enacted federal legislation. While supporting the theoretical right of the people to overthrow a tyrannical regime, Henry reserved this expedient for only the gravest of threats to liberty, and denied that the situation in 1799 constituted such a threat. The several accounts of Randolph's reply agree that he asserted that the Alien and Sedition Acts *did* constitute a sufficient threat to liberty to warrant the interposition of the state. In 1817, remembering the occasion, Randolph said, "I was asked if I justified the establishment of the armory for the purpose of opposing Mr. Adams' administration. I said I did; that I could not conceive any case in which the people could not be intrusted with arms; and that the use of them to oppose oppressive measures was in principle the same, whether those of the administration of Lord North or that of Mr. Adams." Randolph apparently insisted that he was merely following Henry's own illustrious example—Garland's reconstruction is interesting here, even if not verifiable: "But the gentleman has taught me a very different lesson from that he is now disposed to enjoin on us." Randolph's actual argument had been first and most eloquently articulated by Henry in the Revolutionary days. His own response to the Federalist regime followed to the letter Virginia's response to British tyranny. As he said very plausibly in 1817, it does not matter whether the threat be English or federal; if a threat is real, it is the response that matters. Henry himself appears to have acknowledged Randolph's representation of a father-son relationship between them: "Young man, you call me father; then my son, I have something to say unto thee—keep justice, keep truth and you will live to think differently."[19]

It is not stretching the evidence too far to suggest that Randolph's first political argument was at once typical of his continuing political concerns and the logical result of his education. He answered Patrick Henry as a son answers a father, using the father's own example to justify behavior that seemed rash. Their differences *were* generational. Randolph exhibited at Charlotte Courthouse a literalness about what he had been taught. His models, he felt, did not have to be changed with changing circumstance. He understood principle as the inflexible sum of lessons learned.

The Revolution was practical instance enough. Henry's essentially prudential reservations in 1799 made no sense to the eager student of the Henry of 1775. Randolph had indeed caught the mood and tone of the Revolutionary Henry, and expected them to be consistently relevant to the political realities he experienced. There is nothing in his attitude to suggest that his experience thus far had tempered his young man's literalness or trimmed or animated his still-life expectations. As it happened, his particular frame of mind suited that of his Virginian electorate, and he was sent to Congress. There is nothing unusual in itself in this young man's fervent and principled disappointment in Henry's inconsistency. What is unusual—and characteristic of Randolph—is how typical this first encounter was to be of his subsequent career.

❧ 5 ❧

Randolph's First
Congressional Career

John Randolph joined the Sixth Congress at Philadelphia in December 1799. He took his place with the Republican minority. The burden of congressional Republicanism at this time was the attack on Federalist programs and the administration of President John Adams. Randolph joined eagerly in this assault, and in his third congressional appearance demonstrated his peculiar talent for dramatizing an issue of principle and starting a fuss. On January 1, 1800, Randolph addressed the House in support of a bill to reduce the standing army. In the course of his speech, Randolph restated the traditional country-party anxiety about the inherent threat to liberty posed by a standing army:

It is, sir, by a cultivation of your militia alone that you can always be prepared for every species of attack. When citizen and soldier shall be synonymous terms, then will you be safe. When gentlemen attempt to alarm us with foreign dangers, they will permit me to advert to those of a domestic and more serious nature; they will suffer me to warn them against standing armies—against destroying the military spirit of the citizen, by cultivating it only in the soldier by profession; against an institution to which has wrought the downfall of every free state, and rivetted the fetters of despotism. . . .

In addition to voicing this classic republican warning, Randolph characterized the standing army as "ragamuffins." The following day he retracted the word while restating his general point. That evening he was insulted and set upon at the theater by two resentful marine officers. Randolph solemnly demanded redress from their commander in Chief, John Adams: "It is enough for me to state that the independence of the Legislature has been attacked and the majesty of the people, of which you are the principal representative, insulted and your authority contemned. In their name, I demand that a provision, commensurate with the evil be made, and which will be calculated to deter others from any future attempts to introduce the Reign of Terror into our country."[1]

The incredible self-assurance and cockiness of this response have been remarked before; Henry Adams called it "this wonderful piece of bombast." More significantly, it examplifies Randolph's habit of joining public issues to self-dramatization: an insult to his person is not just that but also an attack upon "the independence of the Legislature . . . and the majesty of the people" and the authority of the executive. Some of the preposterous and literal-minded seriousness of Randolph's behavior resulted from his political attitudes and expectations in general. Henry Adams ridiculed Randolph for the "solemnity with which he regards himself," and went on to describe his coterie of friends:

In politics, in love, in friendship, all were equally classic; every boyish scrape was a Greek tragedy and every sharp speech a terror to the enemies of liberty. To treat such effusions in boys of twenty as serious is out of the question, even though their ringleader was a member of Congress; but they are interesting, because they show how solemnly these young reformers of 1800 believed in themselves and in their reforms. The world's great age had for them begun anew, and the golden years returned. They were real Gracchi, Curti, Cassii.

The relevant observation is that Randolph's politics were anchored in these very ideas of himself and his mission. He had been bred and taught to take himself seriously in precisely these ways. Adams believed that initial setbacks (the refusal of his fellow legislators to consider themselves offended when he was) tempered Randolph, providing "a corrective to these ideas." In fact, Randolph was able to express his sense of himself as a classic reformer by co-operating with the Republican opposition and with the first Jefferson administration. When co-operation ceased to offer him those morally secure satisfactions of the independent political man which he expected from politics, he abandoned co-operation for opposition. His first adventures in Congress not only reflected his youthful expectations of political life, they exemplified what always continued to be at the heart of his public life: the literal seriousness with which he understood issues to be most accurately dramatized in and by himself. His attempt to focus in one personal incident opposition to standing armies, to Federalist plans for the army, and to the Adams administration, was typical. He came to Congress with a character and personality already inclined toward this type of thinking, although he took up the method in earnest only after more conventional politics had failed his purposes.[2]

The Jeffersonian opposition in Congress and in the election of 1800 generated Randolph's genuine support. The identification of Federalist politics with England, tyranny, and corruption, encouraged by the Republican leadership, was the very thing necessary to incite Randolph's fervor. He was a convinced Republican, typically taking his stand in favor of the extremes of party principle. Scholars have often used Randolph to represent the most radical segment of the Jeffersonian movement, the Old Republicans. According to Richard Ellis, these Old Republicans were "truly radical. . . . They believed that the principles of the American Revolution had been so perverted that a thorough overhaul of the national government was needed."

This would take more than new officeholders; it would involve the dismantling of the Federalist programs and their bureaucratic embodiment: "With the Federalists, who were tories and monarchists dedicated to the subversion of the principles of 1776, there could be no compromise." As Randolph wrote in 1801, "In this quarter, we think that the great work is only begun; and that without *substantial reform*, we shall have little reason to congratulate ourselves on the mere change of *men*." To Randolph the purpose of the opposition had been to restore the first principles of American independence and republicanism. In this sense he was a Jeffersonian Republican. But his commitment was to retrenchment and reform, not to another man's judgment or prospects. Thus, although he supported Jefferson consistently in 1800, he expressed important reservations about the nature of that support: "I need not say how much *I* would prefer Jefferson to Burr; but I am not like some of our party, who are as much devoted to him as the feds were to George Washington. I am not a *mon*archist in any sense."[3]

His reservations intensified as he witnessed the awe in which many Republicans held Jefferson. His resistance to the adulation of Jefferson, although due in part to his rather perverse temperament and perhaps to personal resentments, described the limits of his political commitments. Randolph committed himself to a program of reform and principle and not to an agency—be it person or party—of that reform. In Henry Adams's words, "if Mr. Jefferson did not prove reformer enough, Randolph would do his own reforming. . . ." This thinking limited sharply the kinds of co-operation and compromise he was willing to engage in; yet these are the metabolism of party politics. His attitude was, first of all, confident, even egocentric—demanding a tremendous degree of self-assurance. Its independence, reserving final judgment on all matters to the individual legislator, exemplified true country doctrine. It also indicated a misunderstanding of the Republican political coalition, a misunderstanding Norman Risjord has seen extending beyond John Randolph: "The weakness in the Virginia doctrine itself was that, though treated as a theology by its more ardent preachers, it was to a large extent a rationale for economic and sectional interests. . . ."[4]

The election of 1800 was won by a practical political coalition in the name of basic reforms and of the often contradictory particular interests of the reformers. Randolph appears not to have grasped the importance of the possible contradictions between reform and the interests of the reformers, except to see individual cases of conflict of interest. He took Jefferson and the Republican movement at their high-minded word and joined them on that basis. He did not think of his commitment to principle as one of the interests in need of compromise. There is no way around this crucial misunderstanding on Randolph's part. His personal and cultural circumstances explain how he came to it and even why its significance repeatedly eluded him, but they do not argue it away. For all his brilliance and self-assurance, Randolph did not understand the central roles of compromise and the prudent exercise of power as American political facts. His failure as a leader in Jefferson's administration was for this reason predestined. In a letter to his friend and fellow enthusiast William Thompson, Randolph offered some personal advice which expressed his deepest political difficulty: "Decision, firmness, independence which equally scorns to yield our own rights as to detract from those of others, are the only guides to the esteem of the world, or of ourselves." These sentiments, the proper and traditional ones, were genuinely Randolph's. They also ran exactly contrary to the assumptions underlying the preferred methods in the world of American republican politics, as Randolph was to find out soon enough.[5]

Randolph took an active leadership role in the first years of Jefferson's presidency. He chaired the House Ways and

Means Committee, served as a principal floor leader for Republican legislation, and at times was the protégé of the Jeffersonian leadership. His energy and brilliant talents soon commanded respect in Congress; he was a very effective and hard-working legislator. Federalist William Plumer wrote in 1803 of his striking presence:

Mr. Randolph goes to the House booted and spurred, with his whip in hand, in imitation, it is said, of members of the British Parliament. He is a very slight man but of the common stature. At a little distance, he does not appear older than you are; but, upon a nearer approach, you perceive his wrinkles and grey hairs. He is, I believe, about thirty. He is a descendant in the right line from the celebrated Indian Princess, Pochahontas. The Federalists ridicule and affect to despise him; but a despised foe often proves a dangerous enemy. His talents are certainly far above mediocrity. As a popular speaker, he is not inferior to any man in the House. I admire his ingenuity and address; but I dislike his politics.

He spoke often and handled much of the administration's program reliably and carefully.[6]

The story of Randolph's disappointment with conventional Jeffersonian hopes, his failure to be the successor the founders of the party had looked for, is well known. Albert Gallatin recalled: "During the twelve years I was at the Treasury I was anxiously looking for some man that could fill my place there and in the general direction of the national concerns; for one indeed that could replace Mr. Jefferson, Mr. Madison and myself. . . . the eccentricities and temper of J. Randolph soon destroyed his influence." Some historians have agreed with Gallatin's succinct judgment and written about Randolph's failure to live up to his promise; others have disagreed with Gallatin, emphasizing instead Jefferson's failure to live up to his own and Randolph's ideals. Each point of departure makes sense; both conclusions are true. Of more interest are the ways in which Randolph's reactions to several important events illuminate the nature of his political stance. He did not change with the times. Rather, he dug in his heels. His story is not one of hope and disappointment, of ambition and just rewards. It is entirely a story of disappointment. Randolph's disappointment in everything resulted in his splendid if peculiar later career as an eccentric prophet in opposition to every American moment, to America itself. It is as they determined this later career and as results of the education he allowed to mislead him that I will examine selected moments in his first congressional stint. This emphasis should make the process which led to Randolph's often remarked failure as a legislative leader more intelligible than it has previously been.[7]

In his highly visible and active position, Randolph was involved with most of the legislative work of Jefferson's first term. He was not always consistent: certainly his support of Jefferson's Louisiana policy constituted an important contradiction of his own states' rights views. In general, he was a hard-working and even disciplined party member as long as he was convinced that Jefferson meant what he said about reforming the government. Randolph's very activity, his restless busyness as a party leader, may well have absorbed some of his temperamental and principled reservations about the course of Jeffersonian reform in power. By 1804, however, Randolph was increasingly less sure that Jefferson did intend reform. The sources of his unease are somewhat difficult to bring into focus. There is no doubt that he was piqued by Jefferson's overwhelming importance to other Republicans. He resented the great influence of others in executive councils, and his intense sensitivity may well have exaggerated this irritation. Randolph was also frustrated by Jefferson's indirect and yet pervasive influence in the House of Representatives. That frustration was fundamentally the result of his inbred fear of executive influence as well as his personal outrage that his, Randolph's, House was being affected. Like so many others, Randolph was confused and angered by Jefferson's influence—subtle, insubstantial, unaccountable, yet undeniably important. Sometime later Randolph complained to Monroe about the president's influence: "It is certainly a melancholy truth that . . . the only question which the major part of [the House of Representatives] inquires into is 'What is the wish of the Executive?' and an intimation of the pleasure of that branch of the government is of equal force with law. There is a proneness to seek office and favors among us which is truly mortifying and distressing to the true republicans, the number of whom, it is to be feared, diminishes every day. . . ." Randolph's ultimate hostility to Jefferson owed its intensity to his feeling that the president not only betrayed his principles, and induced others to follow his lead by his Byzantine influence, but did so to the satisfaction of most Americans. Randolph's furious characterization of Jefferson as "St. Thomas of Cantingbury" got its sting as much from his irritation at Jefferson's overpowering reputation as from his witty characterization of Jefferson's ideological slipperiness. There was in Randolph's opposition to Jefferson an especially heated outrage he reserved for those, in public and private life, who betrayed his original confidence and love—the son's rage once more against the father who turned out not to have meant what he said.[8]

It was, of course, not President Jefferson who seemed to Randolph to be the major obstacle to proper reform in government. He reserved that honor for the federal judiciary and its Federalist judges, who were both personal holdovers and preferees of the repudiated Federalist administration and authoritative obstacles to the house-cleaning work of Republicans and republican reform. Randolph took a major role in the congressional proceedings in 1805 against the extreme partisan Judge Samuel Chase; as chief manager of the case, he was implicated in the ultimate failure of impeachment, which was a bitter disappointment to him. Historians have generally followed Henry Adams in seeing this failure to "get" Judge Chase as the crucial defeat of Jeffersonian reform: "It was here that the Jeffersonian Republicans fought their last aggressive battle, and, wavering under the shock of defeat, broke into factions which slowly abandoned the field and forgot their discipline." If this disaster marked the limit of the forward progress of Republican reform, it was especially galling to Randolph because he, not Jefferson (whose idea it had been to impeach Chase), bore its public brunt. His speeches during the proceedings were poor, and toward the end he broke down altogether, offering no match for the trained advocacy of defense lawyer Luther Martin. His inability to meet the requirements of an impeachment action must have deepened his embarrassed awareness that he had failed to achieve a supreme object of reform. The open amusement of Secretary of State Madison at his distress, and President Jefferson's inconspicuousness as a participant in this matter, worsened his already strained relations with these leaders. The Chase trial, however, for all that it marked the limits of Randolph's own powers in Congress and of the progress of his cause, did not bring about his significant break with Jefferson.[9]

Randolph always remembered Jefferson's first term as the one true republican interlude in American government. Despite some instances of restiveness and suspicion, Randolph was an energetic and important agent in the achievements of that term, and especially in retrospect, it became his own model of what government should be: "Never was there an administration more brilliant than that of Mr. Jefferson up to this period. We were indeed in 'the full tide of successful experiment!' Taxes repealed; the public debt amply provided for, both principal and interest; sinecures abolished; Louisiana acquired; public confidence unbounded." He remembered Thomas Jefferson as "the only man I ever knew or heard of who really, truly, and honestly not only said *'nolo episcopari'* but actually refused the mitre." The contrast between this and "St. Thomas of Cantingbury" illustrates how great Randolph's admiration for Jefferson was, and then how greatly it diminished. The imagery emphasizes Randolph's continuing tendency to look at political matters in an extreme, even religious, manner: things were either right or wrong, men good or bad, presidents tribunes or tyrants. Randolph's political faith was almost unbearably different from Jefferson's "conviction that reason and inquiry would lead men away from whatever was false or capricious or twisted in human affairs toward the truth inherent in the natural order of things." Norman Risjord has written of Randolph: "Politics to him was a religion; upon every issue hung the fate of the republic. To compromise the self-evident principles upon which a free government is based would be to compromise the whole structure. Randolph was never able to compromise or to tolerate those who disagreed with him." Randolph was in the peculiar position of having an un-Jeffersonian commitment of faith to Jefferson's cause. He lacked the flexible spirit which produced and informed that cause. Jefferson never treated his own, or anyone's, *words* as gospel; but Randolph read Jefferson literally. The time came when Randolph was jolted into realizing this difference, and his opposition was founded in rejection of the man who would compromise the integrity of the words.[10]

In 1795 the Georgia legislature had authorized the sale of four immense tracts of western lands to four companies that had effectively bribed the entire body of legislators. Following intense public outrage, a new legislature repealed the sale, removing it from the public record altogether, but not before speculation in the sale and resale of titles to those lands had become considerable and nationwide. The attending legal cases continued until finally settled by Chief Justice Marshall in *Fletcher* v. *Peck* in 1810. In 1796, during the height of the fracas, Randolph had been visiting friends in Georgia and had come face to face with this spectacle of public corruption. It remained in his mind, along with the contemporaneous Federalist regime in Philadelphia, as a firsthand example of the kinds of dangers that might threaten the republic. In 1802 Georgia finally ceded her claims to these lands (Alabama and Mis-

sissippi) to the federal government and with them the contending individual claims to title. The law permitting the
land cession included a provision for the compromise settlement of various private claims. Jefferson appointed Madison, Gallatin, and Attorney General Levi Lincoln as com-
missioners in this settlement. In early 1803 they proposed
an arrangement which gave each of the original Yazoo
claimants a fraction of his claim. The recommendations,
which made the best of a very bad business, were received
well by most concerned parties and were expected to pass
in Congress with strong administration support. This judgment did not reckon with Randolph, who began on February 20, 1804, an attack on the compromise and on its ad-
vocates which he never stopped. His legislative tactics,
which succeeded in delaying action, in themselves have
little importance. His main concern was indicated less by
the states' rights substance of his anti-Yazoo resolutions in
1804 than by his rhetorical attack on corruption. In this
fierce onslaught Randolph began openly to disagree with
his administration and party, not about states' rights, but
about the corruption which he felt might challenge republican liberty in the nation and the states and which his political background and experience had prepared him to recognize. The Yazoo affair, although surely in itself
genuinely repugnant to Randolph, is most significant because it occasioned his expression of a growing and fester-
ing disappointment with Jefferson (although he avoided
direct attacks on the president) and his politics, indeed with
politics altogether. In the speeches about Yazoo Randolph
developed his first characteristic stance.[11]

For Randolph the Yazoo fraud never lost its basic character as an example of wholesale legislative corruption.
The undermining of legislative, and hence republican,
independence by bribery was a classic sign of republican
degeneration and the corruption of liberty, that most dangerous of diseases in a regime. The resemblance of the
Yazoo compromise, suggested by the Jefferson administra-

tion, to an earlier compromise (concerning Revolutionary War debts) that had been a major formative issue for the Jeffersonian Republicans merely underscored Randolph's perception that the party and administration had abandoned principles in a most endangering way. Randolph fixed on the events of Yazoo as the basis for a continuing struggle about honesty in republican government; he had found what we would term a symbolic issue. He apparently did not speak for those directly interested, but to his way of thinking, the "interested" parties in Yazoo were those who had a stake in the freedom of the republic from subverting corruption and in the absolute right of a state or the nation to protect herself from corruption no matter what the effects on contracts or political compromise, on politics or business as usual. The very lapse of time that tended to dull the worries of such men as Madison and Jefferson about the implications of Yazoo, then, appeared to clarify those same worries for Randolph and to inflame him to action.

Henry Adams interpreted Randolph's obsession with the Yazoo fraud as an example of his "vaulting ambition":

Mean ambition does not work in such paths; only a classical over-towering love of rule thus ventures to defy the opinion of others. Had Randolph wanted office he would, like Mr. Jefferson and Mr. Madison, have conciliated the northern democrats and smoothed the processes of corruption. . . . Office he did not want, and he willingly flung his chances away, but only to grasp at the higher, moral authority of a popular tribune. He believed that the administration, backed by northern democrats, was forgetting the principles on which it had claimed and won confidence and power. . . . He told his party that they were going wrong; the time was near at hand when he was to tell them that he could not longer share their offices and honors.

Adams was right as far as he went. Randolph was indeed taking a particular high moral ground, the old country party, American republican ground with its characteristic reflex of seeing the threat of tyranny in conspiratorial corruption. Randolph used his perception of a Republican crisis of conscience in the Yazoo case to express a disen-chantment with his party that had other causes, and to re-affirm his expectations in public life. Randolph's situation was somewhat more complicated than Adams allowed. For four years, he had functioned in Congress as the chief agent of Republican reform, with duties which required him to compromise and bargain with respect to those very notions of proper government which he considered in-violable. As early as 1802, he was writing, albeit gaily, that "as for politics, 'tis a wicked business." As long as this role resulted in real reform, as it did for the first years of the administration, Randolph restrained his unease at having to take some direction and to temper principle to the will of the congressional majority and the executive. But the Yazoo business—a dramatic example of the kind of cor-ruption that he had always been taught was the ruin of lib-erty and republics—could not be ignored. The failure of Jefferson and Madison to recognize this was, from Ran-dolph's point of view, evidence that they and their counsel of compromise had strayed too far from the principles of 1776 and 1800. This conclusion confirmed his tempera-mental and ideological hostility to compromise and there-fore intensified his response. What distinguished his Yazoo speeches was their sudden sustained ferocity and their in-clination to deal with increasing numbers of people and issues within the comfortable moral framework of opposi-tion to corruption. Yazoo allowed him to speak as he liked about the issue he preferred, the dangers to free govern-ment, and for the first time since 1800, allowed him to throw off the burdens of administrative responsibility, which may well have been oppressing him during his years of apparent restraint and party regularity.[12]

The House took up the Yazoo claims on January 29, 1805. Randolph did not take long in his initial speech to get around to what he felt was in fact at stake, "this monstrous sacrifice of the best Interests of the nation on the Altars of corruption." Noting that the compromise was to be considered by a closed session, Randolph drew the traditional inflaming conclusions: "No, sir, the orgies of Yazoo speculation are not to be laid open to the vulgar gaze. . . . When this abomination is to be practiced we go into conclave. Do we apply to the press, that potent engine, the dread of tyrants and of villains, but the shield of freedom and of worth? No, sir, the press is gagged. . . . The demon of speculation at one sweep, has wrested from the nation their best, their only defence, and closed every avenue of information. . . ." The conspiracy founded in speculation was, as was to be expected by anyone familiar with British and American political history, driven by its party spirit and corrupt intent to attack the freedom and independence of the legislature, the liberties of the people, and the free flow of information. The parallels were clear: "When that act of stupendous villainy was passed in 1795 . . . it caused a sensation scarcely less violent than that caused by the passage of the Stamp Act, or the shutting up of the Port of Boston. . . ." And when Randolph turned to the participants in this conspiracy, he drew a portrait of Gideon Granger (the chief agent for the Yazoo claimants and also the postmaster general of the United States) which was at once redolent of traditional villains and the harbinger of characterizations to come:

His gigantic grasp embraces with one hand the shores of Lake Erie, and with the other stretches to the Bay of Mobile. Millions of acres are easily digested by such stomachs. Goaded by avarice, they buy only to sell, and sell only to buy. . . . The deeper the play, the greater their zest for the game; and the stake which is set upon their throw is nothing less than the patrimony of the people. . . . The same agent is at the head of an executive department of our Government, and inferior to none in the influence attached to it. . . . Sir, when I see this tremendous patronage brought to bear upon us, I do confess it strikes me with consternation and dismay. . . . What is the spirit against which we now struggle and which we have vainly endeavored to stifle? A monster generated by fraud, nursed in corruption, that in grim silence awaits his prey. It is the spirit of Federalism.[13]

The Yazoo case represented something much larger than a single instance of corruption. In view of the fact that his own party was in office and he himself was still a central figure in that party—he was still to argue the Chase impeachment—Randolph's escalating overstatements about what Yazoo meant are startling. Without questioning his sincerity, one must inquire into the nature of his perception. How did Randolph come to construe so broadly an arrangement that most observers then and since have regarded as a useful compromise in which all parties made concessions in order to eliminate an intractable and problematic issue? The first answer lies in his political education. Corruption, as we have seen, was regarded as a sign of government tyranny. Involving as it did vast grants of land, the basis of independent citizenship in Randolph's tradition, the Yazoo fraud attacked political independence itself with the weapons of greed, power, and influence. Randolph had been in Georgia in 1796; Yazoo formed part of his own experience. Hence it had for him the personal immediacy which was so much a part of his taking up any issue. Yazoo seemed another example of the kinds of battles he had bred to fight. The language of Revolutionary hysteria informed his speech: tyranny, conspiracy, corruption were endangering liberty; there was no leisure for dealing with such an enemy, such a monster had to be slain! He compared Yazoo to the worst of the tyrannies that Americans had suffered from the British and the Federalists. He would fight the good Republican fight even if his former comrades would not. Unlike the business of effecting reform, this matter presented a clear, dramatic issue of right and wrong, a test of political faith. It was much more to his taste than the taxing, unending process of finding ways and means of compromise. One senses a happy release of personal tension in this explosion. The disinterested, righteous, independent man inhabited the speech. The greater the odds, the more determined his purpose. Randolph exaggerated the danger to justify his own intransigence and underscore the principledness of his stand. Private gain threatened the integrity and independence of the government, and it was up to John Randolph to rescue it.

In this first Yazoo speech, the influence of Randolph's reading also began to reveal itself, not alone in quotations or images, but in his very perception of the matter. Martin Price has written of Augustan satire that "the satirist must prevent Vice from becoming trivial," and so Randolph had to create an overwhelming sense of danger and chaos, which he did, and also an evil genius who could mastermind and effect such skulduggery. Gideon Granger seems to have been such a figure, Randolph's first fully delineated representation of the "enemy." Until this point, Randolph had been only briefly denunciatory of persons. His attacks on Adams and the Federalists were not so totally apocalyptic as his description of the monster Granger. Randolph's Granger was an updated version of the stockjobber or the hated courtier of Augustan days, Cock Robin and Lord North and old John Adams in one. The description applied to both a bad man and a dangerous class of men, menacing and contemptible, gambling with the public lands, with the very guarantee of independence and republican government—"the deeper the play, the greater their zest in the game." Randolph was very good at this. His portrait of Granger was a clever and skillful rendering of a traditional villain, political and fictitious, the monster of selfishness lying over the land. His final identification of the "spirit of Federalism" was an aftercoloring; this monster was at once ageless and contemporary: "Federalism" was fast becoming part of a traditional litany of previous incarnations of present danger. One senses Randolph sensing that the evil was turning out to be rather closer to home.[14]

Another new element in Randolph's Yazoo arguments was his presentation of an alternative to the Jeffersonian party. Although he still maintained that Federalism was at

the bottom of the mess, Randolph had enlarged the definition of "Federalism"; besides applying to a specific administration and set of policies, it now had a generic meaning, referring to the kind of corruption he saw at work in
Congress over Yazoo. Furthermore, he appeared, for the
moment at least, to have abandoned the dichotomy of the
1790's. "Republican" was no longer necessarily the opposite of "Federalist." In 1800, party identification had
coincided with moral identification. Federalist was evil and
Republican good. Now "party spirit" challenged Republican righteousness. The Republican cause was no longer
necessarily either the republican or the good cause. Instead, Randolph talked about men "combined together to
effect some evil purpose," and men of conscience who "will
not stand compromised." The small band of a few good
men, the first refuge of the satirist and the prophet who
still entertain hopes of amendment for the world, appeared here as an alternative to both Federalists and Republicans, foreshadowing Randolph's Quid schism. Nor
did Randolph's antics go unnoticed. His colleagues and vis-
itors began to pay attention to his rhetoric and his sheer
daring, even when they might otherwise have yawned at
his arguments:

In some contests, Randolph has kept the field of argument, alone,
against the whole host of his guards or brethren, and even si-
lenced their batteries. His attacks have been general or personal,
as best suited his purpose; and, in some of his philippics, the gall
of his heart was poured forth without mixture. Epithets have, in
consequence, attached to certain characters, which they cannot
shake off, and which we sometimes think prevents them from *over
much talking*.

The satisfactions of having his say and making his principled points, indeed of obtaining immediate public notice
and effect, must have pleased Randolph. But he was still
denied the political success he yet hoped for; in the letter
describing Randolph's devastating and effective speaking,

Colonel Tallmadge also noted that whenever Randolph attacked the principles of his party, "they will immediately unite as in a common cause."[15]

Randolph's reaction to Yazoo was for a time distinct from the rest of his congressional activities. Soon enough other experiences were to drive him further into opposition, and when they did he continued to use the Yazoo issue to express his swelling disappointment with the Jeffersonian brand of republicanism. This isolation did not occur all at once. A speech on Yazoo in 1805 chronicled Randolph's version of the decline and corruption of republicanism, of which Yazoo was the index. He remembered a similar case of land claims, advanced by the same parties in the 1790's, "when we were then members of a small minority—a poor forlorn hope"; that claim had been rejected despite the petitioner's insinuation that Republican electoral hopes in Connecticut might follow the outcome of the suit:

You, sir, cannot have forgotten the reply he received: "That we did not understand the republicanism that was to be paid for; that we feared it was not of the right sort, but spurious." And, having maintained our principles through the ordeal of that day, shall we now abandon them to act with the men and upon the maxims which we then abjured? Shall we now condescend to means which we disdained to use in the most desperate crisis of our political fortune?[16]

Randolph's description of the golden age of the Republican minority, of pure principles and high hopes, was a significant reflection of his dissatisfaction. He had cast his party's past as a standard the majority were now deserting. He spoke of those days, only a few years before, in the same language he typically used to describe the Revolution. Jefferson's first administration was already the fixed and passing measure of his second. Themes of decline and nostalgia dominated. Randolph talked as if the days of Republican purity were gone:

Mr. Speaker, I had hoped that we should not be content to live upon the principal of our popularity, that we should go on to deserve the public confidence, and the disapprobation of the gentleman over the way; but if everything is to be reversed—if official influence is to become the handmaid of private interest—if the old system is to be revived with the old men, or any that can be picked up,—I may deplore the defection, but never will cease to stigmatize it. Never shall I hesitate between any minority, far less that in which I find myself, and such a majority as is opposed to us. I took my degrees, sir, in this House in a minority, much smaller indeed, but of the same stamp: a minority, whose every act bore the best of vigorous principle, and with them to the last I will exclaim, *Fait justitia ruat caelum.*

Support of the Yazoo compromises had come to be identified with the corruption of power. It was power which had caused the decline of Republican virtue, a decline all the more terrible because the Republicans had come into power on a platform of suspiciousness of power. "I have said, and I repeat it that the aspect in which this thing presents itself would alone determine one to resist it . . . shall political power be made the engine of private interest?"[17]

By 1806 it was clear that talking about the corruption of power meant attacking the Jefferson majority. The spirit of Federalism was still dangerous, but it was no longer principally incarnated by the Federalists. The effect of the Yazoo crisis was to force Randolph into a definition of his stance that made it easy and perhaps necessary for him to break with the administration; it provided moral fuel for his flight. Once Randolph was confronted with an issue that recalled to him his early political lessons, that reimposed categorical moral distinctions on everyday politics, he was bound either to take it up or to change his character. It took an issue like Yazoo to regenerate his lapsed political idealism, to involve him in another replay of the eternal republican crusade, the one he had read and heard about and expected to be able to act out.

That Randolph's response was as much a question of

disposition as of substance is certain. To Jefferson and Gallatin the Yazoo settlement was a necessary if unfortunate compromise, required by the nature of political things. Theirs was surely the reasonable position, in view of the need to keep public business going. But to Randolph that kind of compromise was intolerable. Yazoo came to symbolize for him what was wrong with the Republican party. It was much easier for Randolph to account for his difficulties with the party by seeing a corruption of ideals, in the very literal sense implied by Yazoo, than to recognize that the change of party heart reflected the deeper and more complex requirements of national politics. Hence, he identified Yazoo with the Administration: "The whole Executive Government has had a bias to the Yazoo interest ever since I had a seat here." Yazoo was the cause of Republican divisions. An incident from Randolph's last years illustrates how seriously and broadly he took the Yazoo business. Randolph and Captain William Watkins, a Jackson supporter, disagreed at a public meeting in Charlotte County over Randolph's anti-Jackson resolutions during the nullification controversy:

At the meeting, at which the resolutions were under consideration, Mr. Randolph took occasion to say, addressing himself to Captain Watkins, he did "not expect an old Yazoo speculator to approve of them."

Captain Watkins rose and made a statement denying the charge. Mr. Randolph looked him steadily in the face, and pointing his long bony finger at him, said:

"You are a Yazoo man, Mr. Watkins!"

Mr. Watkins rose a third time, completely overcome with mortification and chagrin. As he rose his savage foe plunged the same dagger into his breast.

"You are a Yazoo man," said he, when Mr. Watkins left the room completely vanquished by the single word "Yazoo."

"Yazoo," clearly, was a way around politics. It kept one from engaging in false issues instead of moral imperatives.[18]

The more obvious and pronounced Randolph's opposition became, the more his speeches reflected his developing personal style. In a letter of April 1805 to Joseph Nicholson, Randolph gave his analysis of the Republican problem, significantly borrowing from Swift:

As Mr. J. is again seated in the saddle for four years, with a prospect of reelection for life, the whole force of the adversaries of the man, and, what is of more moment, of his principles, will be to take advantage of the easy credulity of his temper. . . . I do not like the aspect of affairs. If you have not amused yourself with the Dean of St. Patrick's lately, let me refer you to his "Free Thoughts on the Present State of Affairs" for a description of a race of politicians who have thriven wonderfully since his time. The "whimsicals" advocated the leading measures of their party until they were nearly ripe for execution, when they hung back, condemned the step after it was taken, and on most occasions affected a glorious neutrality.

Randolph's reading of Swift offers interesting evidence of his reliance on books to sort out his position and also of his need in this period to redefine his political stance to accommodate his disgruntlement with the way things were being handled. His particular allusion is instructive because the pamphlet was an attack on politics in the name of principle, and soon after writing it Swift renounced political life in favor of literature and the satirical stance. Swift's disappointment in the ministry of his friends was paralleled by Randolph's, and his description of the "whimsicals" is worth recalling: "Many of those who pretended wholly to be *in* with the Principles upon which her Majesty and her new servants proceeded, either absenting themselves with the utmost Indifference, in those conjectures upon which the whole cause depended, or siding directly with the Enemy. All which indeed arose from a very unjust and perhaps an affected Diffidence towards those of the Helm." Randolph paid Swift careful attention, and his subsequent reactions to the administration demonstrated his conviction that history was repeating itself in a moral sense at least. The circumstances in 1805 and 1806 that got Randolph on an open collision course with the administration came as confirming evidence to this state of mind. The executive attempt to buy Florida secretly, Madison's maneuvering to succeed Jefferson, Gregg's Resolution, and the Embargo, although important historically as individual events, struck Randolph as indications of the expected backsliding betrayal of the principles of 1800. He reacted to them as such, not as independent circumstances.[19]

Randolph's furious opposition to and exposure of the administration's secret attempts to buy Florida were due as much to his objection to the disingenuousness of the scheme as to its substance. The whole tricky business was further proof of the abdication of republican government by its former champions. "I came here prepared to co-operate with the government in all its measures. I told them so. But I soon found there was no choice left, and that to co-operate in them would be to destroy the national character. I found I might co-operate or be an honest man; I have therefore opposed and will oppose them." Randolph framed his announcement of opposition in terms of public and private morality. In response to criticism for breaking the confidence of a secret House deliberation and of private communications with agents of the executive, he declared:

They will not give credit to a private individual as to a conversation had with him. I only stated that conversation was reason for saying I had withdrawn my confidence. And will gentlemen say I am bound when evidence has come to my private knowledge which is sufficient to damn any man, to legislate on a principle of confidence? When I find misrepresentations made to the public, and insinuations of the most despicable kind on this floor, I come out and call on any man to deny what I have stated. They cannot—they dare not. For I take it for granted no man will declare in the face of the nation a willful falsehood.[20]

Randolph was merging private and public honor. He held the government to the strictest code of personal honor to justify keeping it consistent in matters of principle. He was, in fact, addressing a challenge to an entire legislature. The effectiveness of this challenge lay in the power of words, used by Randolph as an alternative to the political pressure he was no longer in a position to exercise with any confidence. In declaring his opposition, Randolph dropped the pretense of playing politics; instead he resorted to the old language of gentlemanly honor. I cannot tell a lie, he was saying, and shall not suffer anyone else to. This attitude did not go unnoticed: "Mr. R. took a very wide range indeed, and pelted the Secretary of State severely. He pronounced him either ignorant of his Duty, or wicked in executing it." Randolph was explicitly assuming the stance of the lone righteous man and was finding the language suitable to that stance in the favorite authors and customs of his youth; literary allusions and references to the code of honor were beginning to blend in his rhetoric. The language of his opposition, now more mature and consistently effective, was his only permanent weapon—he embarrassed, attacked, shamed, and bullied his listeners into agreement. He would not bargain; he talked. (It is interesting that Randolph began at this time to evidence an increasing Anglophilia—especially in matters of style and sympathy.)[21]

Nor was Randolph about to embrace the Federalists to spite Jefferson: the Federalists "will never become good Republicans. . . . they are in opposition from system, and we *quo ad hoc,* as to this particular measure. Like men who have ruffed it together, there is a kind of fellow-feeling between us. There is no doubt of it. But as to political principle, we are as much as ever opposed. There is a most excellent alkali by which to test our principles. The Yazoo business is the beginning and the end, the alpha and omega of our alphabet." All politicians, Federalist or Republican, failed the Yazoo test, because politicians compromised principle. Increasingly it was politics that Randolph saw endangering government. Henry Adams reports that

Jefferson was not impressed by Randolph's literal-minded and extreme position on the sanctity of states' rights. The president characterized Randolph's strict-construction opposition to a bridge over the Potomac as "mere metaphysical subtleties" which "ought to have no weight." In November 1803 Randolph had written to Jefferson to explain that some remarks he had made in Congress were not meant as a personal attack, that he respected Jefferson supremely. Jefferson's response sounds wise and sensible to us, but must have struck Randolph differently: "I see too many proofs of the imperfection of human reason to entertain wonder or intolerance at any difference of opinion on any subject; and acquiesce in that difference as easily as on a difference of feature or form; experience having long taught me the reasonableness of mutual sacrifices of opinion among those who are to act together for any common object and the expediency of doing what good we can when we cannot do all we would wish."[22]

Jefferson's temperate counsel offered a kind of warning, albeit one Randolph was unable to heed. Randolph perceived Jefferson's readiness to compromise as weakness at best and Madison's as evidence of corruption. First Yazoo, then duplicitous foreign policy, convinced Randolph that Madison represented the degeneration of republican principles into Republican politics. In 1806 Randolph complained to George Hay that information was kept from Congress, which was treated "as *we deserve, like children,* told to do as we are bid, and ask no questions. Never did an assembly of the same number exist, so utterly devoid of abilities and independence. Nor it is possible to the present state of things, for any man to obey the suggestions of his own understanding & principles without damning himself and his cause. . . . The *Old* Republican party is already ruined past redemption. New men & new Maxims are the order of the day. . . ." The old patriotic virtues no longer served to advance a public career: "Other qualifications—of a far different nature are requisite to bring men forward now-a-days. The countenance of the government will shine only on such as can render present or promise future service not to the state but to a faction. Revolutionary merit must be its own reward—may starve & be forgotten." The United States was like a chicken with its head wrung off "& whose painful yet awkward contortions excite, at once, our pity & our laughter." Politics would not cure itself: "As for politics I would give them with '*Physic*, to the dogs,' did I not respect the faithful four footed creatures too much." A response to Madison in December 1805 revealed his opinion of Jefferson's advice. When the secretary of state in personal conversation with Randolph expressed a view about Florida which was the opposite of public administration policy, the congressman stalked out: "Good morning, sir! I see I am not calculated for a politician."[23]

Between March 5 and April 21, 1806, Randolph delivered a series of speeches elaborating his opposition to the administration. Henry Adams dates Randolph's "long career of opposition" from the March 5, 1806, speech on Gregg's Resolution to forbid British imports into the United States. The positive content of these addresses was a restatement of the old Republican platform of 1800, with strong overtones of traditional country-party thinking. Randolph alluded directly to the country doctrines and particularist traditions of his stand. Resenting what he saw as the dangerous policies being urged in the narrowest interest of commercial and urban America, he told the House that he was reminded of the words of Sir Robert Walpole—whose ability Randolph defended, in contrast to his honesty—that "the country gentlemen (poor meek souls!) came up every year to be sheared—that they laid mute and patient whilst their fleeces were taking off—but that if he touched a single bristle of the commercial interest, the whole stye was in an uproar. It was indeed shearing the hog—'great cry and little wool.'" His rhetorical thrust was an attack on executive influence and corruption, a call to the Republican Congress to reassert itself as of old. Randolph presented himself in these speeches as the spokesman for a small, embattled minority acting in the name of the ideals of the backsliding majority: "We are what we profess to be—not courtiers but republicans, acting on the broad principles we have heretofore professed—applying the same scale with which we measured John Adams to the present administration. Do gentlemen flinch from this and pretend to be republicans? They cannot be republicans, unless they agree that it shall be measured to them as they measured to others." Parodying Jefferson's First Inaugural Address, he taunted the majority: "But we are perhaps to be told, that we have all become federalists—or that the federalists have become good republicans," and insisted on the vigorous application of the Yazoo alkali test.[24]

Almost from the first, Randolph felt at home in Congress. He spoke freely and often; having always had the habit of personal dominion, and having served as Jefferson's lieutenant, he found it easy to acquire the habit of legislative dominion. He was unusual in the way that he transferred to his behavior in Congress the ease and assurance and insolence that had characterized him in his home places. He had graphic ways of making himself plain. When Madison's pamphlet on the rights of neutrals was placed on each congressional desk, Randolph in the course of a speech opposing administration foreign policy openly attacked the secretary of state, wishing that were he himself "the foe—as I trust I am the friend of this nation—I would exclaim, 'Oh! that mine enemy would write a book!'" Randolph then picked up the pamphlet, threw it onto the floor, and went on speaking. When an older congressman, John Smilie of Pennsylvania, reproved Randolph for this behavior, stating that Madison would be remembered when both of them were dead and forgotten, the Virginian replied that considering Smilie's advanced age and his own ill health, that wasn't much of a compliment to the book or its author. The rough and tumble of debate stimulated

Randolph. He loved to make himself felt. When Barnabas Bidwell, a Republican from Massachusetts who had been preceded to Congress by a reputation for public speaking, made his debut to the House, Randolph found the speaker not to his liking. "Dressed in his usual morning costume— his skeletal legs cased in tight fitting leather breeches and top-boots, with a blue riding coat and thick buckskin gloves from which he was never parted, and a heavily loaded riding whip in his hand," Randolph listened for some minutes and then "rose deliberately, settled his hat on his head, and walked slowly out of the House, striking the handle of his whip emphatically upon the palm of his left hand. . . ." Bidwell, who was expected to be a major administration opponent of Randolph's, was so affected by Randolph's manner during his single term that he apparently found himself unable to speak with confidence in the Virginian's presence. Randolph used what personal advantages he had, attempting to subdue opposition as much by force of personality as by force of argument. He preferred characterization to complicated arguments, having neither the legal nor the rhetorical training to mount such arguments successfully, as his difficulties in the Chase impeachment showed. He relied rather on the models of politics and satire and the principles he had inherited.[25]

His speech on Gregg's Resolution, which marked his break with Jefferson, is noteworthy for the simplicity of his arguments as well for the range and brilliance of his observations. His arguments characteristically pointed up the inconsistency between what was proclaimed publicly and what was proclaimed privately, exposing double standards, catching the administration out, contrasting present deviousness with former principledness. The naïveté of the satirical stance blended with the knowing and vulgar and vicious aphoristic ability for which Randolph was justly famed. Randolph had a gift for attack and for caricature. Thus he warned the great American land animal against tackling the British in a naval encounter: "What! shall this

great mammoth of the American forest leave his native element and plunge into the water in a mad contest with the
shark? Let him beware that his proboscis is not bitten off in
the engagement." The New Englanders who would excite
the country to war for the sake of commercial or maritime
interests were "the mussels and periwinkles on the strand."
The administration forces were "political quacks" dealing
"only in handbills and nostrums." Theirs were false claims.
The thread of his argument was that Spain was the creature of Napoleonic France, the administration forces were
dishonest in pretending to deal with Spain when their di-
plomacy was actually directed at Napoleon, and their focus
on Napoleon was in turn mistaken, given the ironic but saving role of the English navy as inadvertent guardian of
American liberties. The presentation of this view was held
together by the images of false doctors and false remedies;
political truths were asserted baldly, as commonplaces
known to everyone. The result was less an argument than
an outlandish narrative about the political quacks who
knew that Spain was but the creature of France: "There are
no longer Pyrenees. . . . No—you are not such quacks as
not to know where the shoe pinches—. . . . You know, at
least, where the disease lies, and there you apply your remedy. When the nation anxiously demands the result of
your deliberations, you hang your head and blush to tell.
. . . Your mouth is hermetically sealed. Your honor has
received a wound which must not take air." Randolph considered that the administration forces had falsely diagnosed conditions and falsely prescribed remedies to
disguise their incompetence and corruption. Thus Randolph fashioned his images of fraud and deceit and hypocrisy and corruption; the monsters that lurked in his reading of the Augustans sprang to life and peopled his
increasing attacks on the corruption and hypocrisy of his
own age. His message, in contrast to the metaphysical and
misleading nostrums of the administration, was plain and
simple and honest; where the administration was inconsis-

tent and rather hard to pin down, Randolph was straight-forward: "I can readily tell gentlemen what I will not do. I will not propitiate any foreign power with money. I will not launch a naval war with Great Britain, although I am ready to meet her at the Cowpens or at Bunker's Hill . . . ," or "I declare in the face of day that this Government was not instituted for purposes of offensive war." Randolph's behavior and allusions were generally more complex than his arguments. He was essentially looking for striking ways to force or shock his audiences back up onto the simple high ground of what he yet believed were their shared principles.[26]

In these speeches, Randolph revealed a persona akin to the speakers of the English satirists. He was at various times ingenuous naïf, the *vir bonus,* and the public defender. He was honestly appalled at the disparity between principle and practice, increasingly convinced that questions of character underlay political disputes and insistent that his was the moral perception in every case. Randolph spoke out, he said, because he had to; he wanted to cooperate, but the corruption of the administration forced him into opposition.

The drama of the satiric speaker is, in many ways, a stylized one. We are accustomed to read in many "program satires" (those works in which the satirist defends his art and presents his motives) that the satiric speaker cannot write in the high style of poetry, that he has turned from artifice to naked honesty, from "literature" to truth. Decius and Juvenal, too, contrast the dreary public recitations of epic bombast with their own anguished *cris de coeur* and biting coarseness. The satiric writer creates a speaker who is dramatically appropriate, who reveals the ethos which must animate the vision of the world that his satire will disclose.

In a like manner, Randolph turned his self-dramatizing self-absorption to his rhetorical purpose, creating in his opposition speeches a version of himself, a persona, that drew on his own character and experience and that was his great weapon. He spoke extempore, his words being inspired rather than practiced, and had no use for written texts; his were heartfelt opinions: "Speaking, as I always do, from the impulse of the moment, the *verba ardentia* cannot be recalled. The glowing picture fades—the happy epithet, the concise and forcible expression is lost, never again to be retrieved. A miserable shadow is all that remains—nor can I look upon it without disgust." The stance of sensibility here carried over into speaking. His honesty excused his occasional roughness: "Mr. Chairman, if I felt less regard for what I deem the best interests of this nation than for my own reputation I should not on this day have offered to address you; but would have waited to come out, bedecked with flowers and bouquets of rhetoric, in a set speech. . . . I will agree to pass for an idiot if this is not the public sentiment." Increasingly Randolph began his speeches with disclaimers of bad health and ill-preparedness. These, of course, served to exaggerate the importance and patriotism of his speaking. Events compelled him, despite difficulties of body and spirit. The intrusions of his personality that marked Randolph's speeches amplified the satiric ethos—he, himself, Randolph, the speaker, was more and more the dominating presence of his speeches, the persona he opposed to a world of corruption. Was his language too rough, too personal? "I am willing to allow that in the heat of debate, expressions improper for me to use, but not improper in their application to those to whom they referred, may have escaped me—the *verba ardentia* of an honest mind. I scorn to retract them. They were made in the presence of the nation, and in their presence I will defend them. I will never snivel, whatever may be the result."[27]

The drama of Randolph's speeches was his personal drama of confrontation with corruption played out in front of the nation. It was in fact the opposite of backstairs maneuvers. He identified most of the political views or personalities he opposed with one or another form of corruption, because moral corruption, not differences of opinion, was what his public self was best prepared to take on:

The gentleman [Smilie of Pennsylvania] ought to know there are different sorts of corruption. There is a corruption of interest, that is number one; there is a corruption of timidity, which consists in men not saying what they think, that is number two; there is a corruption of court influence—of party—and there is a corruption, which, though last is not least, the corruption of irreconcilable, personal animosity—a corruption which will engage a man to go all lengths to injure him whom he hates and despises, or rather, whom he cannot despise because he hates.

Of course, defined in these ways "corruption" was a term totally inapplicable to Randolph. Indeed, Randolph's speaker was most clearly *not* sullied by any of these corruptions; his every word and action identified him as uncorrupt, even his determination not to hate the enemy, but only to despise him. The indictment of corruption had to be denunciatory and escalating also to keep "vice from becoming trivial," for "if all moral distinctions break down, the lowest will dare to be as vicious as the highest, and social distinctions will go as well. Virtue can do without worldly honor or splendor (since she claims allegiance to another order) but vice cannot tolerate the fall of social status. . . ." Randolph's cause was gentle, even if he himself was not always gentle.[28]

Randolph began to develop a personal style in order to act out this moral position. He had always been flamboyant and self-assured in public. The following incident, reported by Josiah Quincy, demonstrates that there was intentional craft in Randolph's performances:

It was on one of these nights that John Randolph . . . took his turn at talking against time. After midnight, when most of the members [of the Eleventh Congress] had composed themselves to sleep as best they might, Randolph began to utter a disconnected farrago of long words, apropos to nothing in the universe. Gradually the whole House, from Mr. Speaker downwards, awoke and looked with wondering eyes upon the orator, supposing that much speaking had made him mad. His purpose then answered and the ear of the House secured . . .

His method might indeed involve madness, *verba ardentia,* or the famous stinging witticisms. The purpose was straightforward enough: to gain public attention for his self-dramatizing attacks on the discrepancy between administration professions and practices. His opposition went beyond the Old Republican agrarian discontent of Nathaniel Macon and John Taylor. Norman Risjord distinguishes Randolph from this group, noting that he went too far: "Had Randolph stopped at this point he might have erected a stable platform for conservative discontent. He had succeeded in giving voice to many of the fears that had disturbed Southern conservatives for several years. But Randolph was never capable of moderation. He sealed his political fate by provoking an open break with the administration." But sealing his political fate was to some extent the point of Randolph's break. He was objecting to the method of politics, on moral grounds which were in their nature not susceptible to moderation. Risjord is perfectly correct but somewhat beside Randolph's point. There were projects after 1806 that Randolph initiated in order to generate political support—the Quid schism and the Monroe presidential candidacy in 1808—but these were undertaken with the idea of bringing politics and principle together once more. As Risjord has written, the Quids were really a group of friends and cohorts, influenced personally by Randolph. They did not constitute a party or represent an interest, and for all their noise were just "the momentary eddy on the surface that evidenced the stronger current beneath." Their "rebellion failed because Jefferson the idol had not completely lost his power to inspire awe and Randolph was too extremist and erratic to inspire confidence." Similarly, Randolph's attempts to exploit James Monroe's feelings of slighted counsel and thwarted personal ambition by persuading him to oppose Madison for the Republican presidential nomination in 1808 proved abortive. Jefferson and Madison had more solid blandishments and promises to keep the ambitious Monroe in line than that vision of principled republican fellowship that Randolph could offer. Monroe was not about to join Randolph in opposition if that meant joining him in isolation from influence and office. He chose the road which could be relied upon to lead him to power and conventional rewards, first the position of secretary of state and then, in due course, the presidency.[29]

Randolph's attempts at political organization foundered on the rock of his perceptions of the character of the opposition. Friendship, a party of the righteous, was his organizational vision. Urging Caesar Rodney to stand for reelection in 1805, Randolph described the membership of his imagined party: "I speak of those who disdain to make a job of politics. That class of men, throughout America, look forward with much interest & expectation to your reelection to the H of R. You must make this sacrifice, my friend, to your country." Randolph's experience of opposition between 1806 and 1812 indicated to him that his perception of public issues in moral terms was fundamentally different in kind from the perception of most Americans who were not of "that class." His public stance developed as a way of talking across and to that difference, but was only occasionally taken by him or anyone else to be politically palpable. Randolph saw his isolation with ever-increasing clarity, and more and more interpreted it in terms of a general decline of American republicanism from the golden age of the Revolution and its revival in Jefferson's first term. This nostalgic version of declension completed his picture of a public course alternative to practical politics, presented through the personal metaphors of fathers and sons and inheritances so important to him: "We are proscribed and put to the ban; and if we do not feel, and feeling do not act, we are bastards to those fathers who achieved the Revolution; then shall we deserve to make our bricks without straw." Again: "I look upon the embargo as the most fatal measure that ever happened in this country—as the most calamitous event. . . . We have lifted the veil which concealed our weakness—We have exposed our imbecility. The veil of the temple of the Constitution is rent in twain, the nakedness of the fathers of the country, has been exposed to their unnatural impious children." As for Randolph himself: "I practise the doctrines now that I practised in 1798. Gentlemen may hunt up the journals if they please; I voted against all such projects under the Administration of John Adams, and I will continue to do so under that of Thomas Jefferson."[30]

∾ 6 ∾

Breakdown and
Reaction

Randolph's determined opposition to the administrations of Jefferson and Madison finally resulted in his defeat for re-election to Congress, in 1813. The victor was John W. Eppes, Jefferson's son-in-law. Randolph's opposition to the War of 1812 probably was the decisive factor in this defeat. He claimed to be relieved that the burdens of public life were at last to be lifted, and referred to his "disappointment, if a man can be said to be disappointed when things happen according to his expectations." He regretted the loss of some friends, but declared:

On every other account, I have cause of self-congratulation at being disenthralled from a servitude at once irksome and degrading. . . . To say the truth, a mere sense of my duty alone might have been insufficient to restrain me from indulging the very strong inclination I have felt for many years to return to private life. . . . No man can reproach me with the desertion of my friends, or the abandonment of my post in a time of danger and trial. "I have fought the good fight, I have kept the faith." I owe the public nothing. . . .

His letters reflect a profound bitterness and disgust with politics, despite their flippant and relieved tone. This profession of being tired of politics had become an increasingly prominent theme during Randolph's congressional career. Such an attitude enabled him to answer his frequent political disappointments with aloof indifference, as in his letter to James Monroe in 1811, written after Monroe had rejoined the Madison wing of the Republican party: "Accept my earnest wishes for your prosperity and happiness. I have long since abandoned all thoughts of politics except so far as is strictly necessary to the execution of my legislative duty." It also expressed his genuine exhaustion with the battles of opposition and, perhaps most centrally, his pervasive disillusion with American politics altogether:

I had taken so strong a disgust against public business, conducted as it has been for years past, that I doubt my fitness for the situation from which I have been dismissed. The House of R. was as odious to me as ever a schoolroom was to a truant boy.

And later:

It is paying very dear for elective government to suffer all the mischief and miseries of parliament and I think it would not be difficult to demonstrate that such a government as ours, so far from deserving the name of free is a mere engine worked by numbers, against property and talents and is to the weaker party the most hateful of all tyrannies. My relish for public life is gone.

He returned to Virginia "disappointed [as he had anticipated he would be] of every rational hope of my life and looking forward to nothing better in this world," and began a life of solitude and retirement. "For weeks together I never see a new face."[1]

Pessimistic about America's future and about his capacity to correct its tendencies, Randolph sounded note after gloomy note in his correspondence. To Josiah Quincy he wrote that he would attempt a history of the government of the country except that "if faithfully written" it "would sound like romance in the ears of succeeding generations." The apostasy of the Republican majority seemed to Randolph worse than British tyranny: "The oppression of Lord North's administration was lenity and compassion to the *regime* of the last six years." The hopeful American experiment had failed: "We fondly thought we were about to become an exception to the general laws of political philosophy, and our disgrace and punishment is like to be proportionate to our vanity and presumption".[2]

Corrupting "party spirit" had decimated the ranks of true Republicans: "If we exclude every 'party man and man of ambition' from our church, I fear we shall have as thin a congregation as Dean Swift had when he addressed his clerk, 'Dearly Beloved Roger.'" The trouble with politics as practiced in America was that they required a man to be immoral, to avoid consistent principled stands. Writing to Francis Scott Key about a mutual acquaintance, Randolph praised this man as being too good for politics: "He is too honest, too unsuspicious, too deficient in *cunning*. I would as soon recommend a man to a hazard-table and a gang of sharpers, as to a seat in any deliberative assembly in America." Disappointed idealism and personal bitterness combined in Randolph's indictment of politics to push him to a new stance of disenchantment with America. He took his failure to arouse the public conscience as evidence of the degeneracy of the people of "my delirious country" and despaired of doing much to change the situation: "How can a foolish spendthrift young man be prevented from ruining himself? How can you appoint a guardian to a people bent on self-destruction?" It was a "radically vicious" American society itself which was at fault. Here, in disillusionment, is the origin of Randolph's subsequent antidemocratic attitude, the belief that the moral insufficiency of government reflected the moral problems of a libertine people, lacking the necessary institutional checks of church and aristocracy and tradition. "It is there, if at all, that the remedy should be applied."[3]

Randolph characteristically looked for explanations and remedies for these problems in what he understood to be the Anglo-American tradition, the principles and books of his youth. To describe his malaise and bitterness, Randolph compared himself to Lemuel Gulliver looking with disgust upon his fellow creatures: "For weeks together I never see a new face; and to tell you the truth, I am so much of Captain Gulliver's way of thinking respecting my fellow-Yahoos (a few excepted, whose souls must have transmigrated from the generous Houyhnhnms), that I have as much of their company as is agreeable to me. . . ." There is in Randolph's correspondence of this period a rising tide of bitterness against others, together with professions of unhappiness and depressed spirits about the future. Randolph attributed his unhappy state and the unhappy state of the nation to the demands of politics: "My nature has become so degenerate and grovelling, during a double apprenticeship to the *art, mystery,* or *craft* of politics. . . ." His personal and ideological disappointments together fed a bitter and satiric view of American society that began to develop into something like coherence during his period of retirement. It was a vision of America compounded of nostalgia for the Revolutionary and English past as well as for a *personal* past. Animated by furious disillusionment with the present, it was occasioned by Randolph's political failure to effect reforms and by his personal unhappiness. It was a platform of opposition, characterized by the coming together of private and public into Randolph's sense of himself, a process already typical of him but suddenly in retirement accelerated into a personal and self-centered understanding of history since 1800:

I would not give the reflection that, under every circumstance of discouragement, I never faltered or wavered in my opposition to them (the Administration), to be president for life. Nearly eight years ago the *real views and true character* of the Executive were disclosed to me, and I made up my mind as to the course which my duty called upon me to follow. I predicted the result which has ensued. The length of time and vast efforts which were required to hunt me down, convince me that the cordial co-operation of a few friends would have saved the republic. . . . But the delicacy and timidity of some, and the versatility of others, insured the triumph of the court and the ruin of the country.[4]

The terms Randolph chose to describe his first legislative career varied significantly in some respects from the feelings he expressed at the time of the events. To begin with, he was now telling a story of decline, not warning of possible decline. His own role emerged as that of an embattled and unheeded prophet. He borrowed his terms from the old English country vocabulary; the past years had witnessed one more chapter in the struggle of court and country. The increasing prominence of this language had charted his move into opposition. The hysteria and urgency of his statements was diminished. Political hope, the expectation of reform, had been blasted. Instead, Randolph returned to the language of eighteenth-century political disillusion—the language of retirement, of nostalgia and declension, of bitterness and satire, of a jaundiced Cassandra and an embittered Gulliver. He renewed his acquaintance (it was a slight one) with Horace. The state of American society was beyond the remedy of political action. War fever was paramount: ". . . the people will not hear, cannot hear, and if they could, cannot understand, until the paroxysm of drunkenness is over. Wanting your faith I cannot repress *my* forebodings." He speculated on "the tendency of a certain state of society to deaden the feelings, ossify the heart, and sharpen the sense of ridicule." *Difficile est non saturam scribere.*[5]

Randolph turned from extravagant hopes of reform to a searing indictment of the government which had disappointed him and the people who supported it. His hopes, like those of the Augustans, turned to the young: ". . . it seems to me, to work any material change in the state of things, we must begin (as some logicians lay their premises) a great way off. I mean with the children; the old folks have taken their *ply*, and will neither bend nor break." Randolph might have taken his failure to be re-elected in 1813 as a sign that he should revise his estimate of political possibilities downward and re-enter public life on a somewhat more modest platform of reasonable hopes and diminished expectations. He might have learned how to co-operate with the "adult" political world on the basis of what it did, not what it said. Instead, he furiously rejected the whole business of compromise and co-operation in favor of the purity of principle he had learned as a boy to prefer. In temporary retirement, he retreated to the old familiar high ground. His exploration of the old lessons was drastically affected by a dreadful series of private griefs which uncannily struck him during this period of retirement and decisively shaped his subsequent career.[6]

Randolph's health was never very good. He was almost continually afflicted with some illness or other. The old saw had it that if he had really suffered from all those diseases, he would have been dead a hundred times. His letters abounded with complaints and lamentations about his health. These began to be more frequent in 1813, as he merged descriptions of his physical and his emotional states into miserable effusions of gloom and self-pity: "Since the hot weather set in, I have been in a state of collapse, and am as feeble as an infant—with all this I am tortured with rheumatism or gout, a wretched cripple, and my mind is yet more weak and diseased than my body. I hardly know myself, so irresolute and timid have I become. In short, I hope that there is not another creature in the world as unhappy as myself." Randolph's self-dramatizing fashioned a figure of poetic pathos out of his considerable sufferings. He was sick and lonely, and his defeat had left him humiliated and bitter. Congressional life had "deṣtroyed" him, he believed; although in public he tried "to put on a different countenance, and hold a bolder language," it was "sheer hypocrisy, assumed to guard against the pity of mankind."[7]

Worse awaited him. Randolph's private life was not especially happy. He had no wife and no children of his own. His brother's sons, St. George and Tudor, were his main objects of affection and concern. By 1810, he had broken with his stepfather, St. George Tucker. The reason for their quarrel is difficult to determine. Bruce assigns it to political differences and Garland to financial. Both agree on the following account of the actual break: Randolph and Tucker were discussing the passing of a great Virginia estate to the half brother of the family line. Randolph denounced this usage, whereupon Judge Tucker replied:

"Why, Jack, you ought not to be against that law, for you know if you were to die without issue, you would wish your half-brothers to have your estate."
"I'll be damned, sir, if I do know it," said Randolph; and from that day ceased with his good and venerable stepfather all friendly intercourse."

Randolph's extreme sensitivity on the question of inheritance is easy to comprehend. He was the last of John Randolph's sons and unlikely to have any sons of his own. His nephews St. George, who was deaf and dumb, and Tudor were all that remained of his family. To one so diligently schooled in family pride and tradition, the question of collateral heirs was peculiarly painful. Undertones of decline and degeneration were difficult to avoid. The colloquy with Tucker distilled these concerns into resentment.[8]

In June 1814, Randolph received word in Richmond that St. George had suffered some kind of breakdown. Returning to Roanoke, he found his nephew "a frantic maniac" beyond hope of restoration: "He has become manageable with little trouble. His memory for words, persons, and events is unimpaired, but he cannot *combine.* He has dwelt a great deal on the terror of future punishment also, and often mentioned the devil, but that was subsequent to his total derangement." St. George's illness was compounded by a crisis in the management of Randolph's plantation: "My plantation affairs, always irksome, are now revolting. I have lost three-fourths of the finest and largest crop I ever had." In the same letter, Randolph revealed the strain he was under: ". . . on the terms by which I hold it, life is a curse, from which I would willingly escape, *if I knew where to fly.*" Tudor Randolph, then in New York, had developed consumption. "He was the pride, the sole hope of our family." Tudor's would be a dreadful homecoming: "His birthplace in ashes [Bizarre had burned down in 1813], his mother worn to a skeleton with disease and grief, his brother cut off from all that distinguishes man to his advantage from the brute beast. I do assure you that my own reason has staggered under this cruel blow."[9]

July ended with floods, famine, a draft of men from his country to serve in the war with England. Randolph struggled to feed his "family of more than two hundred mouths looking up to me for food." Later that summer, the British threatened Washington and Randolph rushed pell-mell into action: ". . . I heard news of Washington, and, without delay, proceeded thither." The immediate danger over, Randolph went to New York in October to fetch the ailing Tudor home. On the way he suffered several mishaps, "one of which had nearly put an end to my unprosperous life." He found Tudor in the home of Gouverneur Morris and his wife, Nancy Randolph Morris. The shock of meeting once more the woman Randolph blamed for his brother Richard's disgrace and death resulted in a searingly vicious correspondence and the reawakening of bitter memories. Tudor died in England in 1815. Judith Randolph, Richard's widow, died in 1816.[10]

This series of calamities, coming one after another, constituted the central crisis in Randolph's adult life. The catastrophes, terrible in themselves, also involved an incredible range of challenges to Randolph in his various adult roles. In the space of two years, between 1813 and 1815, he lost his seat in Congress, his family, his posterity, his harvest, and, for a time, his reason. Each of the circumstances assumed a special kind of personal horror; taken all together, they seemed to Randolph to be a judgment on him, and this view informed his own subsequent judgment of the world. Tudor's illness and death recalled Richard's. St. George's madness prefigured his own. The natural disasters mocked his fatherhood of his slave family as the fates of Tudor and St. George mocked his fatherhood of the clan and sealed the fate of his line. The burning of Washington seemed a judgment on the republic which would not heed him. The personal events all seemed to refer to the unsettled past, and in order to comprehend and survive them, Randolph systematically if unself-consciously plunged deeper and deeper into his past, personal and cultural, finding there the point of view he required to understand what had happened to him and to the country. His misfortunes threatened to destroy his reason; his correspondence abounded in exclamations of misery and melancholy. He himself feared for his sanity, and others were of the opinion that he was periodically mad. Randolph's letters during and immediately after the crisis period reflect the several ways in which he sought to understand and thereby survive the chain of tragedies. He remembered; he read; he mortified himself and was converted. The common thread that ran through all these activities was Randolph's attempt to comprehend, to make sense of what had befallen him. He emerged with the story about himself and the world that he told until his death. Each of the crises directed him along lines of thought he had already begun to follow.

The unhappiness of his life was not the only reason for Randolph to look backward. To some extent, his character was nostalgic, as were his politics. In 1814 Randolph was forty-one, and his forced retirement from Congress marked the end of a period in his life. The lesson of that period reinforced his backward looking, because Randolph viewed it as the lesson of a fall from high principle, a lesson made clear by the likeness of this to previous falls. The "country" knew that life repeated itself in cycles of renewal and death. Randolph's retirement was the occasion of some reflection about his past. In March 1814, he revisited his birthplace at Cawsons. The "sad and desolate" present heightened his memories of childhood and turned his thoughts to his English and Indian forbears. The contrast between the dismantled present and the recollected glories of the past caused him to think about what lay in store for Tudor in a Virginia whose social fabric was "uprooted." "I am under great uneasiness for Tudor. There is no field for him in his native country." The life of a country lawyer was difficult and degrading. "Country life with us has few charms." New York City offered opportunity but also its own dangers.[11]

Randolph was convinced that Virginia had declined. The desolation of Cawsons, indeed of the whole Tidewater, symbolized the depressing change in society and the dismal future. In July, after St. George's breakdown, Randolph wrote to Josiah Quincy, reflecting further on the changes in Virginia in answer to Quincy's questions about the Old Dominion. Thinking about Virginia's glorious past, Randolph emphasized the treasured connection with England, the Old Home:

Before the Revolution the lower country of Virginia, pierced for more than a hundred miles from the seaboard by numerous bold and navigable rivers, was inhabited by a race of planters, of English descent, who dwelt on their principal estates on the borders of those noble streams. The proprietors were generally well educated—some of them at the best schools of the mother country, the rest at William and Mary, then a seminary of *learning*, under able classical masters. Their habitations and establishments, for the most part spacious and costly, in some instances displayed taste and elegance. They were the seats of hospitality. The possessors were gentlemen, better-bred men were not to be found in the British dominions. . . . Even now the old folks talk of going home to England.

This pleasant memory of Virginia's golden age indicates how strong a hold on Randolph's imagination the "good old days" exercised. *Then* was a kind of nostalgic dream, his father's day, when the Randolphs were at the center of a pleasant and burnished world of ladies and gentlemen. The association of that world with pre-Revolutionary Englishness was interesting. It emphasized how long distant Virginia's good days were and framed the story of Virginia's decline in a new way: the Revolution, democracy, *America,* had ended the old days. What had happened to Virginia, Randolph wrote Quincy, was due to "free living, the war, docking entails (by one sweeping act of Assembly), but chiefly the statute of distributions. . . . Bad agriculture, too, contributed its share." Unlike New England,

we had a *church* to pull down, and its destruction contributed to swell the general ruin. The temples of the living God were abandoned, the *glebe* sold, the University pillaged. The old mansions, where they have been spared by fire (the consequence of the poverty and carelessness of their present tenants) are fast falling to decay; the families, with a few exceptions, dispersed from St. Mary's to St. Louis; such as remain here sunk into obscurity. They whose fathers rode in coaches and drank the choicest wines now ride on saddlebags, and drink grog, when they can get it. What enterprise or capital there was in the country retired westward. . . . Deer and wild turkeys are nowhere so plentiful in Kentucky as near Williamsburg.[12]

It is surprising to find Randolph attributing the decline of Virginia to the Revolution and the changes it wrought in American society, but that is what he was doing. "The brutality of the present age" offended him and filled him with despair. Certainly his political disappointments, his accumulated feeling that the Founding Fathers had unknowingly exchanged one tyranny for another—Lord North for St. Thomas of Cantingbury—softened his hatred of British rule, in retrospect, and allowed him explicitly to identify Virginia's greatest moments as English. In so doing, Randolph was vindicating his upbringing and his taste, and also his politics. This change in Randolph's attitude (which did not cause him to abandon his notions concerning the political principles of the War of Independence, though he now rejected the concomitant nationalist overtones) did not originate in his period of personal crisis. Earlier, he had bitterly opposed the nationalistic spirit that sought a new war with Mother England. In a speech in which he tried to prevent the War of 1812, he invoked the common English heritage:

Name, however, but England, and all our antipathies are up in arms against her. Against whom? Against those whose blood runs in our veins; in common with whom we claim Shakespeare, and Newton, and Chatham for our countrymen; whose form of government is the freest on earth, our own only excepted; from whom every valuable principle of our own institutions has been borrowed; . . . against our fellow Protestants, identified in blood, in language, in religion with ourselves.

Driven by his opposition to the impending war, his hatred of the would-be warriors and what they represented in American politics, and his passionate loathing for Napoleonic France, Randolph began to develop in 1811 and 1812 his new version of the American Revolution. It was responsive to his identification with Virginia's less disturbing English past, increasingly a happy contrast to the changing American present. And it was then intensified by what he thought the disaster of the 1812 war. However, it did not cause him to side with England against America. It was not a brief for the Hartford Convention. The effect of his political and personal woes was to confirm him and fix him in his changed opinions, his revision of recent history, according to which British tyranny was the work of a minority of corrupt ministers: "It ought to be remembered that the heart of the English people was with us. It was a selfish and corrupt ministry and their servile tools by whom we were not more oppressed than they were." This explanation was the literal conclusion from the Virginian independence movement. It is the argument for independence without the positive thrust of American nationalism that taught us to hate the British, not merely a corrupt ministry. Randolph's nature, his education, and his own first principles were driving him, under the pressure of events, into the past. The circumstances of his life from 1813 to 1815 did not originate but did focus and fix his need and disposition to move in this direction.[13]

Randolph's private tragedies, then, sharpened his general sense of Virginia's decline. Personal loss converted the present into an even more hateful and desolate time, exaggerating what had changed in the world and insisting that all had changed for the worse. The coincidence between his own experiences and the experiences of his class intensified his already strong disposition to see his particular circumstances as part of a generalized fate. Thus, St. George's madness was a judgment on the Randolph line, not an accident: "Poor St. George, ill-starred, unfortunate boy!—his destiny was sealed before his birth, or conception." Randolph identified with his nephew's madness, recognizing himself in it. The complex associations of family, self, and destiny this madness prompted in him are eerily contained in Randolph's signature to an 1819 business letter, ordering a saddle. "John St. George Randolph of Bizarre." In a man so punctilious about his name, this is a significant manifestation of his disturbed state, intelligible in terms of the concerns which unbalanced him and which plagued his sanity and his madness. The difference between "John Randolph of Roanoke" and "John St. George Randolph of Bizarre" was one of degree not of fundamental perceptions. Seen from the ordering perspective of a doom or curse, the events of 1813–15 began to make sense. Randolph understood his personal life to be working out of some tragic design which paralleled the declining fortunes of his people. The floods, famines, and invasions, the disastrous war with the mother country, were calamities not only for him but for Virginia. Bizarre burned down, but all the old mansions were in ruins. The Randolph line was petering out, but so were all the old families. The identification was easy, and characteristic for Randolph, and—it must be remembered—there was considerable truth in it. In subsequent years, Randolph returned again and again to the theme of decline, public and private.[14]

Tudor's death was the crowning blow. Tudor had been Randolph's "son": "Permit me to introduce you to my nephew—let the father say my son—for he has known no other father and is the child of my heart and my adoption—Mr. Tudor Randolph." Tudor had been the recipient of Randolph's most interested advice; it was Tudor who was to avoid those mistakes of temper and undiscipline that plagued Randolph about himself. Tudor was the future of the family, the vindication of Richard's name and John's life. Randolph had worried that Virginia was no place for this young man:

He promises to possess all his father's genius. He cannot have a better. . . . All my dread is that his temper may prove too soft—so as to give to his inferiors in other respects an ascendant over him. The boy is no coward—far from it; but is meekness himself, overflowing with the milk of human kindness. This would do admirably for Robinson Crusoe's Island or the Golden Age, or even for a Moravian Brotherhood, but it will not suit these times. This, as Mr. Talleyrand has shrewdly remarked, is the age of upstarts, and you must take your choice to crush them or be crushed by them.

Randolph had intended that Tudor should avoid the decay and stagnation of his race and his class. His death offered incontrovertible proof of the unalterable fate of his kind. In reply to a letter informing him of Tudor's death, Randolph wrote, "Your kind and considerate letter contained the first intelligence of an event which I have long expected, yet dreaded to hear. I can make no comment upon it. To attempt to describe the situation of my mind would be vain, even if it were practicable. May God bless you: to Him alone I look for comfort on this side of the grave; there alone, if at all, I shall find it." The loss of Tudor was the loss of the future. Randolph had suffered wounds "in the three great concerns of man, mind, body, & estate." He could yet counsel others not to permit their minds "to be twisted by despondency. When the infection is once taken there is, I fear, no remedy."[15]

Randolph sought consolation in religion. During this period he underwent a conversion, and spelled out his personal grief in the language of religious enthusiasm. Upon examination, however, his conversion turns out to have been a return to the scenes of his childhood, an attempt to avoid the consciousness of his lone survival of the calamity that had overtaken his race. In 1826, Randolph wrote to his half brother Henry Tucker a letter of consolation upon the death of Tucker's eldest son. He reflected in that letter on his own crisis of loss a decade before:

Had I remained a successful political leader, I might never have been a Christian. But it pleased God that my pride should be mortified; that by death and desertion, I should lose my friends; that, except in the veins of a maniac, and he too possessed "of a deaf and dumb spirit," there should not run one drop of my father's blood in any living creature besides myself. The death of Tudor finished my humiliation. I had tried all things but the refuge of Christ, and to that, with parental stripes was I driven.

This is pretty much what happened after 1815. Randolph plunged with enthusiasm and literalness into a period of frenzied religious feeling. His return to the faith was an involved and sincere experience in its own terms. However, it also had motivations which were independent of religion—although expressed by Randolph in the feverish language of belief and repentance. To begin with, Randolph's was literally a return to the faith of his fathers, as his mother had taught it to him. Randolph's image of his mother as the gentle conveyor of paternal lessons dates from this period, and his reunion with his Lord and his Savior was transparently a reunion with his mother, and with the old, vanished world of his father, as well:

When I could first remember, I slept in the same bed with my widowed mother—each night before putting me to bed, I repeated on my knees before her the Lord's Prayer and the Apostle's Creed—each morning kneeling in the bed I put up my little hands in prayer in the same form. Years have since passed away; I have been a skeptic, a professed scoffer, glorying in my infidelity, and vain of the ingenuity with which I could defend it. Prayers never crossed my mind, but in scorn, I am now conscious that the lessons above mentioned, taught me by my dear and revered mother, are of more value to me than all I have learned from my preceptors and compeers. On Sunday I said my catechism, a great part of which at the distance of thirty-five years I can yet repeat.

When Randolph wrote to Dr. John Brockenbrough in 1815 of the "rich inheritance of an imperishable palace, of which we are the immortal heirs," he was surely talking as much about the recovery of a past world as about the certainty of the next. Randolph's "heaven," with its reconciled fathers and sons, its inheriting heirs, and its connection to his mother's love, stood for all that he had lost on earth; heaven was Virginia's golden age.[16]

Randolph's conversion provided more than the recovery of the lost world of his childhood; it soothed his bitter disillusionment at the collapse of his expectations. In his 1826 letter to Henry Tucker he explicitly contrasted a success in politics with religion (in what are again familiar tones): "Had I been a successful political leader, I might never have been a Christian." His distaste for what he took to be the corruption of politics found heavenly sanction. He had God's approbation in his political unsuccess. Christianity justified Randolph's politics in a peculiar way. He knew he should be dependent on God and love his fellow men. The fact that he had not done so troubled him sorely. Religion would help him to overcome his failings of temper and charity, if not to moderate his ambition: "I feel my stubborn and rebellious nature to be softened, and that it is essential to my comfort here, as well as to my future welfare, to cultivate and cherish feelings of good will towards all mankind; to strive against envy, malice, and all my enemies. There is not a human being that I would hurt if it were in my power; not even Bonaparte."[17]

With that extreme literalness that always characterized his espousal of opinions, Randolph turned to God. The independent terror of Congress was now the humble lover of God and man. The role had changed; the actor had not. Disappointed idealism had become disappointed resignation. Randolph spoke of his resignation, his world-weariness, with the same exaggerated, excited accents found in his other speeches. The voice was unchanged. He struck the "submissive" chord of dependency as violently as he had struck that of independence. He could do nothing by halves: "My sensations are such as become a dependent creature, whose only hope of salvation rests upon the free grace of Him to whom we must look for peace in this world, as well in the world to come. . . ." Randolph carried on his repentant change of heart in the old pose of sensibility. He had not learned moderation or resignation; rather, he uttered resigned sentiments, acknowledged the necessity of moderate expectations in the world, in his old enthusiastic, ferocious way. In a letter to Dr. Brockenbrough, urging his friend to "experience the most delightful of all sensations that springs from a well grounded home of reconciliation with God!" Randolph talked of friendships and kindred spirits in salvation as he had talked of them in the Old Republican cause.[18]

Randolph's Christianity vindicated his politics, but at the same time it seems to have pushed political concerns aside. Religious thoughts and political thoughts were incompatible; they could not coexist in his mind. His account of his conversion, written in May 1815 to Francis Scott Key, shows how tricky their rivalry was. Randolph confessed to a long period of doubt: "For a long time the thoughts that now occupy me, came and went out of my mind." Business and pleasure interfered with serious reflection. "But heavy afflictions fell upon me," and these serious thoughts "came more frequently and stayed longer—pressing upon me, until, at last, I never went to sleep nor awoke but they were last and first in my recollection." The problem, Randolph wrote, was that normal life in the world disturbed his religious complacency:

I cannot repress the feelings which the conduct of our fellow-men too often excites; yet I hate nobody, and I have endeavored to forgive all who have done me an injury, as I have asked forgiveness of those whom I may have wronged, in thought or deed. If I could have my way, I would retire to some retreat, far from the strife of the world, and pass the remnant of my days in meditation and praying; and yet this would be a life of ignoble security. But, my good friend, I am not qualified (as yet, at least) to bear the heat of the battle. I seek for rest, for peace. . . .

If he had to go out into the world and see how corrupt and evil men were, he would have to stop forgiving. The only way to love God, and for His sake to love men, was to be all alone in some cave. This was a marvelous moment of self-knowledge, however incomplete. Randolph expressed the two contradictory attitudes that sprang from his basic literal-minded unwillingness or inability to compromise. If you were going to be religious, you had to forgive everything and everybody and be a monk; if you were going to be in politics, you had to be a scourge. As long as men and conditions continued as bad as they were, charity was impossible when you had to look them in the face. Only theoretically, as a hermit from a distance, could you forgive. Randolph did not take back anything important that he had said. What his conversion meant was that leaving the world was the best solution for someone unable to stand it. There was no hint of genuine resignation or moderation. Randolph's idealism and his disillusionment remained intact.[19]

Underlying Randolph's religious experience was unhappiness and profound disgust with life. He sought an explanation of "those wonderful coincidences, which men call chance, but which manifest the hand of God," so many of which had characterized his life. He was not always sure of his own mind, knowing that he might "be reduced to the condition of some unhappy fanatics who mistake the perversion of their intellects for the conversion of their hearts." Even here Randolph showed that his new-found beliefs had not altered his dichotomous, one-or-the-other way of seeing things. He was either saved or mad. Randolph's profoundest religious sensation, like his profoundest secular one, was triggered by his detection and exposure of hypocrisy or compromise—he could not distinguish between them:

> We would serve God provided we may serve mammon at the same time. For my part, could I be brought to believe that this life must be the end of my being, I should be disposed to get rid of it as an incumbrance. If what is to come be anything like what is passed, it would be wise to abandon the hulk to the underwriters, the worms. I am more and more convinced that, with few exceptions, this world of ours is a vast madhouse.

In fact, there were real limits to Randolph's conversion. In a letter to Key he declared that he considered its ultimate effect on him as "giving me better views than I have had of the most important of all subjects. . . . I do not hate my brethren of the human family. I fear, however, that I cannot love them as I ought. . . ."[20]

Randolph did not leave the world. In 1815 he returned to active political life. The lasting meaning of his conversion lay in its nostalgic, backward-looking thrust. His was an old-fashioned kind of experience, having more to do with the sensibility of Cowper than with the emotionalism of Finney. Christianity was a vehicle for emotional self-indulgence, a step on the way to melancholy egotism. Randolph had returned to Anglicanism, the church of his forefathers. His religious feelings ultimately reinforced his growing commitment to his own past, to the days *before* the Revolution, to the life style of Virginia's golden age. The cutting off of his blood connections to the future, the spectacle of desolate Virginia, the humiliation of isolation and defeat, had brought him into the disestablished Anglican fold. His Christian belief, once the wave of emotionalism had passed, was essentially ancestor worship. The better world, the more stately mansions of Christian promise meant quite literally his father's house. Randolph's conversion to his own misleading tradition was indeed a way of finding an alternative to this world of suffering and humiliation, a return to the values and emotional surroundings of his youth: "I was born and baptized in the Church of England. . . . When I speak of my country, I mean the Commonwealth of Virginia. I was born in allegiance to George III; the Bishop of London (Terrick!) was my diocesan. My ancestors threw off the oppressive yoke of the mother country. . . ."[21]

During this difficult time Randolph also sought comfort and guidance from books. His nonreligious reading, in English works, as was his custom, helped him to order his disheveled reactions. What emerged was a rendering of his world view that gave lasting shape to his earlier inclinations and opinions. The most important reading of this period was an intense study of the political writings of Edmund Burke. Burke was not new to Randolph. He had read the *Reflections on the French Revolution* when it first appeared but was not much impressed, being still at that time an enthusiast of the French revolutionary cause. Nathaniel Beverley Tucker placed his half brother's serious reading of Burke in the second half of Jefferson's presidency, when Randolph's political disillusionment with the Republicans and his revulsion at Napoleon led him to become more receptive to Burke's skepticism about innovation, democracy, and revolution. Tucker wrote that this coincidence of events and a second reading of Burke led Randolph "to suspect that there may be something in the enjoyment of liberty which soon disqualifies a people for self government, which is but another name for freedom." In 1814, Randolph wrote to a friend that "except for Burke and Lord Byron's poems I have read nothing for a long time past." Randolph's increasing openness to Burke's suspicions of democracy and to his general political outlook was confirmed by his real alienation from the course of political events leading up to and including the second war with England and his own removal from Congress. By 1813, Randolph was referring to Burke as "the Newton of political philosophy," "the great master of political philosophy," and declaring that "if I am an enthusiast in anything, it is in admiration of Burke." This admiration, explicit and plentifully illustrated in allusion, acknowledgment, and agreement, lasted for the rest of Randolph's life and caused contemporaries and subsequent historians to compare him to Burke, or even to call him an American Burke. Francis Walker Gilmer, for example, remarked upon the similarity of Randolph's speaking to Burke's: "His invective, which is always piquant, is frequently achieved with the beautiful metaphors of Burke."[22]

Reading Burke first confirmed Randolph's repudiation of his enthusiasm for the French Revolution. Like so many young Americans of the 1790's, Randolph had followed Jefferson's lead in transferring his own Revolutionary ardor to the cause of the French people. In 1806, in his speech on Gregg's Resolution, Randolph recalled the enthusiasm of that struggle, paying it tribute as misguided nobility:

Then every heart beat high with sympathy for France, for *Republican France!* I am not prepared to say, with my friend from Pennsylvania, that we were all ready to draw our swords in her cause, but I affirm that we were prepared to have gone great lengths. I am not ashamed to pay this compliment to the hearts of the American people, even at the expense of their understandings. It was a noble and generous sentiment, which nations like individuals, are never the worse for having felt. They were, I repeat it, ready to make great sacrifices for France. And why ready? Because she was fighting the battles of the human race against the combined enemies of their liberty. . . ."

Randolph turned hostile toward that episode with time, however, coming to identify the French Revolution not as the misguided and betrayed child of America's Revolution but as the great modern example of the dangers to American independence. In 1816 he honored Washington for keeping America out of the "vortex" of that struggle: "The liberty of the world was said to be in jeopardy; the tyrants of the world, it was said, had conspired against liberty, and we ought no longer to withhold our aid. . . . By the wisdom of that man who alone, at that juncture, could have held the reins of empire, who alone could have reined in the public madness, by his wisdom we have been saved from being involved in the vortex of that tremendous comet." In time the French experiment came to symbolize for Randolph all that was leveling, innovative, popular, and dangerous in politics; it was a negative reference point. Although he did not learn from Burke to hate the French Revolution, he did learn from him how to organize and express his hatred. Ultimately, for Randolph as for Burke, the French Revolution came to stand as the image of attacks on the stable, inherited order in the name of abstract political principle: "If you want to know the effect of metaphysical madness, look to the history of the French Revolution and the undoing of the country."[23]

This repudiation of his earlier commitment to the French Revolution was part of Randolph's break with Jefferson. He redefined the French commitment to place it outside of the republican creed, considering it a dangerous excess of Republican enthusiasm. He let it stand for the dangers he saw in Jefferson's temporizing with Old Republican doctrine. His stance thus had double force, being directed at the centralizing, democratizing trends in American politics, against which he set himself, and also at the theorizing and innovating side of Jefferson's politics, which he found intolerable. Napoleon became for Randolph a titanic and meaningful figure of danger, a political anti-

Christ. His move into opposition was triggered by events abroad and by his feeling that Bonaparte posed a danger to free institutions. In a public letter to his constituents upon being returned to Congress in 1815, modeled on an address by Burke to his constituents, Randolph presented his conclusions concerning the French Revolution and its lesson for American politics, revealing how united the two subjects had become in his mind and also how completely he had accepted the Burkean argument:

In the virtue, the moderation, the fortitude of the People is (under God) our last resource. Let them ever bear in mind that from their present institutions there is no transition but to military despotism; and that there is none more easy. Anarchy is the chrysalis state of despotism; and to that state have the measures of this government long tended, amidst professions, such as we have heard in France and seen the effects of, of Liberty, Equality, Fraternity. None but the people can forge their own chains; and to flatter the people and delude them by promises never meant to be performed is the stale but successful practice of the demagogue, as of the seducer in private life.

The events in France had become a part, an instructive counterpart, of American history. The lessons of power and corruption, the indictment against first the Federalists and then the accommodating Republicans, the causes and motives for Randolph's opposition, merged in this Burkean reading of the French Revolution. The conservatism, the hostility to popular democracy, the mistrust of change on the basis of abstract principle, which characterized Randolph's position from about 1815 on were not new elements in his thinking. What his crisis-inspired re-evaluation of his thinking and simultaneous rereading of Burke had produced was a new story, a completed position on the disquieting events of his first Congressional career. Using Burke, Randolph interpreted the recent past and arrived at a new way to describe his already existing views.[24]

Randolph's identification of himself with Burke was a public process. In 1811, he compared his own opposition to the English war with Burke's stand during the American Revolution: "As Chatham and Burke, and the whole band of her patriots, prayed for her defeat in 1776, so must some of the truest friends to their country deprecate the success of our arms against the only Power that holds in check the arch-enemy of mankind." Increasingly he associated himself with Burke, whose presence in his speeches, as the "master of political philosophy" or "that eminent statesman" symbolized his constant presence in the language and formulation of Randolph's political ideas. In reading Randolph's speeches, it is impossible not to see, as Russell Kirk has done, the profound influence of Burke in his political expressions: "To call Randolph 'the American Burke' is no great exaggeration." But it is not entirely clear what ought to be made of Randolph's heavy borrowing from Burke. Kirk would have them almost partners in "solemnly noble conservatism." There is little evidence, however, that Randolph did more than learn from Burke how to express beliefs which were his. It was not Burke who turned him from the French cause; instead, having turned away on his own, Randolph found good and sympathetic reasons in Burke for having done so. Furthermore, Randolph never learned certain fundamental Burkean lessons. Even Kirk admits that Randolph "did not share Burke's admiration for the party system and lacked Burke's veneration of the state." The role of Randolph's reading of Burke was fundamentally organizing and confirming. It lent weight and authority and patina to his thoughts and expressions.[25]

A most important effect of this reading of Burke during the years leading up to and including his retirement and crisis was the reconciliation of England and America in Randolph's mind. Randolph had come to see England rather than France as the bulwark of American international policy. He was bitterly opposed to the War of 1812 not least because it pitted two harmonious nations against their own better interests, to the benefit of the tyrant

France. On December 10, 1811, Randolph expressed his feeling that England and America were naturally allies; he did not minimize the injustices of British commercial policy but wondered if they were worth such an unnatural war:

Against those whose blood runs in our veins; in common with whom we can claim Shakespeare, and Newton and Chatham for our countrymen; whose form of government is the freest on earth, our own only excepted; from whom every valuable principle of our own institutions has been borrowed—representation, jury trial, voting the supplies, writs of habeas corpus—our whole civil and criminal jurisprudence; against our *fellow-protestants*, identified in blood, in language, in religion with ourselves. In what school did the worthies of our land, the Washingtons, Henrys, Hancocks, Franklins, Rutledges, of America, learn those principles of civil liberty which were so nobly asserted by their wisdom and valor? And American resistance to British usurpation had not been more warmly cherished by these great men and their compatriots; not more by Washington, Hancock, and Henry, than by Chatham, and his illustrious associates in the British parliament. It ought to be remembered that the *heart* of the *English people* was with us. . . . But the outrages and injuries of England, bred up in the principles of the Revolution, I can never palliate, much less defend them. I well remember flying with my mother, and her new-born child, from Arnold and Phillips; and they had been driven by Tarleton, and other British pandours, from pillar to post, while her husband was fighting the battle of his country. The impression is indelible in my memory. . . . I call upon those professing to be republicans, to make good the promises held out by their republican predecessors when they came into power; promises, which for years afterward, they honestly faithfully fulfilled. We vaunted of paying off the national debt, of retrenching useless establishments; and yet we have now become as infatuated with standing armies, loans, taxes, navies, and war, as ever were the Essex junto. What republicanism is this?[26]

Here Randolph can be seen working on the process of reinterpretation that crisis would complete. It is a version of American history that is in fact the history of Virginia and her two mother countries. Its contradictory notions are familiar to the reader of the American Revolutionaries. It represents but does not resolve their thinking. It is at once Virginian, national, and prenational, an unfinished colonial argument which seeks to use English tradition to moderate a worrisome national American present and future. English men, customs, and ideas are seen to form the thread and standard of American history. The Revolution is enshrined as a vindication of English history. The War of 1812 threatens to destroy liberty and the English nations that alone cultivate it. Personal loss and an intense reading of Burke enabled Randolph to develop even more completely the vision of a consistent, continuous English and American past from which he chose to reason. The French Revolution, the unrepublican American innovations of recent times, the new war with England, all of these were discontinuous events; reading Burke helped Randolph recreate a version of the Anglo-American past—a tradition, authority, aristocracy—with alternative values, more favorable to his politics and his view of the world than those of democratic America.

Randolph's reading of Burke was problematic, however. Randolph was not an adherent of tradition and custom over the letter in constitutional matters. He did not grant that sovereignty was indivisible. His famous remark that a state could no more surrender a part of her sovereignty than a lady surrender part of her chastity was not Burkean, as Kirk would have it, but rather reflected his prior view of sovereignty as divided between the states and the federal government:

But ours is a system composed of two distinct governments—the one general in its nature, the other internal. Now, sir, a government may be admirable for external, and yet execrable for internal purposes. And when the question of power in the Government arises, this is the problem which every honest man has to work. The powers of Government are divided, in our system, between the General and State Governments, except some powers, which the people have very wisely retained to themselves. With these exceptions, all the power is divided between the two Governments.

Randolph was like the American revolutionaries in his belief that sovereignty was divisible and subject to systematic
arrangement. He did indeed detest innovation and
change, and was explicitly Burkean in his mockery of political abstractions and metaphysics. He resented bitterly the
passing of the old ways and tried to revive, in himself at
least, the customs and attitudes of the English and Virginian past. Burke was his cherished authority and preceptor
in this effort. Essentially, Randolph was in control of his
use of Burke. His was an acknowledged and indeed a
pleasant debt. However, despite all that they shared, it is
not clear that in the deepest sense Randolph was Burkean.[27]

Burke's delineation of the importance and necessity of
tradition and continuity in political thought was not meant
to take place in a vacuum. His particulars applied to England and might not easily be transferred to America.
J. G. A. Pocock has described Burke's thought as "the habit
of interpreting English politics and society not with the
word of any political theory designed for the explanation of
society in general, but in light of those assumptions about
English society which were already contained in its most
distinctive and characteristic body of rules." The appeal
of this kind of thought to Randolph was obvious. To his
literal-minded, tradition-bound, and increasingly skeptical
political sensibility, the notion that politics should expound
and conserve the traditional was persuasive. The question
remains, however, as to whether his understanding of what
was characteristically American was Burkean. The particulars were often the same. One must ask if Randolph was
not trying to explicate an English tradition of American
politics—the codes of eighteenth-century Virginia—seen in
the relief of changing conditions. This may not have been
the tradition an American Burkean would nurture and assert. In fact, Randolph may have been *imagining* a tradition—reactionary, but still at one remove from the then
current traditions of American politics. This is a difficult

matter to state clearly, but it seems evident that although Randolph agreed with Burke's ideas and applied their strictures, often to the point and with great shrewdness, he failed to go beyond those particulars to present a more coherent Burkean interpretation of American history. His versions always go back to English America. His taste for Burke, like his other tastes, was an expression of his feelings for the old home. It was in this period that he began to travel regularly to England and refer to his English ancestral past and convictions, to see the Founders as figures in an English tradition and create his own personal version of the English country gentleman. His miseries and dillusions seem to have liberated him from the necessity of dealing in a consistent, realistic way with the present. It is hard to regard writings which are so willful, so dismissive of contemporary political conditions, so escapist, as truly Burkean.[28]

Randolph's best use of Burke's views lay in adapting them to particular criticisms of the absurdities and dangers of American politics. Thus, at the Virginia constitutional convention in 1829, Randolph employed the anti-theoretical, common-sense Burkean notions to ridicule unnecessary changes in the Virginia order. Arguing within the context of Virginia politics and with a firm grounding in practical political knowledge, Randolph did produce a speech that was genuinely Burkean in its approach to political matters. It was moving and a sensible statement based on a very clear use of Burke:

As long as I have had any fixed opinions, I have been in the habit of considering the Constitution of Virginia, under which I have lived for more than half a century, with all its faults and failings, and with all the objections which practical men—not theorists and visionary speculators, have urged or can urge against it, as the very best Constitution; not for Japan; not for China; not for New England; or for Old England; but for this our ancient Commonwealth of Virginia.

But I am not such a bigot as to be unwilling, under any circumstances, however imperious, to change the Constitution under which I was born, I may say, certainly under which I was brought up, and under which, I had hoped to be carried to my grave. . . .

I have by experience learned that changes, even in the ordinary law of the land, do not always operate as the drawer of the bill, or the Legislative body may have anticipated; and of all things in the world, a Government, whether ready made to suit casual customers, or made to order, is the very last that operates as its framers intended. Governments are like revolutions; you may put them in motion, but I defy you to control them after they are in motion. . . .

Here his argument in support of tradition was based more or less on facts, the facts of his own life and of the ruling class of Virginia, still strong. His reading of Burke helped him to express his attitude with greater clarity and more general applicability than might otherwise have been the case.[29]

During his time of loss and crisis, Randolph was unusually receptive to the emphasis Burke placed on tradition and inheritance and continuity—indeed, on resistance to change—as political principles. Pocock has written that "it cannot be quite coincidental that in these passages Burke is telling of the advantages which accrue when a people lay claim to their liberties on exactly the same principles as those on which they inherit their estates." The importance to Randolph of this context for thinking about politics is obvious. The general drift of Burke's thinking, the emphasis on tradition, on looking to the past for standards by which to judge the world, suited Randolph's needs during his time of backward glancing and loss, providing him with the means to reconstruct a vantage point from which to look at things once more. Burke offered him a rhetoric and reasoning for the reassertion of the old values of land, family, and church in spite of their evident ruin. Reading Burke and remembering, Randolph put together his own version of the decline of American society, one which explained his own fate and circumstances at the same time that it supported his lonely politics. The language of inheritance, of tradition, which distinguishes Burke, the insis-

tence that liberties are a precious inheritance, that a nation's past is the source of its wisdom, these were already
clear in Randolph's letters and speeches. Burke offered authoritative (and not accidentally, English) confirmation of
his already established habits of mind.[30]

Randolph's reading of Burke ordered his thinking toward the past which Jefferson and Madison had violated.
One of Randolph's most successful and cutting Burkean
forays concerned Jefferson's *philosophe*-ical plow. During
the Virginia constitutional convention of 1829, Randolph
defended the traditional order and structure of Virginia
government against change, especially equalitarian and reforming change. "Change is not reform" became his motto,
and he attacked "tinkering" with political institutions and
practical realities, especially on the basis of abstract principles. Jefferson had designed a model plow, based on the
scientific principles of the Enlightenment, and intended to
improve the cultivation of Virginia land. The plow was
greeted with enthusiasm in Paris and exhibited publicly in
the Jardin des Plantes. Randolph used the plow as a symbol
of Jefferson's abstract tendencies in political matters and
reminded his audience that an ordinary, common-sense
plow, unhonored by the Paris *savants,* "beat Mr. Jefferson's
plough as much as common sense will always beat theories
and reveries. . . ." Burke guided Randolph to a principled
disagreement with Jefferson, one that raised to a dignified
level their quarrel over shared political ideals. The chaste
past was for Randolph personally imagined, a subject for
nostalgia. Under the influence of Burke, Randolph organized his thinking about the decadence of Virginia and the
decline of virtue in America in a way that matched them to
the vivid outlines of his own history. Randolph surfaced
with a version of an American tradition, heavily Anglo-
phile, explicitly based on Burke, which at its truest level
vindicated the assumptions of his upbringing and blamed a
new, innovative, and vicious time for their obvious failings
and for the ruin of the world they were meant to describe.

It was an emotional, generalizing, and literal reading, different from his explicit use of Burke in particular arguments in that it was not after all Burkean. Imagining a tradition is not at all the same thing as explicating one. The difficulty with saying, as Kirk does, that Randolph was an American Burke and had always been one is that so long as Randolph was the proponent of a successful and hopeful republican ideology, his belief was inactive and superficial. Spurred on by disillusion with his party and then by the urgent need to re-examine his own life, Randolph came again to Burke and was converted. In the process, however, he took Burke's substance, not his method, and he came up with a reactionary, self-willed, nostalgic, and personal tradition which he expounded as if it were indeed the kind of nurturing political custom to which Burke referred. The status of tradition in post-Founding America was not certain; some sort of innovation and change may well have become the substance of American tradition. What is certain is that Randolph's attempt was foredoomed when he arbitrarily and, as has been suggested, idiosyncratically sought to name the moment and location of a Burkean standard by which to measure and inform the progress of American political life. Randolph was searching for a past moment of superior excellence by which to judge a society generally committed to a vision of progress. His quest shares the dignity of similar attempts by such unheeded prophets of decline as the Puritans, but its Burkean essence, as a method, is difficult to define. It does not appear to respect what was becoming, what had become, the indigenous political genius, good and evil, of American politics—a genius which, among other things, held that change was reform, and sought change in every event. As always with Randolph, these passionate and necessary readings of Burke made the most lasting impression. What emerged, however, was Burkean only in an ordering and referential sense. The real echoes were of Randolph's education and his despairing insistence upon an imagined past.[31]

Randolph's crisis receded only gradually. The melancholy, the religious enthusiasm, and the emotional instability it engendered remained with him. The self-pitying morbidness which had always been his failing became all too characteristic. Randolph sensed this, and also his imperfect self-control, and developed an attitude toward these aspects of himself which allowed him to play out his self-indulgence and at the same time maintain some distance from it. His old habit of fragmenting his roles served him well here. He was able to act out his feelings and then comment upon himself as if he were someone else. A note of apology, of self-explanatoriness, became increasingly frequent in his letters after 1813. The effect of this self-awareness was not to palliate or restrain his excesses. On the contrary, it existed on a separate plane from his egotism and by explaining served to license the wilder acting out of his feelings. In this sense, Randolph's self-consciousness, arising from and shaped by his losses, became the fellow traveler of his swollen self-centeredness. The effect of the combination was to fix his attention permanently on himself and his own needs and ideas. Public issues and private ones had to survive the tricky passage through his self-involvement, and the resulting characteristic attitudes about politics and society were just that—*characteristic*. The Randolph who survived 1813–15 turned everything in life to his own account, seeing first its relation to him. His person, his self, was increasingly and irrevocably both the lens and the focus of his views.

Randolph was aware of his voracious self-centeredness and of his proneness to act out his thinking, to assume the role of his opinions in any particular instance and to do so in an exaggerated fashion. As early as 1813, he wrote to his protégé Theodore Dudley, "Do not misconstrue me, whatever you may observe in my conduct or observations before others." This warning referred to more than the commonplace division between one's public and private selves. It showed Randolph's recognition that he not infrequently behaved unusually and fiercely, that he was not always the master of himself. Perhaps making statements like this was another way for him to question his own sanity, something he often did when among his intimates. It is an instructive guide to his self-awareness, that redeeming note of consciousness that lurked in his increasingly frequent and intense carryings-on. Another example of this elusive process of self-explanation came in an 1816 letter to Key. Randolph described his bitter and lonely sense that "the world is a vast desert, and there is no merit in renouncing it, since there is no difficulty," and continued, "I look back upon the havoc of the past year as upon a bloody field of battle, where my friends have perished. I look out towards the world, and find a wilderness, peopled indeed, but not with flesh and blood—with monsters tearing one another to pieces for money or power, or some other vile lust." His private and public griefs merged into one disappointed, fearful image of the world—the decadent, chaotic vision of the disillusioned idealist. This familiar stance of despair is militantly self-absorbed: the world reflects my misery and disappointment in it. What saved the outburst in the letter to Key was a curious moment of parenthetical self-awareness: "My own case (*everybody, no doubt, thinks the same*) appears to be peculiarly miserable." Randolph continued to believe that his situation was peculiarly miserable, and to act on that assumption. The disclaimer may have been *pro forma* and certainly did nothing to temper his statement of the case, but its presence indicated that Randolph had not simply surrendered to his self-indulgence. He indulged his morbid feelings with an eye on himself.[32]

Randolph's sense of himself, his willingness to talk about himself as a being already formed, in the emotional third person, was evident in another letter to Key, written in

1814. He was reacting to a comparison between himself and Lord Chatham:

No man is more sensible than I am of the distance between myself and Lord Chatham; but I would scorn to imitate even him. My powers, such as they are, have not been improved by culture. . . . My manner is spontaneous, flowing, like my matter, from the impulse of moment; and when I do not feel strongly, I cannot speak to any purpose. These fits are independent of my volition. . . . I had as lief be accused of any crime, not forbidden by the decalogue, as of *imitation*. If these critics choose to say that I have neglected, or thrown away, or buried my talent, I will acquiesce in the censure; but amongst the herd of imitators I will not be ranked, because I feel I could not descend to imitate any human being.

There are familiar elements in this statement: we recognize Randolph's accustomed stance of sensibility, of affectedness, taken beyond literature and natural life to define his attitude toward himself. He insisted on the authenticity and specialness of his untutored impulses and, what is more, on their originality. He still retained the old remorse about his undiscipline, but he identified this weakness with his public success. Discipline was good, but he was incapable of it—in the same natural sense as an *inability*—just as he might prove lacking certain particular talents or aptitudes. Discipline was like craft and guile; Randolph associated adult self-control, which he officially and in moments of self-reproach claimed to value, with those compromising and corrupt moral attitudes he had rejected in political life. "Imitation," in his letter to Key, has two meanings, both referring to kinds of dependence—emulation of someone else as a model, and simulation of a feeling or a state of mind. Both involve dishonest renderings of one's self and compromises with one's true feelings. Randolph insisted on his independence by rejecting self-control, which he conveniently associated with disingenuousness and a loss of integrity. Here, once again, can be seen the stance of sensibility unchecked, indeed dominating. The danger of imitation was that one would accept the corrupt world's standards for one's own.[33]

Randolph's version of himself was lonely but also self-serving and self-congratulatory. He defined himself and his character in such a way as to guard his moral position, that literal adherence to principle he cared for so dearly, against the assaults of a world willing to settle for something less than principle. His earlier method had been simply to hold up the discrepancy between principle and practice to public view, expecting it thereupon to be remedied. Randolph emerged from his retirement with a more baroque method: the elaborate presentation not only of the perception of inconstancy to principle but of himself, the perceiver of that inconstancy. The habits of mind which kept him from joining the adult world in its disappointed but realistic ventures determined how he would oppose, by opposing himself to, a corrupt world. Randolph anticipated the censure of critics almost eagerly. He had indeed wasted his promise; the years of political frustration were precisely the years spent defining his moral position—his apprenticeship. Randolph had come to look for sustenance and support not from anyone or anything, but, as they say, within himself. He was his own party. He himself, ingenuous and refreshed by the purest wells of moral sense, was all he had to rely on.

Randolph's comments on the publication of a speech he had delivered bear remark in this regard. He always detested the published versions of his speeches as dry distortions of his spontaneity: "The skeleton of the speech has been mounted by some bungler who knows nothing of political osteology. I feel ashamed of myself—not only stripped of my muscle, but my very bones disjointed." The metaphor may have been intended mockingly, but it contained the very special truth of Randolph's understanding of his political role. More than anyone else in his day, Randolph stood defiantly, insistently alone. He would not and did not co-operate. He said finally that he could not (for reasons of principle commonly, but sometimes of temper). He usually refused to edit and authorize publication of his speeches. They were, he said, absolute reflections of himself—not just of his opinions but of his whole being. His point had become the presentation of himself as the embodiment of a moral and a cultural position, and therein lay the folly of imitation for Randolph. It presented a false self. In a very real sense, his speeches were his flesh and blood, lifeless except in delivery. Reading one of his speeches could make him ashamed of himself. The complicated happenings of his public and private life, acting upon his self-involved, self-dramatizing, literal-minded nature, resulted in his at least partially self-conscious offering of "Randolph of Roanoke," the public man, as an alternative to bad democratic times: "It is too late in the day to vindicate my public character before a people whom I represented fourteen years, and whom, if they do not now know me, never will." It was a question of knowing Randolph and liking him or not. His tone was self-assured, as always, but newly explicit about the fact that at the core of his politics was a version of himself. This perceptible change in emphasis indicated something of the change in Randolph. He returned to Congress more committed than ever to the old ways but also committed to a version of himself embodying them as the text to be explicated.[34]

In an open letter to his constituents published on April 1, 1815, in the *Richmond Enquirer,* Randolph delineated his position on the state of public affairs at revealing length. His letter was first and foremost a defense of himself, reminding his people that he had been right all along, about the world and the disastrous turn of government and society away from the old republican standards. Randolph emphasized the prophetic role he had for nine years carried on: "Nine years have now elapsed since he raised his voice against the commencement of a system of measures, which although artfully disguised, were calculated, as he believed, to produce what we have all seen, and are fated long to feel." The disastrous consequences of administration treachery were but too evident, disunion and anarchy were in the air. "Anarchy is the chyrsalis state of despotism; and to that state have the measures of the government long tended. . . ." The letter sounded a new note, critical of popular democracy and strongly Burkean: "None but the people can forge their own chains; and to flatter the people and delude them by promises never meant to be performed is the stale but successful practice of the demagogue, as of the seducer in private life." The war had burdened the people with repression, debt, and taxation: ". . . disease and vice, in new unheard-of forms, spread from the camp throughout society. Not a village, not a neighborhood, hardly a family escapes the infection." Randolph's list of the horrors let loose upon the country paralleled the list of his own misfortunes: land threatened and encumbered, natural disasters, starving slaves and hard-pressed masters, the loss of sons and heirs: "His eldest son has perished in the tentless camp, the bloodless but fatal fields of the enemy country." The state of government bitterly reflected a chaotic and burdened and degenerate society; the war was carried on by sharpsters and would-be tyrants. Men had but two choices, a military career or a career at court. "In a little while, men of all parties will insensibly slide into the support of the Cabal at Washington; will be seen dangling in the ante-chamber of the Secretary of War, dancing attendance for a commission." Even the opposition was enfeebled: a little time would see them "very good courtiers" while their younger ranks will be at once "thorough Janissaries." Randolph drew a picture of American society in the colors and shadings of the country-party style—showing court and country, threatened independence and insinuating dependence. It was a more complete and self-contained version than any of his previous attacks. He took his stand explicitly on the traditional distinctions: "I was not born into this order of things, and I never will consent, voluntarily, to become the vassal of a privileged order of military and monied men, by whom, as by a swarm of locusts, the produce of my land is to be devoured, and its possessors consigned to indigence and scorn."

Randolph's cry of alarm was almost a set piece—the terrible state of things had become his personal vindication. There was a note of complacency in his assertions of declension, the peril to civil liberty, and the futility of opposition. He had not urged his own election: "I was satisfied with having stood an eight years' siege against the whole power and patronage of Government and the incessant roar of the press exclusively devoted to the administration. To fall in such a cause was no mean glory." Randolph treated his being in opposition now as the badge of his righteousness. He was self-congratulatory and self-regarding in his references to conditions. He did not appeal to his constituents; he merely reminded them that time had proven him right on all counts all along and that his prophetic principledness was, as ever, at their service. He promised nothing except that he would continue to go on his own way, which he hoped they had learned not to question. He acknowledged the "egotism" of his position: "But, as I am the subject, I know not how to write about it without mention of myself." Randolph had added to his principled opposition at Washington, a self-proclaimed, self-willed and Burkean independence of his constituents:

I have heretofore trod the path of public duty, fearless of consequences; secure of that confidence which furnished at once the motive and means of exertion. Are you not afraid that, when I should seize some state felon by the throat and drag him to the bar of public justice, I shall be throwing many a homeward look, doubtful of your support? Respect for the opinions, even for the prejudices of his constituents, a common interest and common feeling with them, are essential to the character of a fit and fruitful representative of the people. But none can be more unfit, and, in fact, unfaithful than he who is ever trembling for his influence at home, and in the general wreck of the state, is alive only to the risk of his own paltry popularity.

The people were free to join with him in righteousness, but the judgment and direction were to be Randolph's.

The whole declaration was a confirmation of his previous attitudes, with the difference that here Randolph said explicitly that he stood alone, in opposition, on the traditional grounds. His Burkean language and analysis of conditions successfully and altogether conflated the American situation with the imaginary (although possible) conditions country doctrine warned about. The effect of his retirement appears here to have been one of confirmation. His adherence to the old ways had become, if anything, more explicit, more complete. He had even adopted the Old Republicans' anti-democratic strain, something he had previously stayed clear of. The will of the people as they expressed it, like the majority decisions of government, might ratify Randolph's independent good sense but not shake it. This letter revealed the completeness with which Randolph had accepted the consequences of his own position, assuming the public self that it demanded. Toward the close he alluded to Shakespeare in an interesting fashion, reminding his readers that "this is not the language of an American libel but of a dramatic writer who flourished under an English Queen, the glory of whose reign and the sagacity of whose ministers we are barbarous enough to think not eclipsed by those of the Prince Regent." Finding American tradition insufficiently stable ground for explaining his own life and what he took to be his country's serious danger, Randolph with characteristic literalness and transparent arrogance attached his critique to an older tradition, the one he had grown up within, a restatement of the country doctrine. Resting his opposition on this foundation, he fashioned himself into its deliberately obtrusive human version. Within himself he contained all his politics, and he pursued them independent of party or people.

Randolph's opposition to the National Bank during the Fourteenth Congress exemplified his attitudes in action. The principal theme of his argument in opposition to the

Bank was straight country doctrine. The Bank served as a focus for a more pervasive concern—with the degenerate state of society, which endangered the Republic. Randolph treated the Bank less as a specific substantive issue than as the symbol of what was wrong in general. The consciousness of decay informed his entire presentation, framing the specific issues, adding urgency and legitimacy to his argument: "Let us not disguise the fact, Sir. We think we are living in the better times of the Republic. We deceive ourselves; we are almost in the days of Sulla and Marius." The Bank was an evil which reflected the corrupt and greedy spirit of the times: "The evil of the times is a spirit engendered in this republic, fatal to Republican principles; fatal to Republican virtue." Looking around the chambers of the Republic, Randolph saw "a stockholder, president, cashier, clerk or doorkeeper, runner, engraver, papermaker, or mechanic in some other way to a bank." There was no way of escaping "this mammoth." "The banks are so linked together with the business of the world that there are very few men except for their influence." At the head of the few stood Randolph. He compared the Bank to the East India scandal and both to the "spirit of party." In a subsequent debate, Randolph again expressed his point of view:

I am the holder of no stock whatever, except livestock, and had determined never to own any, but, if this bill passes, I will not only be a stockholder to the utmost of my power, but will advise every man over whom I have any influence, to do the same, because it is the creation of a great privileged order of the most hateful kind to my feelings, and because I would rather be the master than the slave. If I must have a master, let him be one with epaulettes, something I can fear and respect, something I can look up to—but not a master with a quill behind his ear.[35]

What Randolph perceived to be at stake in the Bank fray was nothing less than the morals and manners of the society. He had taken over the old country habit of seeing in every particular conflict the ultimate general struggle. The question was the survival of republican institutions, which Randolph saw imperiled by the centralizing commercial pull of the democratic spirit of progress and entrepreneurial daring. The heightened warning language he used referred not so much to the Bank as to the underlying situation he took it to signify. Reflecting on this issue in 1823, Randolph revealed the train of thought it started:

Sir, that act, and one other which I will not name, bring forcibly home to my mind a train of melancholy reflections on the miserable state of our moral being;

> *'In life's last scene what prodigies surprise,*
> *Fears of the brave, and follies of the wise?*
> *From Marlb'rough's eyes the streams of dotage flow,*
> *And Swift expires a driv'ler and a show.'*

Such is the state of the case, sir. It is miserable to think of it—and we have nothing left to us but to weep over it.

The overtones and undertones of this passage show how Randolph had come to identify his public and private concerns so that they informed and embittered one another. He might as easily have said these things (and did say very like things) about himself and his race as about his country. Personal crisis following on the heels of the astonishing disillusionment of his first years in Congress had attached Randolph even more stubbornly to the ideas and manners of his boyhood, as he now—older, disappointed but still self-involved, self-dramatizing, and literal-minded—understood and applied them. His was a deliberately evocative, allusive, and anachronistic posture. He assumed it out of need and, folks said, out of madness. In examining it, two things must be remembered; it frequently worked, and as Randolph often reminded his friends, he "had method in my madness."[36]

7

Randolph of Roanoke: "The Warden on the Lonely Hill"

> His was a nature that would have made for itself a hell even though fate had put a heaven about it.
>
> HENRY ADAMS

In his second public career as congressman, sometime senator, and ambassador to Russia, John Randolph continued to espouse the principles of his upbringing with literalness and vehemence. He acted out more completely and with greater abandon than he had previously the ideas he held about politics and society. The style of his later years was an aggressive and insistent assertion of an eccentric self. This eccentricity was not altogether new, but now it engrossed his public capacity to the exclusion of other means of political communication. It also carried Randolph to extremes of behavior, bizarre and unrestrained even by his idiosyncratic standards. There were some opportunities for a revival of his political fortunes, but because of his alienation from the political process and the social climate of American society, his feints at politics were halfhearted and foredoomed. His way of making the most of his opportunities was to address himself to what he thought was a headstrong and self-destructive country, finally preferring to prophesy its destruction rather than to save it.

For Randolph this was an era of blasted hopes. The reasons for his disillusionment have been examined previously. Fundamentally, however, his disappointment resulted from the literalness and naïveté of his commitment to what he had been taught as a boy, to lessons inappropriate and misleading in nineteenth-century America. True to his mother's injunctions he passionately kept to the land, accumulating and cultivating it, and—the proof of his unusually strong commitment—made it keep him. Similarly, he returned to his mother's words in matters of religion, professing to have become in his middle age a devout Anglican. In public matters he kept himself firmly to the old ways too: anti-Federalist, American Revolutionary, country-party, *republican*. Public life presented a problem, however. To hold to the traditional line oneself was not enough; a nation of people remained to be disciplined, argued, or terrorized into republican correctness. This task had proved Randolph's downfall in his first congressional career, and he no longer seriously expected to succeed in it. Upon his return to Congress in 1815, he understood himself to be returning to opposition, and so defined his posture. In each new assault he included references to his previous career in opposition, again and again making it very clear that his contemporary particular stance had its sources in himself as he had stood before. "I bore some humble part in putting down the dynasty of John the First, and, by the grace of God, I hope to aid in putting down the dynasty of John the second," he announced when John Quincy Adams became president. He played on his feud with the Adams presidents not merely to emphasize a political point but to create that aura of old-fashioned politics in which the disputes of interest and character, and the standards, were unchanging: "The cub was a greater bear than the old one." The stuff of American politics became under Randolph's masterful and determined direction a Shakespearean drama, a grand and fateful quarrel, a noble fight to the death, as if it were being staged in a long-distant and tangential time, a time when different regions produced different kinds of men, defending certain clearly opposing interests. The Randolph who rallied the southern sectional cause did not differ in political substance all that much from the boy who had criticized the southern members of the first federal Congress for their inattention to the concerns of their region. New England was still New England and an Adams still an Adams—indeed they had to be for Randolph to be Randolph still.[1]

The isolation, righteousness, and independence of the opposition stance suited him. And so Randolph developed, or perhaps completed, his public style in the expectation of isolation. It was a personal creation, the invention, intermittently self-conscious, of a public self to represent the fast-evaporating world to whose values Randolph was irrevocably tied and to attack the democracy and its attendant social mores, which appalled him. Martin Van Buren recollected the subjects of Randolph's conversation during the 1820's, the subjects upon which his mind commonly ran:

He avoided, as a general rule, the subjects under discussion in Congress, apparently glad to drop them and to recreate his mind in fresh fields, except when something of unusual piquancy was afoot, and when left to himself, Virginia, her public men of earlier days, her people and her past condition, the character and life of his deceased brother Richard, with England and the English, were commonly the themes on which he talked better than I have ever heard another man talk. Nothing could be more interesting than his descriptions of the former prosperity of the Old Dominion, the extent and magnificience of the baronial establishments, as he called them, especially on the James River and the Appomattox, the honorable pride and splendid hospitality and true quality of their proprietors and the contrasts he depicted between those halcyon days and the times in which he spoke.

As Constance Rourke has reminded us in *American Humor,* this was an age of boldly drawn public figures, legendary and less legendary, conceived for a newly interested mass of equal men. "Characters in public life were indeed one of the great creations of the time; and they seemed to gain their emphasis less from closely packed individualism than from bold and conscious self-picturization." This observation applies especially and perhaps quintessentially to John Randolph. He made an impact. In his last years, Randolph abandoned himself to the character we have come to know as "Randolph of Roanoke," the eccentric and prophetic figure of the old-fashioned times which democratic America was fast supplanting. Randolph of Roanoke concentrated his many talents in a distracted delaying tactic, a harrying of the American present and tendency in the name of an ever more remote and obscured past age. Sometimes he made nonsense and sometimes he made common sense and on a few issues he made startling sense; what remained constant was not the value of what he said but its source—the character, the persona, Randolph of Roanoke. "As Calanthe died dancing, so must I die speaking."[2]

Randolph returned to a Congress in which he was continually outnumbered and habitually alone on those matters he most deeply cared about. Within a few years new times brought him some new and some old allies. The Missouri crisis seemed to revitalize Randolph's states' rights purism. Missouri and postwar mercantilism together brought the southern states to a more general awareness of the threat that a centralized and democratic national regime might pose to their most cherished interests and institutions. Strict construction, states' rights, and the determined defense of slavery became again common, southern grounds of political allegiance, and their most consistent champion again rose in sectional esteem. Soon even Thomas Jefferson was referring to John Randolph as his old "companion in sentiments." This revival of Old Republican doctrines and language, which was intermittently to characterize southern sectionalism did not really capture the religious and literal tone of the original run. Norman Risjord concludes that as the position "became less a matter of the Virginia conscience and more a matter of economics, it underwent a gradual, yet perceptible, change." No longer a statement of conscience and principle, strict construction became a standpoint from which to oppose particular national administrations by raising general arguments. It was a useful theoretical way of expressing political dissent, with a very respectable tradition behind it. It was also very often an appropriate and necessary substantive argument.[3]

Randolph contributed to the revived perception of the southern interest in two ways. He said outright what others had tended to avoid, eschewing euphemism for dire, inflammatory warning, as in a speech on internal improvements on January 31, 1824:

There is one other power which may be exercised in case the power now contended for be conceded, to which I ask the attention of every gentleman who happens to stand in the same unfortunate predicament with myself—of every man who has the misfortune to be and to have been born a slaveholder. If Congress possess the power to do what is proposed by this bill, they may not only enact a sedition law—for which there is precedent—but they may emancipate every slave in the United States and with stronger color of reason than they can exercise the power now contended for. . . . I ask gentlemen who stand in the same predicament as I do to look well to what they are now doing, to the colossal power with which they are now arming the government. The power to do what I allude to is, I aver, more honestly inferable from the warmaking power than the power we are now about to exercise. Let them look forward to such a time when such a question shall arise, and tremble with me at the thought that that question is to be decided by a majority of votes in this House, of whom not one possess the slightest tie of common interest or common feeling with us.

Having made his point about what might constitute the real common interest within this union, Randolph illustrated in himself, personified, a reminder of it. He captured in his bearing the ideal, the story, the ancestry, the legend, and the warning—most poignantly the warning—of sectional interest. He stood on that common ground of southern particularism to which he summoned his fellows. It was a high and mighty ground and an ancestral one, fed by the literary and historical and fantastic sources that fed the developing southern imagination and self-consciousness. His attacks were reminders and promises of glory as well as warnings of decline and defeat. The country had always preached suspiciousness, and Randolph in his arguments and in himself lent a solidity of specification to that suspiciousness; he provided a really shared rallying ground, hallowed by his capers, soon enough to be hallowed by blood. What energies of reform and improvement, working as they must against a clear material and racial interest, could compete with the show of Randolph of Roanoke? His didacticism recalled the deepest sentiments and shrines of his audience, the old household gods and even the unspoken cultural taboos; it was a preserving didacticism, embodying the old lessons and the old warnings. It was a symbol offered for a cause reluctantly but perhaps irresistibly in the making. Randolph may not have converted Calhoun, but he opened the way for more conventionally expressed agreement.[4]

The politically motivated rehabilitation of Randolph did him no lasting political good. He was too difficult, too extreme, as always, and his friends proved insufficiently attached to his view of their common beliefs. The occasional revivals in his political fortunes were brief—his eccentric and isolating behavior continued to stand in the way of co-operation. Randolph's story remained one of opposition and disagreement. His behavior reflected the depth of his convictions, which made impossible his co-operation with others of apparently similar principles. Eccentricity in his case had become a metaphor for the *how*, which of necessity modified and sanctioned the *what*, of political belief.[5]

Randolph's behavior was legendary in his own day. If people listened to him, it was because they were watching him. He aroused interest among his constituents, his colleagues, the American public, and (when he traveled) foreigners. He cut an intriguing, unusual, and memorable figure. According to William Cabell Bruce, no one spoke of Randolph, even years later, without attempting to mimic his unique presence. There is ovewhelming evidence of his theatrical public personality, especially during his later career, and of the popularity of his performances. Bruce admits that the thousands went to hear Randolph not for instruction, but "to be startled and entertained." When he appeared in public, by all accounts, he packed them in; the crowds always came. His speeches were more performances than oratory. Hugh Blair Grigsby typically describes Randolph as an actor: "He was, too, though he had the art to conceal his art from common observers, a consummate actor. In the philosophy of voice and gesture, and in the use of pause, he was as perfect an adept as ever trod the boards of Covent Garden or Drury Lane." His feuding neighbor Henry Carrington agreed; describing a public business dealing with Randolph he said, "The scene was highly dramatic; the acting, if it could be so regarded, unsurpassed." It is impossible to recreate the Randolph performance. He did not rest on the text he was speaking. "His words were only a part of his performance; the uttering of but few of these showed that he was an *actor*. They were few. So were his gestures. But his gestures were as expressive as his words." Randolph cast a great actor's spell, combining the statement of his meaning with vivid and cunning self-presentation. He may have seemed out of control, about to burst, thundering and roving through the disparate estates of his concern, but his appreciative contemporaries, whatever the stripe of their opinion, knew good talking when they heard it: "This combination required deliberation for its display; otherwise, it cannot be conceived how so much time was consumed in uttering so few words, without any apparent impatience of his hearers, or that throbbing twitter which is felt when expectation is excited and held too long in suspense." Randolph knew the limits of most situations, taking advantage of them with exasperating exactness: he knew with whom he could or could not duel, whom he could or could not intimidate, whom he could or could not entrance; in the Senate he took full and mighty advantage of his right to talk at length to no particular purpose outside of his own, and on the stump he knew how to entertain his people. He could rise with pantomime mischief to his own perception of what more solemn occasions might require. At the Virginia constitutional convention, Randolph was in the company of the living pantheon of Virginian patriots; Madison, Monroe, and Marshall set a very high tone for the proceedings, and yet Randolph managed to make not only his argued points but his other kinds of points as well:

But Mr. Randolph, who was a great *actor,* drew many eyes to himself. At first he leaned forward, gazed as if in wonder and in awe. For two or three moments he looked and acted as if he expected something great. By degrees he seemed to lose interest in the speaker, and finally sank back into his seat with a strong expression of contempt on his countenance. He had said not a word nor violated any parliamentary law. The acting was perfect. It had its effect.

By the 1820's, Randolph had mastered, if not himself, the display of himself.[6]

The drama of his appearance was as careful and effective as that of his speaking. A James Whittle described Randolph's appearance on the way home from Congress at Prince Edward County Court in 1821:

In a short time, after reaching the courthouse, groups of people were seen hurrying to a spot down the road some hundred yards off. Joining the throng, I followed on, and discovered a dense crowd surrounding a person in a sulky, drawn by a gray horse, and behind it, a negro seated on another of the same color, apparently its match. The heads of these animals were lifted high above the spectators, and looked down upon them with disdainful pride. On approaching, it was observed that the sulky and harness were deep black, with brilliant plated mountings, the shafts bent to a painful segment of a circle, the horses of the best keep, as doubtless they were of the highest blood. The servant, who was of the profoundest sable, carried a high black portmanteau behind him, and was attired in clothing of the same hue. Quite a strong contrast—possibly designed—was exhibited between the masses of intense darkness and the plating, the horses,

the teeth and shirt collar of the servant. The order of the whole
equipage was complete. . . .

Randolph's personal drama was in keeping with the drama
of his gear. Of his bow, Whittle observed, "It may be
doubted whether there lives in America a man who can do
this as he did it. His countenance and manner were solemn—funeral. . . ." And then of Randolph himself:

He appeared to be the Englishman and Indian mixed; the latter
assuming the outer, the former, the larger part of the inner, man.
His dress was all English—all over. His hat was black; his coat was
blue, with brilliant metallic buttons and velvet collar; his breeches
and vest drab, with fair-topped English boots and massive silver
spurs—likely they were ancestral; his watch ribbon sustained a
group of small seals—heirlooms it may be, from times beyond
Cromwell. His age must have been about forty-three; his hair was
bright-brown, straight, not perceptibly gray, thrown back from
his forehead and tied into a queue, neither long nor thick. His
complexion was swarthy; his face beardless, full, round and
plump; his eyes hazel, brilliant, inquisitive, moody. . . . Every part
of his dress and person was evidently accustomed to the utmost
care.

Randolph made a vivid public showing. Always expressive
in his dress and accessories, the young stripling in Revolutionary buff and blue who rode alone to Congress, where
bespattered and muddy he walked, riding crop in hand,
hounds at heel, had matured into this outlandishly anachronistic picture of olden elegance, stepping, as it were,
out of a tableau of vanished glory. That seems to have been
his point. Randolph's person and his behavior made his
message clear to all observers. It was not essential to be literate to understand him; it was not even necessary to *hear*
him. One look.[7]

All of the reminiscences of Randolph convey the same
sense of his keen and effective self-presentation: he was the
dramatization of his ideas. Randolph's behavior worsened
with age. My attempt to make sense of his positions and
offer reasons for his carryings-on ought not to be con-

strued as an effort to palliate or mitigate his excesses; I am trying only to discover what in them must be understood to take the meaning of their shapely point. Randolph offered his people an embodiment of his difference from them, broad enough for all to apprehend and dramatic enough to constitute a good show. Personifying the bygone days, now kindly recalled because they were gone, his aristocratic showing appealed to the shared nostalgic sense of community in a changing democratic America, and thereby avoided the offense that might have been taken by an independent people. His public gestures and actions were all about mastery—the kind of aristocratic mastery that had largely disappeared from relations between white men and was curiously regretted by the 1820's. The English and Indian elements in his bearing heightened the old-fashionedness of it all. We can only conclude that the people he so grandly entertained shared some part of his nostalgia for the good old days. They all knew those days were done for, and they could safely enjoy Randolph's impersonation of them, easing their obscure sense that perhaps all had not changed for the better. Bruce concludes that "few men have ever so completely enslaved the imagination of a people as Randolph did that of the people among whom he lived. They felt in him such a degree of curious interest as they felt in no other man." The trick was to be the subject of interest without arousing too much resentment. Randolph turned that trick, in his own native country at least. Nor were his more cosmopolitan and nationalistically inclined contemporaries immune to the effect of a Randolph performance, as a letter to Gideon Welles from John M. Niles reporting on the Virginia constitutional convention of 1829 reveals. Niles, his feet firmly planted in the real political and democratic and American world of his day, perceived Randolph as the shade of old Virginia:

You will perceive that I am in the capital of the "Ancient Dominion" and in the headquarters, if not of correct principle, at least of those principles which have, and hitherto do, sustain the ancient political regimen of this great commonwealth. This regimen, however, of the slave holder and tobacco grower, is gradually giving way, and this very day a great victory has been gained, by what the orator of Roanok [*sic*] calls "King Numbers." . . . The Virginians are so fond of speechmaking and of long speeches too, that it is impossible to tell when the convention will be brought to a close. It appears to me it will require the whole winter to finish the work before them, unless they take John Randolph's advice who told them "that the best and the only service they could render the state was to go home and advise the people to be satisfied with the blessing which they enjoyed."

The association of Randolph with the political analysis of the disappearance of Old Dominion ways, which Niles made, was the response the "orator of Roanoke" had in mind.[8]

Randolph's public offering was a version of himself as a vessel for his thoughts on public questions. Here again, observers agreed that the older Randolph had no other principle of organization in public than himself: "Again, I must decline any analysis or compendium of his speech, it was controllingly personal, personal in both aspects of the term, as relating to himself, and as relating to other individuals." This method, of course, fashioned theater from public questions. Randolph associated measures with men, and not just his own measures with himself. This approach suited his view of public issues—bad deeds were done by bad men and resulted in bad times for the people. It also suited his uncanny sense of the nature of his public appeal. He brought into view his personal relations with other well-known figures in order to dramatize his politics. The role of the man of honor attracted him because it evoked the values he wished to restore, and dramatized in the right way the only kind of political struggle he was willing to admit—the struggle of principle on a field of honor. Thus his duel with Henry Clay occurred over a personal remark in which Randolph expressed his political hostility to Clay and John Quincy Adams. A Dr. Kirkpatrick characterized his speeches as self-promptings: "For the most part, his remarks followed one another on no principle governing them than that of involuting suggestion. They seemed to run riot, without any act of the will to control the selection, the order of the limits. . . . So he went on from hour to hour, a 'freelance,' challenging all comers." He appeared the involuntary mouthpiece of his inner self, uncontrolled from within and uncontrollable from without. And yet Mr. Whittle considered it "obvious that the supreme mastery which he had over himself was essential to the deadly aim of his arrow, and the fatal mixing of the poison in which he dipped it." Randolph's were calculated excesses. His insults and his personalizing of issues made them easier to understand in his terms. He disciplined himself to appear carried away with the moment.[9]

Was Randolph aware of himself as a public person—did he intend the effect he had? At such a distance and in the absence of concrete evidence that he presented a conscious image in the way contemporary Americans might, this question is difficult to answer with assurance. Such evidence as we have, however, suggests strongly that there was conscious if intermittent method in all of his public wildness. A study of his character indicates that Randolph's literal-minded and self-dramatizing disposition drove him to the extreme of impersonating his ideas as a solution to personal and political difficulties. His ideas were the kind that depended on personal action. He insisted on a coincidence of profession and behavior that only impersonation could satisfy. He had to act out his uncorrupted independence, live the values of his tradition, behave according to his old lights, if only to distinguish himself from the practices he deplored in society and government. His peculiarly intimate sense that what he valued was threatened with decline and loss made his choice of behavior a matter of utter seriousness. The political problem he faced was that, as he saw it, American government had come to that point where co-operation in public measures involved one in cor-

ruption with terrible regularity. Randolph felt himself irrevocably committed to opposition, to a role outside party
and caucus. Thus left to himself, he had only the resources
of his own personality from which to fashion his impact on
public life. He had come to identify his personal isolation
with the cause of civic virtue. He had acquiesced in a solitary role, deciding that whatever else might fail him, his
principles would not, and however and wherever he might
fail, his would not be a failure of principles. In 1821 he
wrote:

My days of business, of active employment, are over. My judgment, I believe, has not deserted me, and when it does, as old
George Mason said, I shall be the last person in the world to find
it out; my principles I am *sure* have not; and if, which God forbid,
they should, I shall be the first person to find it out. Till that shall
happen, I will be "the warden on the lonely hill."

And in a speech in Congress: "I am contented to act the
part of Cassandra, to lift up my voice, whether it will be
heeded, or heard only to be disregarded, until too late."[10]

Content to be fool or prophet, resigned to being proven
right by later events, Randolph was forced to dramatize
himself as a *persona,* the embodiment of his warnings. It
might be said at this point that if Randolph appeared to
present a sprawling, cascading, and indiscreet public self,
this was in part because he had to include not only his
warning but the example of his warning. Thus Randolph
of Roanoke illustrated the process of declension and not
merely the staid apprehension of decline. His excesses
were among his chief examples of what had changed. His
anachronistic, exaggerated demeanor and behavior were
as essential in making his point as were the pungent things
he had to say about other people. One cannot separate
Randolph's meaning from his cantankerous inflections, as
Beverley Tucker and Russell Kirk tried to do, even for the
sake of upholding his opinions. A restrained adherence to
Randolph's positions, however attractive, must sacrifice the

clamor and height of his feeling. Picturesqueness had a shrewd claim on his intention. Randolph knew how to summon up his particular associations, the ones he needed in order to show as well as tell the people his story. As he saw it, there really was no other way, and one suspects that for someone of Randolph's inclinations it was a sympathetic choice. With all its frustrations, this role seems to have been the one preferred in his heart and soul. Certainly, it was the one in which is gifts served him most nobly and with the least reproach. All those disabilities of temper and eccentricities of spirit that Gallatin worried over in a successor to Jefferson suited the self-dramatizer of opposition. In the same way, his wide-ranging reading served his search for models; his literal-minded attachment to the past informed the impersonation of the vanished glory of Virginia; his lack of self-discipline facilitated his studied and undisciplined appearances. The role suited him all right, and that is possibly explanation enough of why he took it up.

The question of self-awareness persists. Without some hint that Randolph saw himself with some clarity in his public persona, it is hard to believe that he could have meant anything by it. If he was to be more than a dervish, there must have been some self-consciousness. Two avenues lead to the conclusion that this self-consciousness did exist: his staged behavior, which always had an intelligible point, and the regular references to his public performance in private letters. The second first. Randolph's letters after 1815 contain frequent references that can reliably be read as acknowledgments of the existence of a public persona that was his own creation; in some moods, however, it was a creation that misled the friend who wished to know him, *as he really was.* One consistent strain was of protest: he would proclaim that "they" were putting words into his mouth, although he could not always remember what he did say in public. Embarrassed protest was a way in which Randolph distinguished himself from his public performances and in effect acknowledged them. These morning-after protests were either confused or confusing, but all in all they seem to indicate both awareness and embarrassment. Writing in 1820 to Dr. John Brockenbrough, who headed the Bank at Richmond and was perhaps his closest friend, Randolph talked of his private needs and the inseparable public ones:

The situation of public affairs, and of my own more especially, disturb my daily and nightly thoughts. I believe I must even make up my mind to "overdraw" or to be "an unfortunate man." Can you put me in no way to become a successful rogue to an amount that may throw an air of dignity over the transaction, and divert the attention of the gaping spectators from the enormity of the offense, to that of the sum?

He understood his public quite well, one feels. He was always complaining of being misquoted and misrepresented. "All the bastard wit of the country is fathered on me":

I must be a very uncommon personage "to astonish all the world" with what I *do not do*. Since I am not able to astonish them with my exploits, it is very good in them to be negatively charged on my account. I heartily wish that I had never given them any other cause of wonder. [1822]

The morning ride, my affairs, my horses and dogs afford me deeper occupation, and over my coffee and wine I look with pity upon this frumpery world, where my actions are being watched and words set down to be repeated, not always as they are uttered. [1828]

Randolph would write texts for his appearances; he continued to make those appearances although he was aware that his behavior was noticed and exaggerated. In fact, one eyewitness account has him telling a stenographer who was to record one of his speeches that since it was impracticable to take the whole business down, the sharpest parts, "the biting parts at least, should be preserved; and in conclusion saying: 'When I say anything that *tickles under the tail,* be sure to put it down.' "[11]

Randolph's way of distinguishing himself from the extravagance of his public actions, especially to his few good friends, was to claim that he was being misrepresented. It is a venerable means by which the popular performer can distinguish himself from his embarrassing acceptance by the vulgar public. (It is not unknown today and is not so outrageous when one considers that the alternative is complete self-deception; demagoguery of any sort is unpleasant, but it is an interesting question as to whether the sincere form is preferable.) Randolph sometimes dealt with the problem of his public representation through philosophical strategies, finding justification, for example, in the conclusion that all the world is like that: "We dare not trust ourselves with the truth. It is too terrible. Hence the whole world is in masquerade. ... Hence a conventional language in which it is understood that things are never to be called by their right names, and which at least ceases to answer its original design, except with the vulgar, great and small." Randolph's consistent uneasiness with his public self did not particularly restrain him and worried him only after the fact, among friends to whom he wished always to appear indifferent to the public roar. When he had to own up to a speech, Randolph tended to blame the enthusiasm of the occasion, whatever the occasion: "But the truth is, that after the occasion passes away, I can seldom recall what I said until I am put in mind, by what I did not say, or by some catch word." There is no doubt that the necessity of public exposure galled him even as he delighted in it. That contrariness is again a not unfamiliar American reaction. Writing to Elizabeth Coalter in 1828, he declared, "I can hardly bear the gaze of the multitude, but I shrink from the eyes of those who know me only by person or reputation." He railed against the "dense crowd" even as he sought its repellent attention, and crying out in irritation "that he was no *wild beast* intended for public exhibition," he implicitly acknowledged that he was and that he had insisted upon being one. The ample testimony by witnesses of every opinion about Randolph confirms the inescapable sense that he sought and exploited the very attention he professed to despise, for its effect on him was unvarying and in the most literal sense inspiring: "As he saw the people gather around the stand, his eye began to kindle, his color to rise; and as he became more and more animated, his eyes sparkled brighter and brighter, and his cheeks grew rosy, the wrinkles on his face seemed to disappear with the sallowness and languor, and he became almost transfigured." That is to say, he became "himself" under the intoxicating influence of the stimulant he despised and needed.[12]

The particulars of Randolph's "eccentric" carryings-on offer another kind of evidence that there was more than a little self-consciousness in his public role. Almost every anecdote about his public behavior exhibits a core of witty, clearheaded intelligibility, as well as keen judgment of the effect on his audience. His notorious challenges expressed more fully than any conventional politics could the range of his disagreement with the measures and methods of the government. In an age of equality and self-interested compromise, Randolph succeeded in forcing some of his antagonists onto the field of honor.

The famous episode of Randolph's duel with Henry Clay exemplifies this intelligibility. Their quarrel was an old one—Clay's charismatic dominion over the House of Representatives in the years of war with England was of the kind Randolph had once exercised and in that cause had isolated and defeated him. Clay's western ease and hardheaded guile succeeded where Randolph might have liked to succeed. In politics, Clay stood for a nationalism and a spirit of accommodation of conflicting principles that could not have been more repugnant to Randolph. It was probably Randolph who would rather have been right. There was a spirit of contest between them. One of Randolph's demented episodes concerned his refusal to board a ship called the *Henry Clay*. It is said that he was buried facing west, contrary to the custom of the country, so that he could keep an eye on Henry Clay. It is certainly true that on his last trip to Washington, Randolph commanded that he be brought to the Senate so that he could hear Clay speak one last time. In a letter of 1820, Randolph bragged that he had celebrated Washington's birthday by forcing Speaker Clay to pay him strict attention through dramatic parliamentary punctiliousness: "a memorable day in the history of my life." Randolph enjoyed twitting and humbling Clay—personally and politically—for he knew the Speaker to be the current engine of what he disapproved of in American government:

He replied in a subdued tone of voice, and with a manner quite changed from his usual petulance and arrogance (for it is generally one or t'other, sometimes both) that he had paid all possible attention &c., which was not true, in fact: for from the time that I entered upon the subject of his conduct in relation to the bank in 1811 (the new bank) and or internal improvements, &c (quoting his words in his last speech that "this was a limited, *cautiously restricted* government") and held up the "compromise" in its true colors, he never once glanced his eye upon me but to withdraw it, as if he had seen a basilisk.

Some of the pretenders to the throne, if not the present incumbent, will hold me from that day forth in cherished remembrance. I have not yet done, however, with the pope or the pretenders, their name is legion.

Randolph considered Clay a proper enemy—one who was worthy of his hostility and to whom he had things to say. In the presidential election of 1824, since no candidate received a majority of the vote in the Electoral College, the choice was made by the House of Representatives; Clay, who was then Speaker, cast his influence for the hated John Quincy Adams. Thus when Clay joined with Adams in the new administration, the circumstances were easily misconstrued, and Randolph seized the opportunity to attack the men and their measures. In the course of a Senate debate (for Randolph had at that time been elevated to the Senate) on a matter involving both the Panama Congress and the proper relations between Senate and chief executive, Randolph took out after Secretary of State Clay. Randolph accused Clay of attempting to "influence" the Senate with his misleading charm, and succeeding. He topped off his attack with this famous provocation: "I was defeated, horse, foot, and dragoons—cut up, and clean broke down by the coalition of Blifil and Black George—and by the combination, unheard of til then, of the puritan with the blackleg." The sally was brilliant, witty, and effective: Clay challenged him and their duel ensued.[13]

What is most noteworthy about Randolph's remark is how faithfully it encapsulated his political quarrel with Clay—a deal for the presidency by a legislative leader was the ultimate in the corruption he so feared, and he saw the combination as even more substantially dangerous because of the shared centralizing nationalism of Adams and Clay—and how effectively it shifted the level of discourse to the one he preferred. Randolph had his own way of forcing Clay not merely to pay attention to him but to accept his own terms altogether. Yet as Henry Adams wrote in apparent disparagement, Randolph was not literally after blood: "He never pressed a quarrel to the end, or resented an insult further than was necessary to repel it. . . . His insulting language and manner came not from the heart, but from the head." His political terrorism was theater—effective theater, as his encounter with Clay demonstrated. They settled their difference as Randolph felt they should have conducted public business, like gentlemen, in accordance with a system which was generally honored, like his opinions, in the breach. Though Randolph's conduct was eccentric, it is certainly intelligible. Thomas Hart Benton's account shows how theatrical the affair was for Randolph—if not for Clay—and how strong its impact might have been on a democratic politician and people. A critic's comment on the source of Randolph's offensive allusion, Fielding's *Tom Jones*, suggests a possible reconciliation of Randolph's utter self-seriousness and the apparently eccentric impression he made but could not have intended:

Fielding the novelist, is consistent with Fielding the moralist. The novelist plays against forms just as much as the moralist. "Play against" may need a word of explanation. The comic writer and the comic actor achieve some of their bests effects by maintaining the traditional forms of heroism or morality—which provide their world with a stable and secure familiar meaning—but treating them with an excess of gravity, curiously upsetting literalness, a pleasure in the dilemmas they pose.[14]

Randolph was no funnyman—his "excess of gravity" and "upsetting literalness" were aspects of his character, not means to a literary end. But his single-minded pursuit of what he knew was already old-fashioned constituted the kind of comedy Fielding would have appreciated, a serious comedy of the disparity of norms. Randolph's borrowings from books remind us that it was from them that he learned how to express his ideas in the absence of contemporary norms that he agreed with, and that much of his personal dramatics may have had revealing literary sources. For in picking up quotations he absorbed the deeper play of ideas. The intelligibility in terms of intention, situation, and source of Randolph's eccentric behavior does establish that he habitually expressed in words and actions those of his ideas which more conventional politics ignored. The degree of intention is somewhat beside the point. He might well have resorted to *ad hominem* witticisms and duels, as other politicians did, had he been equally of their mind about the conduct of government. He was not, and his carryings-on, which were the source of so much interest in him, reflected his very different notions. They constituted an alternative to the world of compromise, nationalism, and "corruption" which he rejected. Just how much and in what ways he understood his own conduct in this respect is beyond certain answer. He was assuredly

aware enough of his differences from others and his disagreements with them, of his interest for others and his effect on them, and of the necessity of acting things out consistently to dramatize his point: as he himself put it, "I have
been an idiosyncracy all my life."[15]

There were duels Randolph could not fight, however;
indeed, most of his challenges went unanswered because
most were delivered to the times or the processes which
governed the times. It took a Clay to foil a Randolph. Daniel Webster simply ignored Randolph's provocation. The
failure to bring Webster onto the old fields of honor stood
for the deeper frustration of eccentric politics as practiced
by Randolph. The new men, the transcendent Yankees like
Webster, lived too completely in their own time to fool
around with Randolph. It took a Calhoun to challenge
Webster and to carry on the prolonged and high-toned
series of debates about issues in which personal excess was
left to the drawing room and the ordered flow of gran-
diloquent or at least formal public statement absorbed the
energies of politics. Bully Brooks (who caned Charles
Sumner on the Senate floor) was no Randolph, although a
sport of those politics of terror the Virginian pioneered.
Webster and Calhoun were the figures who came to stand
for the sectional debate. They were very much new men,
unconcerned with summoning up the colonial, aristocrat
past. Randolph was a good talker and could manage an
exchange, but the public business of the nineteenth century proceeded by means of the sustained encounter of
rhetorically adorned argument, systematic confrontations
to and fro of a sort he had neither the training nor the inclination to master. The legal language that came to characterize American politics in the middle period was beyond
Randolph. The debate over the *theory* of the federal government was truly outside of his comprehension. He had
no patience with theory, indeed hated it and saw no need
for the terms it created. He relied on a politics so ingrained
that to be understood and to form a basis for decisions it

had merely to be alluded to; his was a politics summoned up from a shrinking common consciousness, depending on taboo and assumption, on understanding without argument. It took Yankees, the high-minded and the sharp-minded, northern and southern, to set out the boundaries of argument, and it was the Yankee/American of the new Midwest who decided the issue in the end. Randolph had little liking for the silver age of American statesmen, though he suffered Clay's charm and had moments of admiration for Jackson's bravado. And the time came when he was no longer counted as regards the men and measures that were to absorb America. Even Calhoun learned the connection between states' rights and slavery without understanding Randolph's subtext of the old ways. Melville was right to pit a Yankee monomaniac so like Calhoun against the transcendent leviathan so like Webster in his story of Man and Whale, of America. Randolph's politics in the end left him isolated in a society more concerned with itself and its material future, and the kinds of men and measures that would involve, than with his complicated attempts to keep alive what was dead and gone and irretrievable. Randolph's words in other mouths summoned up Dixie, not Virginia.[16]

The books Randolph continued to read provided a substructure of reference in his letters and speeches. He was incapable of keeping to himself anything so important as an apt allusion or a great poem. His insistent literateness, although mixed with a pungent, even crude, homeliness, seems to the reader of his letters and speeches almost compulsive. Benton's description of his dueling style as "high-toned" applies powerfully to his general style. He made a point of his erudition, although affecting to belittle his education, and would as soon correct a man's grammar and information as his politics. For Randolph, style described politics. Good books made good men, and barbarities of personal style, bearing, or manners, and especially of opinion and expression, were sure tokens of a moral barbarian.

This attitude distinguished him in crude democratic times, as he very well knew. Books remained a source, perhaps unconscious, of this thinking about America.

In his years of personal trial after 1815, Randolph turned once more to some admired authors to find diversion and guidance. His reading of Burke has already been examined: it helped him to organize his reactions and gave him an external framework for his personally experienced ideas. His reading of Lord Byron and of certain works of Shakespeare functioned with equal seriousness to help him collect and order his thoughts. Randolph was not the only American, not even the only American legislator of his day, who was genuinely well read and publicly high-toned. Literary and classical allusions were part of the rhetorical style of the time. Randolph was not unique in his habit of using standards of high culture to judge other people and to distinguish himself from them. His determined and at times sycophantic attachment to English culture exemplifies precisely the sort of prevailing taste which frustrated the native American literary genius for so long. In exploring his reading one need not necessarily defend it. His literary opinions were commonplace and derivative. He read the reviews and generally followed them. His idea of a good talk about books comprehended on the surface a good deal of quoting and a rather bluestocking primness.

What intrigues is the emotional component in his reading and the self-centeredness with which he devoured certain strains of writing. His commitment was more interesting than his opinions. Randolph was no Poe; his criticism is not really worth rediscovering. The use to which he put literature is. The need to define himself and his relation to his country impelled and colored his reading. In this I suspect he was not alone, so he may serve as a revealing, if exaggerated, case study. Randolph did not read Byron or Shakespeare as Jefferson did Bacon, because he found the author useful, or simply, as Benton did, to become a cultured and well-rounded democratic man. Beneath the complacency of his allusions was a craving that apparently only certain books could satisfy. To understand how they did so is to understand something more about the version of himself that Randolph offered to the public, the version in which we are most interested and with which we are stuck.

Randolph did not read the English poets of the Romantic period with the same encompassing enthusiasm with which he read Pope and Cowper and Thomson, but he was extremely fond of Scott and of Lord Byron. In 1821 he wrote that he had not and likely would not read the Lake poets. He did not think of himself as a Romantic and found no need to improve on the tender sensitivities to nature of Cowper and Thomson. In 1828 he declared, "Neither am I painter nor poet; and Heaven knows I am not romantic. Yet, like you, I am an enthusiastic devotee of nature, and this is my favorite season. . . . There is a pleasure in the pathless woods. . . . The trees are half leafless, and, as they shed their remaining honors, they forcibly remind me of my own approaching destiny." He never went beyond this fairly traditional attitude, drawn from and satisfactorily expressed by the poets of the Age of Sensibility. In the appreciation of nature, Randolph was drawn to older poets; his favorite contemporaries—Scott, Byron, Moore—were not essentially nature poets, even as Wordsworth was. None of Randolph's surviving letters includes any substantial reason for his dislike of the Lake poets. Perhaps it was due to his provincial's attachment to the conservative and safe taste of the English critical establishment. He may have disliked the Lake poets because they disliked his beloved Byron: "In sheer distress what to do with myself, I yesterday read *Don Juan*—the 3, 4 and 5 cantos for the first time—fact I assure you. It is diabolically good, the ablest I am inclined to think of all his performances. I now fully comprehend the case of the *odium plus quam theologicum* of the Lake School toward this wayward genius." Also, there may have been elements in the Lake poets, notably Wordsworth, that proved uncongenial to a reader like Randolph.

Especially interesting in this regard is that part of Wordsworth's poetry which subverted the treatment of nature
common in the Age of Sensibility, the imitation of which
was a source of some pride to Randolph. According to
Geoffrey Hartman, Wordsworth's poems "combat the melancholy use of nature and . . . for Wordsworth this melancholy is symptomatic of a morbidly self-centered mind.
Nature should aid us to go out of ourselves, to broaden our
feelings by mediation, and to recover original joy." Randolph cultivated melancholy and was morbidly self-centered. He did read not to escape his fascination with himself and his moods, but to feed it.[17]

Hence, he preferred the poets more conducive to his
self-absorption—Scott and above all, Lord Byron. In 1813
he questioned Francis Scott Key: "Have you read Lord
Byron's Giaour? I have been delighted with it. He *is* a poet,
as was emphatically said of our P. Henry. 'He is an orator.' " By 1814 Randolph was proclaiming to the recalci-
trant Key, who continued to prefer Scott, that Bryon was
the best of modern poets:

I cannot yield the precedence of Lord Byron to Walter Scott. . . .
No poet in our language (the exception is unnecessary) Shakespeare and Milton apart, has the same power over my feelings as
Byron. He is, like Scott, *careless,* and indulges himself in great
license; but he does not, like your favorite, write by the piece. I
am persuaded that his fragments are thrown out by the true spirit
of inspiration, and that he never goads his pen to work.

Randolph did not need Scott (as perhaps later southern
yearners did) to furnish his picture of a vanished squire's
paradise. His admiration for Byron persisted unabated. In
1824 he observed that *Don Juan* was "diabolically good."
Byron was a source of allusion, explanation, and delight. "I
am got up safe with Lord Byron."[18]

Why did Byron so captivate Randolph? The poet was a
dashing and romantic figure—his scandalous exploits excited the emulation and interest of the literate. But there

was more to it in Randolph's case: Randolph was interested by the person presented in the poetry—that contradictory individual ego whose moods and exploits Byron chronicled. Recent scholarship has tended to minimize the differences between Byron's voices in his early and later poems, emphasizing the "unity and consistency that embraces all his moods and styles." The satiric and the romantic, gloomy poems are now regarded as not necessarily distinct in attitude. The same expectations of life which informed his romances also underlay his satires and melancholy poems. Byron's individualism had eighteenth-century roots: "With respect to the human mind, we could say that the eighteenth century tended both to imprison each man in an individual consciousness and to reduce everything to experience within that consciousness. Each condition can in itself induce anxiety, and the relation between them is trying." The difficulties that plagued this imprisoned individualist formed much of Byron's subject; the expression of them released the poet's "alternate cries of helplessness and mastery, solitude and union."

"His vision of melancholy is a vision painfully clear and unillusioned. . . ." The poet of serious, explorative disappointment and melancholy was also, according to Edmund Wilson, a man whose "gift was for living rather than for literature":

The truth is that Bryon was a man of picturesque and violent moods, who reacted to life with extraordinary vividness, but without discipline or order. He never knew where he stood nor what he wanted—he was a force of enormous energy running amuck through a world in which he could not find peace. His compromises with civilized society, were doomed to disaster from the beginning, though in them he was surely sincere in seeking tranquility or discipline.

The vivid impersonation of conflicting impulses in poem and poet must surely have constituted a good measure of Byron's appeal to Randolph.[19]

Reading this inspired wayward genius nourished Randolph's self-conceit. "In all Lord Byron's description of the ocean, I recognize my own feelings." The highest satisfaction of style Randolph experienced was always to see himself mirrored in the poet and the poem. Rare indeed was the writer who could thus match him. "The necessity of *loving* and *being be-loved* was never felt by the imaginary beings of Rousseau and Byron's creation more imperiously than by myself." The highest compliment Randolph could pay a writer was this to Byron: "Madness, suicide or Piety— (perhaps both the first) in some of these must Lord Byron take refuge. I think I see passages that shadow out my own story." Criticizing Hugh Garland's *Life,* Beverley Tucker compared writing about his brother to writing about Bryon: "*The life of his mind,* the thing that they *really,* though unconsciously wished to know, could only be written by himself." Tucker picked up on Randolph's similarity, self-perceived and probably self-induced, to the Byronic pose. It is a shrewd and telling comment on Randolph's reading of Byron. Randolph's own estimation of himself, already quoted in another context, is interesting as a comment on what he looked for in identifying with Bryon: "I have been all my life the creature of impulse, the sport of chance, the victim of my own uncontrolled and uncontrollable sensations: of a poetic temperament. I admire and pity all who possess this temperament." His statement of identification with Byron involved elements of admiration and pity in fellow feeling.[20]

Of all Byron's shifting moods, Randolph was most commonly comfortable with his self-absorbed melancholy. Randolph's own unhappiness and egotism—"that vein of egotism to which I am too prone"—were wearyingly frequent themes in his letters. Effusions of melancholy haunted his correspondence. The causes of his despair were real enough; its virtuoso expression was closely related to his identification with Byron. The poet offered a legitimate and high-toned justification for the self-centered morbidity Randolph understood rightly as self-indulgence. Byron was the key to Randolph's melancholy egotism, as Burke was to his nostalgic conservatism. The most serious sources of Randolph's feeling were not entirely personal. His despair was one way he could express the depth of his disillusionment with the fate of his principles and his mores in a democratic society. The personal and the political were inseparable in his mind—politics could as easily drive him to the edge as personal misfortune. In Byron's poetry, moreover, things happened. Action took place from the point of view Randolph shared. Byron nurtured the illusion of action, an illusion that mattered to Randolph. It was closely related to his satisfactions in reading and in presenting himself. The sources of the Byronic mode of melancholy egotism, taking the world on one's shoulders defiantly and then pitying oneself for carrying so heavy a load, were similar to those of Randolph's feeling, and adopting this mode served as a kind of solution for Randolph, a means by which he would express his unhappiness in the personal way in which he could perceive it. That was the basis for his deepest identification with the poet. "The satirist is perforce a judge, and he is nothing unless he can speak with the voice of righteousness. The darkness of his gloom is the measure of his indignation and a sense of isolation is inevitable in his calling."[21]

However, recognition of this eighteenth-century connection between the ideal and the melancholy by way of egotism is insufficient for an understanding of Randolph. His misery was not that of Pope or of his youthful self. It had moved beyond the righteous to the piteous. His identification with and reliance on Lord Byron announced this change without explaining it. During the years 1813–15 a break with the old world on which Randolph's ideals were based had occurred. The literal death and destruction of that world had turned Randolph from the simple, literal-minded application of its ideal standards to a romantic, reactionary quest to re-establish or, perhaps, only to commemorate this vanishing world. He applied the old-fashioned standards even as he bemoaned the passing of the old-fashioned society. After 1815, Randolph spoke more from memory than from experience. Analyzing Lord Bolingbroke's conservatism, Isaac Kramnick has made a distinction which plausibly defines Randolph's case:

The "primitive conservative" Bolingbroke experienced the beginning of a challenge to the old order. This order, not yet behind him, was an integral part of his life; it was not yet only a memory. His defense of an aristocratic England was an intensified experience of something he still possessed but felt himself in great danger of losing. It is of paramount significance that his idealized order was not yet totally lost. Because this order was not merely an object of reflection, he was not led to the introspection of romantic conservatism.[22]

Randolph *was* led to the "introspection of romantic conservatism" in the loss of his "idealized order." The old days were over—he knew that. Writing from Paris in 1824, he used the following illustrations to emphasize the *impossibility* of something occurring:

It would be just as possible to restore the state of society and manners which existed in Virginia a half a century ago; I should as soon expect to see the Nelsons, and Pages, and Byrds, and Fairfaxes, living in their palaces and driving their coaches and sixes; or the good old Virginia gentlemen or the assembly, drinking their twenty and forty bowls of rack punches, and madeira and claret, in lieu of a knot of empty sheriffs and hack attorneys, each with his cruet of whiskey before him, and puddle of tobacco-spittle between his legs.

Randolph's melancholy egotism, Byronic and deafening, was the companion piece of his resignation to the passing of the old days. His own exaggerated personification of those days and their principles and ideals was also Byronic. Randolph's identification with the poet was steady and revealing. He was like Byron's "Queen of a fantastic realm":

> . . . *her thoughts*
> *Were combinations of disjointed things;*
> *And Forms, impalpable and unperceived*
> *Of other's sight, familiar were to hers,*
> *And this the world calls frenzy; but the wise*
> *Have a far deeper madness—and the glance*
> *Of melancholy is a fearful gift;*
> *What is it but the telescope of truth?*
> *Which strips the distance of its fantasies,*
> *And brings life near in utter nakedness,*
> *Making the cold reality too real!*

In an 1829 letter to his friend Dr. Brockenbrough, Randolph quoted approvingly: "It is difficult to conceive any situation more painful than that of a great man condemned to watch the death agony of an exhausted country. . . ."[23]

Randolph's melancholy more than once gave way to what contemporary observers and subsequent biographers have agreed were fits of insanity. He himself lived in fear of derangement: his letters frequently included references to his apprehensions, and after-the-fact confessions of madness. Around 1819 he wrote Dr. Brockenbrough that "perhaps a strait waistcoat would not be amiss"; his misery was getting the better of him:

There are to be sure, a few, a very few, who are what they seem to be. . . . You can have no conception of the intenseness of this wretchedness. . . . I had hoped to divert the gloom that overhangs me by writing this letter . . . but I struggle against it in vain. Is it not Dr. Johnson who says that to attempt "to think it down is madness."

Randolph's undiscipline, his emotional self-indulgence and his fancied poetic poses, likely encouraged his fears and his spells. He freely discussed his worst wearies. In 1833 he told a friend that he had been "struck mad, as well entitled to a cell in Swift's hospital as anyone who had ever occupied one." He would even fashion funny stories out of his distress: "I was quite delirious, but had method in my madness; for they tell me that I ordered Juba to load my gun, and to shoot the first 'doctor' that should enter the room; adding, they are only mustard seed, and will serve just to sting him."[24]

Randolph appears to have been less of two minds about his so-called mad behavior than about his public excesses. His anxiety about his depression and his struggles against it are moving and bitter testimony to his inner division. He knew what he was doing most of the time, and it is as if his transports of rage, madness, or excitement relieved him of his responsibility to discipline his fragmented self. His self-confessed attacks were usually somehow related to "the world"—they centered on deceptive appearances, lurking dangers, and above all, angry, sorrowful disappointment in men and events. For Randolph, claiming insanity was usually tantamount to declaring that the world was beyond improvement and men were beyond redemption—his guilt over loving too little the world and his fellow men took over at these times. Often, he explicitly connected public and private madness:

I am more than satiated with the world. It is to me a fearful prison house of guilt and misery. I fear that my feelings toward it are not always sufficiently charitable. . . . In short, I have lost all hope of public service, and whithersoever I direct my eyes a dark cloud seems to impend. . . . Cases of insanity and suicide (although not so numerous as might have been expected, judging from the effects of the South Seas and Mississippi bubbles) have not been unfrequent in this quarter. . . .[25]

There is incomplete agreement about just when Randolph was indeed insane. His opinions did not severely change in those periods where one or another authority has called him mad. In fact, these episodes were often marked by a heightened awareness and expression of his usual opinions. It is not always easy to tell whether Randolph was acting a madman's part or a fool's. Drink, dope, and crowds excited him to similar excesses. In the legal dispute over Randolph's will, no less a model of Scotch-Irish sanity than

John Calhoun testified that Randolph had not been very crazy: "Mr. Randolph was generally regarded as a man of remarkable genius and great brilliancy, with uncommon sagacity and keeness in debate, and distinguished colloquial powers." Most opinions as to Randolph's sanity tell us more about the author's agreements and disagreements with him than about Randolph. It did not matter to Calhoun how crazy Randolph's actions were, or to Henry Adams how sane: the reason for their interest and the indicator of his sanity was their assessment of his politics.[26]

Indeed, much of his mad behavior—that is to say, the actions that Randolph or his intimates considered out-and-out crazy—was not so very far removed in message or manner from the eccentricities of his public career. On occasion, these mad episodes seem to solve or resolve tricky points that had been perplexing him. Randolph's fevered apprehensions that the ordinary things of life might be dangerous—poisoned, haunted by devils, alive with menace, really dead and just pretending to life, tormenting him with false appearances—were certainly deranged. But they also make a certain kind of sense when one remembers that the discrepancy between the proclaimed and the real in all areas of life constituted the central issue of his "real" life. Milk did go bad, too many people had died, one's youthful high-spiritedness had turned into raving. During his sieges, apparently, Randolph turned against almost all his friends for periods of time, but again, as with St. George Tucker, these vendettas expressed a part of his always complicated feelings—the mad part constituting the domination of the emotions of jealousy or hostility or anger or suspicion which in his less mad moments he had drowned in exaggerated professions of love and friendship or religious passion or public righteousness. Like most of us, Randolph was capable of social dissimulation and covert feelings, of judging his friends harshly in the privacy of correspondence, of all the gray and white lies social life seems to demand. Indeed, Randolph was adept at the accepted behavior of what he thought of as society, relishing the high drama of social intercourse. His breakdowns, however, encompassed a failure to achieve even that baroque accommodation of inner and outer selves, and issued in a oneness of fury and suspicion, reducing complexity and doubt to a solid certainty, unhappy, dangerous, deathly—but with relief, sure and certainly *so*. They also solved real problems, thus Randolph's claim that Clay had cut his throat with his own tongue.

Surviving testimony concerning Randolph's demented doings confirms the suspicion that in his alienation he went further along familiar roads. After his return from his aborted mission to Russia, he wrote to Henry A. Watkins, "I write with a blotting pen, upon greasy paper—unclean, all offensive in the eye of God. I am under the powerful influence of the Prince of Darkness, who tempts me with a beautiful mulatress." At the same time, his usually fond treatment of his slaves became harsh and abusive. One need not be a sensationalist to see in this image a loosing of the restraints on his power, as a slaveholder, restraints so necessary to a man like Randolph who lived under the double demand that he be a successful and disciplining master and at the same time prevent himself from sinking into those enjoyments of his dominion which would dull his keen awareness of the moral injustice of having slaves at all. His upbringing had provided for this contradiction, but the new agitation, the new climate of sectional relations, the spread and growth of slavery and the challenges being posed to it, made it ever more difficult to maintain. The "beautiful mulatress," representing a desire triply denied to Randolph, has personal echoes which excite at once our curiosity and perforce our restraint—there is no way of getting through to the heart of this particular passage. It is evident, however, that the mad vision solved by simplifying the complex sane reality. Mad, Randolph could tyrannize, could *master* his slaves, and in that mastery, we might add, could achieve in fantasy the actual degeneracy his life apparently did not allow him. Crazy, Randolph could be a man, a southern man, a master, without the hindrances of the conflicting realities of his difficult life. Randolph's disorder floated the debris of his concerns, borne along by the swift current to resolutions otherwise too distant and too direct for the real flow of his life. In a letter to President Jackson, Randolph wrote:

I am resolute not to assist in the subjugation of South Carolina; but, if she does move (as I fear she will), to make common cause with her against the usurpations of the Federal Government and the Supreme Court especially. The late infamous decision of those minions of arbitrary power will give us Georgia. Everything south of Ohio except perhaps Kentucky and the western district of Virginia, must be with us. With this noble country and Cuba, where we can make a hogshead of sugar as easily as a pound can be grown on the Mississippi or in Florida, we shall have a vast empire capable of indefinite improvement and of supporting easily 40,000,000 of people.

A mad fantasy perhaps, but not to a later generation. Here as elsewhere, Randolph's madness projected the clear implications of his sane vision. For all sorts of reasons, the balanced, normal Randolph did not envision this southern slaveholding empire, but like the mulatress, it was a figure of his imagination that cut through the knot of his custom and his attachments to resolve a troubling issue directly, heedless of real consequences, madly. Randolph returned to his ideals of friendship while deranged, and his manner of doing so again suggests how his genuine affliction served to unravel some of his cares. He venerated friendship among men and must often have experienced the pangs of one condemned to feel only friendly love with his fellows. His exaggerated letters offering friendship and solicitude to the wives of his intimates betray his anxiety to preserve the intensity of friendship even after other claims have asserted themselves. Writing to Jackson, from whom he wished favors and attention, during what is usually regarded as a mad time, Randolph assured the president of his friendship in extravagant terms, like but not quite like the terms of his letters to his associates in earlier years. He compared Jackson to Alexander and himself to Hephaestus, adding, "I trust that I am something better than his minion (the nature of their connection, if I forget not, was Greek love).. . ." This was a very strange thing for Randolph to write, but it betrayed his anxiety about friendship and the extravagance of his mood and, by the way, indicated a subtler worry about the nature of the only attachments he seemed to maintain. This is not to say that Randolph was a homosexual any more than that he was in fact a Legree toward his women slaves. Rather it suggests that mad John Randolph desired the whole where life had forced him to settle for only a part. He knew the limits of friendship and there is no call to think he was anything more or less than a passionate friend. But he did understand the depth of his feelings for his friends, perhaps worried about them, and when his affliction released him from the obligation of responsible speech, that may reflect his deepest worries. Thus Calhoun, whose powerful and charismatic dominion over the young political men Randolph resented, was a "He-Bawd." Madness simplified.[27]

Only slightly more restrained versions of the qualities labeled mad formed the stuff of his public career. Is a prophet "mad" only when people do not realize he will be or has been proven accurate? Randolph's insanity heightened but did not alter his ways. At times there was even the suspicion that Randolph cultivated the impression of madness. It was a romantic way to escape the strains of living. He compared himself to every mad genius he knew of—to Swift, Byron, and Cowper:"But there are times when . . . the chaos of my mind can be compared with nothing but the state that poor Cowper was in before he found peace. . . ." Thomas Hart Benton heard Randolph apply Dr. Johnson's verses from "The Vanity of Human Wishes" to himself:

In life's last scene what prodigies surprise,
Fears of the brave, and follies of the wise?
From Marlb'rough's eyes the streams of dotage flow,
And Swift expires a driv'ler and a show.

"Mr. Randolph, I have several times heard you repeat those lines, as if they could have an application to yourself, while no person can have less reason to fear the fate of Swift."

"I have lived in dread of insanity," replied Mr. Randolph.

There was a familiar boast in all of this. Randolph's affliction was the curse of his specialness, his genius, his poetic temperament, and was presumably subject to the same extenuation. It is entirely reasonable to suppose that Randolph came to exploit his marked instability as he did his other misfortunes, turning them into badges of his particularity. Again, this is to deny neither his real derangement nor his sincerity in exposing it to sympathetic view.[28]

Randolph came to understand his afflicted mental state in part through his reading of *King Lear* and *Timon of Athens*—a remarkable instance of the way in which he continued to read about others and understand himself. Randolph claimed Shakespeare among his most treasured inheritances from his English and Virginian ancestry. Like Henry Crawford in *Mansfield Park* he considered the dramatist "part of an Englishman's constitution. His thoughts and beauties are so spread abroad that one touches them every where, one is intimate with him by instinct." In January 1817, Randolph wrote that he had been reading *King Lear* "and incline to prefer it to all Shakespeare's plays. In that and Timon only, it has been said, was the bard in earnest." Indeed, his references to *Lear* abound. On the floor of Congress, during the debate over the Compensation Bill, Randolph dismissed the angry response to his accusation that those legislators who voted for a bill by which they would benefit in increased salaries were no better than thieves in this fashion: "The little dogs and all, Tray, Blanch and Sweetheart. See, they bark at me!" The quota-

tion is from the third act of the play, where the mad Lear
reviles his ungrateful daughters. Beleagured, besieged,
and beset by thankless enemies, he dismisses his harrying
furies. Thus Randolph chose to echo a madman's disclaimer upon his return to Congress. A few days after his
duel with Henry Clay, Randolph wrote to Dr. Broken-
brough that he had tried previously to write but "my pen
choked. The *hysterica passio* of poor old Lear came over me. I
left a letter for you in case of the worst . . . I am a fatalist."
Another allusion to *Lear* occurred in one of his more exces-
sive speeches on the Tariff, a speech famous for his fevered and extreme presentation of the defiant southern interest and including this vaunted cry: "A fig for the
Constitution! When the scorpion's sting is probing us to the
quick shall we stop to chop logic?" In this speech Randolph
spoke of his fellow slaveholding southerners as follows:
"We are the eel that is being flayed while the cook-maid
pats us on the head and cries with the clown in *King Lear,*
'Down wantons, down.' " All of these quotations suggested
a feeling of identity between Randolph and the mad King
Lear, driven from his senses by his disappointment at the
ingratitude of those he loved.[29]

Like Randolph's identification with Byron, this identification with Lear is revealing. *Lear* and also *Timon* tell the
stories of powerful and gifted men who go mad in disillusionment with mankind—thinking in their moments of bitter disappointment that the worst in men which they so
clearly see represents also the truth about man. Their naïve
and false original hopes of mankind betray them into unreasonable disappointment. That Lear recovers his wits
and Timon does not is less important than the common
source of their unreasonable and insane bitterness against
their fellows, their refusal to recognize themslves in those
others. Randolph had previously resorted to less extreme
metaphors for his disillusionment and on occasion continued so to do. After 1815, however, he felt the need for
something more intense than the feelings of righteous let-

down that had served him hitherto. *Lear* offered a much more extreme statement of one's position in this sense than Randolph had adopted; it substituted a direct allusion to madness for what had previously been a playing with that possibility. Like his assumptions of the prophetic role and of the Byronic mode of melancholy, Randolph's use of *Lear* exaggerated his accustomed stances to include madness among the other griefs to which his staunch, righteous politics had exposed him. His use of *Lear* was a statement of degree and also a fairly direct inclusion of his madness within his politics.[30]

At the Virginia constitutional convention, Randolph closed his majestic speech warning of the dangers posed by innovation in the name of majoritarian democratic impulse and rule with the following personal statement, among the last and most serious statements he ever made:

Sir, I have exhausted myself, and tired you. I am physically unable to recall or to express the few thoughts I brought with me to this Assembly. Sir, that great master of the human heart, I mean Shakespeare—when he brings before our eyes an old and feeble monarch, not only deserted, but oppressed by his own pampered and ungrateful offspring, describes him as finding solace and succour, only in his discarded and disinherited child. If this our venerable parent, must perish, deal the blow who will, it shall never be given by my hand. I will avert it if I can, and if I cannot, in the sincerity of my heart I declare, I am ready to perish with it. . . . I am too old a man to remove; my associations, my habits, and my property, nail me to the Commonwealth. But, were I a young man, I would, in case this monstrous tyranny shall be imposed upon us, do what a few years ago I should have thought parricidal. I would withdraw from your jurisdiction. I would not live under King Numbers. I would not be his steward, nor make him my task-master. I would obey the principle of self-preservation, a principle we find even in the brute creation, in flying from his mischief.

Lear manifests the Virginia constitution, the old regime it maintained, and its gallant defender, united and enfeebled all. This is perhaps Randolph's most dramatic and telling conflation: he has at last found the figure of his age and disappointment without having to sacrifice his stubborn attachment to the old ways. Lear is Virginia and Randolph both, and Randolph is Cordelia and Lear—the innocence and disappointment, the freshness and the madness, the expectations and the lessons of his life hand in hand facing their cruel end:

> *Upon such sacrifices, my Cordelia,*
> *The gods themselves throw incense. Have I caught thee?*
> *He that parts us shall bring a brand from heaven,*
> *And fire us hence like foxes. Wipe thine eyes;*
> *The good-years shall devour them, flesh and fell,*
> *Ere they shall make us weep!*

Randolph's statement is rich with the ruling concerns of his life. Shakespeare offered the metaphors he required, and the result was magnificent and dignified. How sharper than the serpent's tooth indeed![31]

Randolph did not analyze his own reading of *Lear* and *Timon,* but his letters of that period, and intermittently for the rest of his life, show the confirming effect of the plays on his unhappy mind. In 1817 he wrote to Theodore Dudley:

I feel that in this world, I am alone—that all my efforts (ill-judged and misdirected I am willing to allow they must have been) have proved abortive. What remains of my life must be spent in a cold and heartless intercourse with mankind, compared with which the solitude of Robinson Crusoe was bliss. I have no longer a friend. . . . I know neither how to conciliate the love nor to command the esteem of mankind. . . .

Alone and afflicted in the isolation of Roanoke, Randolph often sounded this chord of alienated despair, railing against the corruption of the world. These transports of hatred were sometimes closely followed by religious contrition and usually by some saving self-awareness. But in the depths of his "madness," Randolph found his echo in the disappointed, unrealistic expectations of Lear and Timon.[32]

Apemantus's rebuke of Timon, that "the middle of humanity thou never knewest, but the extremity of both ends," serves for Randolph also. There is a likeness between Timon's scene with his servant Flavius in act 4 and one of Randolph's with his servants. Flavius contradicts his master's verdict on mankind with his own insistent fidelity—prompting a reluctant Timon to admit:

> How fain would I have hated all mankind,
> And thou redeem'st thyself. But all save thee
> I fell with curses.
> Me thinks thou art more honest now than wise.

In 1831 Randolph recounted this incident: "I was so moved by the ingratitude of my servants, and my destitute and forlorn condition, that I lifted up my voice and wept; wept most bitterly. Yet I am now inclined to think that I did the poor creatures some injustice, by ascribing to ingratitude, what was the insensibility of their condition in life." Randolph's madness was like Lear's and Timon's in its rational cause and in its expression, and rage against mankind was part of its course. He felt disappointed, isolated, an outcast; and he alternately pitied himself and turned on his tormentors. This attitude became important finally because it colored his portrayals of the decline and degeneration of American society. His perception of that degeneracy owes as much to Shakespeare and to Randolph's apprehension of his own madness as it does to Burke. His reading of Shakespeare's plays at such a time throws significant light on the kinds of strategies he developed to comprehend and use his derangement. This reading, especially in view of his characteristic way of reading books, is even more important to his historian than the initial fact of his misfortune. The drama of declension Randolph played out for American audiences in the 1820's got much of its passion and expression from his excited, mad, but literal reading of Shakespeare during his own worst despair.[33]

If tragedy framed Randolph's madness, comedy circumstanced his presentation of himself. It is difficult to see him as a comedian, in the sense of a prankster or a wise guy; he took himself too seriously. But there was apparently irresistibly comic interest in Randolph's impersonation of "Randolph of Roanoke." Consciously or not, Randolph behaved so that his appeal to his audience, legislative or public, included the kind of comedy found in the eighteenth-century pastoral and novel. Randolph lived as if in an old-fashioned place where distinctions of rank were preserved. William Empson reminds us that pastoral, comedic self-presentation is an integral part of such class systems: "Clearly it is important for a nation with a strong class-system to have an art-form that not merely evades but breaks through it, that makes the classes feel part of a larger unity or simply at home with each other." Randolph's public performance, though framed within the outlines of such roles as that of the aristocratic lord visiting his village, retained a strong element both of playing to the crowd and of self-exposure.[34]

Two aspects of Randolph's self-presentation are especially remarkable (if not unique)—first, his endless comments on his own illness, sickness, pain; and second, the fact that the first person is the organizing reference of all his talk. His protestations of illness became a ritual. Representative William H. Roane recalled an encounter with Randolph in 1816. One morning in the Capitol, informed that Randolph was dying and wanted his attendance, he and some others hurried to Georgetown. There they found Randolph, by his own account, "Dying, dying, dying! in a dreadful state." He asked what was afoot in Congress and was told the galleries were full of expectant people. Then he launched into a eulogy of the great Patrick Henry, and sent them away still "Dying, sir, dying." A few hours later he appeared in Congress, and rose to address the body: "Mr. Speaker, this is shrove Tuesday. Many a gallant cock has died in the pit on this day, and I have to die in the pit also." He then spoke for some time— dying sixteen years later. Randolph was often truly sick, with assorted diseases, but sickness was something he appeared to relish, if not exactly enjoy. He certainly made a great deal out of it.[35]

His egotism and self-absorption have been amply discussed. The recollection of one W. B. Green helps to focus these two elements in a very suggestive way: commenting at length on Randolph's stumping style, Green concluded, "This coincidence of manner and thought between the speeches of Mr. Randolph and the writings of Lawrence Sterne has always appealed to my mind so striking that I have not been able to resist the belief that he had, without making the acknowledgment, appropriated the manner and thought of that great writer." It is a powerful comparison. Randolph had read some Sterne but did not like him much. The comparison remains telling because knowingly or not, he was practicing the kind of comedy of self that is at the core of Sterne's work. "Sterne sought refuge deliberately in illusions when life became unbearable, especially in the imaginative dramatization which is Shandeism, and which is too frequently taken as a complete self-portrait." It is a comedy of disillusioned idealism in which the discrepancy between expectations and the way things turn out is seen to be funny. "Throughout the work Sterne plays off the crippled body or temperament, seen from the outside as the ludicrous victim of circumstance, with the expansive mind, which tries to convert all it apprehends into the stuff of its obsessions." Play-acting, even of oneself in real life, is involved. Such play-acting is a logical response to a period "when the metaphors men live by have become detached from old systems of belief and have not yet been absorbed into new structures." Viewing Randolph's histrionics, his illness and self-absorption in terms of Shandeism is a help toward understanding his irresistibly comic appeal, although there is not enough evidence to justify arguing a causal connection. The point is that what is funny and publicly appealing and distinctive in Randolph has sources similar to those for his more serious self-exposure. Like Tristram Shandy, Randolph played "the comedy of the mind locking itself up in its own world" and then forcing it on this one.[36]

Randolph's stunning public theatrics, and their varied sources, are finally only as interesting as their substantive result. Having gotten her attention, what did Randolph have to say to America? Much has been made of his prophetic attack on big government, antislavery, and mass democracy, and surely he did see these more clearly than others because he was more intensely disposed to see them. He was a brilliant advocate of the states' rights cause and of the continuing importance of the English and conservative roots of American politics. The cumulative effect of his self-presentation, however, was to make these substantive points less important than his generalized, impersonated critique of American society. His was a presence that evoked certain political points. One thinks of these points—of how far from her Founding, in a literal sense, America had and has traveled—when one thinks of him. There is no question that he could, almost to the end of his career, scare or charm legislators to accept his views on specific subjects, nor would one question the many significant perceptions he had about the practice of American politics. Nevertheless, he sacrificed a politically acceptable course for a personally satisfactory dissent, removing his views from a context where they could be consistently effective and substituting a personal, dramatic context. His later speeches, riveting and exciting though they occasionally might be, were also personal, rambling, and not always germane to the issues. Randolph himself, not any abstracted opinions, constituted his politics. The twists and turns of argument in his famous speech on retrenchment and reform, for example, defy organization from a political standpoint. He moved without apparent system from subject to subject, in a marvelous and compelling way no doubt, but one which referred to himself and to the role he had created for himself, not to the issues discussed. It is a mistake to treat Randolph as a systematic thinker, even as a systematic interpreter of Burke. He often made sense politically; indeed, he was sharp and shrewd and effective in his critiques. But he was not a political thinker, he was a political reactor. His theory echoed his education, the old-fashioned mix of values he clung to as an anachronistic standard. John Calhoun, whom conservative scholars like Russell Kirk would like to associate with Randolph in the formation and carrying on of the American Burkean tradition, and who himself came to claim Randolph as a master in matters sectional, put Randolph's problem as a logical thinker succinctly: "Upon a single point . . . Randolph reasoned admirably; it was only when he came to deal with a combination of points that his ratiocination fell short." On a given issue, momentous or not, Randolph's eccentric perceptions might strike sparks and inflame attention. His statements concerning the sectional issue, especially the relationship between states' rights and slavery, demonstrated his ability to make a bold connection and hold others to it. The demanding stuff of forging agreement, the regular business of politics, was beyond him.

What organized all his political thoughts in the later years, the point of his act, seems to have been the horror with which he viewed what had come to pass in America. Each particular of his indictment only served to document his general conviction of the degeneracy of his times. During a speech given at Prince Edward Courthouse in 1831, Randolph framed his remarks in the context of the degeneration of the present race of Virginian sons, among whom he included the unworthy descendants of Patrick Henry, John Marshall, and John Taylor of Caroline, concluding, ". . . in short, look at the Lees, Washingtons, Randolphs— what woeful degeneracy." It was a conviction his upbringing and personal circumstances had prepared him to hold. Every particular, even of material life, reinforced Randolph's sense of the dimming lights by which Virginia was living:

On my road to Buckingham, I passed a night in Farmville. Wherever I stop, it is the same—walls black and filthy—bed and furniture sordid—furniture scanty and mean, generally broken—no mirror—no fire-irons—in short, dirt and discomfort universally prevail, and in most private houses the matter is not mended. . . . in fact, the old gentry are gone and the *nouveaux riches,* where they have the inclination, do not know how to live.

He took the disappearance of his own world, the one he had been born into, as evidence that the whole world was gone to ruin. Even politics in such a circumstance was absurd: "We hug our lousy cloaks around us, take another *chaw of tubbacker,* float the room with nastiness, or ruin the grate and fire-irons, where they happen not to be rusty, and try conclusions upon constitutional points." Prepared by so much in his life to expect decline, he recognized it all around him and disclaimed any but a seer's role. There was no helping the situation because "we are arrived at that pitch of degeneracy when the mere lust of power, the retention of place and patronage, can prevail not only over every consideration of public duty but stifle the suggestions of personal honor, which even the ministers of the decayed governments of Europe have not yet learned entirely to disregard." One might see clearly enough what would result and why things had come to such a pass: "The old families of Virginia will form connections with low people and sink into the mass of overseers' sons and daughters. And this is the legitimate, nay inevitable, conclusion to which Mr. Jefferson and his leveling system has brought us." Randolph wrapped his lavish perceptions of decadence and fall around a central criticism of democracy, majority rule, leveling, and materialism. The one meant the other, and the critique of democracy was inevitably broached in the cause of the example dearest to Randolph's senses, the survival and then the veneration of the old-fashioned Virginian ways of his youth. Once it appeared to him that those times, the colonial heyday of the landed elite in English North America, were in fact gone beyond recall in the nation at large, he left off instructive for corrosive perceptions, preferring denunciatory warning to illustrate the evils of the present age over constructive political thinking about how democracy might best be guided. Only at the Virginia constitutional convention did he try to restrain himself and make sense, keeping the lid, as it were, on his extravagance, because he seems to have thought that there was something in the Commonwealth that might be saved or venerated. In effect, Randolph had become so disenchanted with America that he forsook allegiance to it for allegiance to Virginia, to the past, and to England.[37]

Randolph visited Europe in 1822, 1824, 1826, and 1830. He was happiest in England, where he reveled in visits to the ancestral counties, in the recognition of landmarks, and in participation in the customs and social life of the English great. ". . . have we not been steering on the same course ever since we left you without touching or taking in sail? Only we have thrown the King overboard, God bless him," he remarked upon arrival in England for one of his visits. Randolph took pride in his knowledge of things and places English, making a point of displaying his expertise and his mastery of polite usage. Upon being urged by a more cautious friend not to make use of a special order of admission to the House of Lords on the day of a momentous debate on the Roman Catholic Peers Bill, Randolph bristled: "What, Sir! do you suppose *I* would consent to struggle with, and push through, the crowd of persons who for two long hours must fight their way in at the *lower* door. Oh, no, Sir! I shall do no such thing, and, if I cannot enter as a *gentleman commoner,* I go not at all!" Sure enough, his timid companion observed from a modest place in the gallery Randolph's proper entrance through the private entrance with Canning, Castlereagh, Peel, and other distinguished Commoners. In England, he redeemed at last his provincial's unease by consorting with celebrities. Most of the stories about Randolph in England reflect his insistence on experiencing the England of his traditions and his reading. He delighted in the company of lords and such. Apparently he enjoyed some vogue in high circles as an entertaining and curious sample of the American. The poet Thomas Moore observed him sitting with Lord Limerick, and identifying him as "the famous American orator," described him this way:

... a singular-looking man with a young-old face, and a short, small body, mounted upon a pair of high crane legs and thighs, so that, when he stood up, you did not know when he was to end, and a squeaking voice like a boy's just before breaking into manhood. His manner too strange and pedantic, but his powers of eloquence (Irving tells me) wonderful.

Many of Randolph's English acquaintances shared Moore's sense of his oddness and regarded him as something of a show, but the result was a kind of acceptance into the genteel circles he aspired to, which made his London trips a pleasure. Washington Irving wrote in 1822 of Randolph's impact:

John Randolph is here and has attracted much attention. He has been sought after by people of the first distinction. I have met him repeatedly in company and his eccentricity of appearance and manner make him the more current and interesting; for, in high life here, they are always eager after anything strange and peculiar. There is a vast deal too of the old school in Randolph's manner, the turn of his thoughts and the style of his conversation, which seems to please very much.

England appears to have accepted Randolph as an American, as an oddity, and as an interesting if peculiar visitor; his were not the last American charms to gain a somewhat left-handed entry into English high society.[38]

If Randolph appeared odd to England, England suited Randolph just fine. His letters and journal notes do not betray any feelings of discomfort. Indeed it would appear that he was very well contented there and vastly pleased with his success. He did not change his behavior to suit the clime. Perhaps his routine performance struck the English ear differently than the Virginian or American, but the evidence is that he did not restrain himself; one critical observer reported:

It was a scene *sui generis,* novel even for London. Repeated it was with variations: "Hoby's boots forever, so help him Heaven and Manton's guns—his rascally overseer who had cheated him—the roundheads, how he hated them—the cavaliers, how he loved them—Virginia, old Virginia, true to Charles—the vermin in his own country that fattened on the public crib; he gave it to them—that he did and would; Bladensburg; Yazoo; the Yankees; the Negroes; Mason's and Dixon's line; the man in the moon; everything danced in the astounding gallimaufry." To the sensibilities, to the restraints, bodily and of mind, to the multiplied obligations and habitudes, to all the anxious and assiduous cultivation that go to make up the gentleman he was a stranger. His irregular and undisciplined temper was the parent of rudeness in him, and his vanity hurried him into offences against good sense and decorum.

Here was Randolph abroad very much like Randolph at home. And he really enjoyed himself. England, long becoming the home of his memories and his taste, was now a concrete reference point, a place from which to view American events. Thus, in speaking of Rufus King, Randolph regretted his vote on the Missouri question; but for that *"he* would be our man for the presidency. He is, sir, a genuine English gentleman of the old school; just the right man for these degenerate times." England was increasingly his most favored nation: ". . . there never was such a country on the face of the earth, as England; and it is utterly impossible that there ever can be any combination of circumstances hereafter, to make such another country as old England now is—God bless her." The implied reproach to his own country, founded to reform and refound old England, is telling indeed.[39]

To be sure, Randolph did not think England free of problems. His letters from England indicate that he was well aware of the troubles of that realm and was unrestrained in his criticisms: "If you see the English newspapers, you will see what a horrible state of society exists in this strange country, where one class is dying of hunger and another with surfeit. The amount of crime is fearful; and the cases of extreme atrocity are not wanting." It was not the England of the 1820's that so captivated Randolph, but the England of his imagination, represented to him by the titled, the landmarks, the accents and customs he encountered. What he saw did not surprise him, except perhaps for the unpleasant sights. He carried on a constant process of location and confirmation, seeking and finding the objective correlatives to his mind's image of the old home. From *that* England he looked at America and Virginia, and using *that* England as a standard, he found both wanting:

I know not what to think of these times, and of the state of things in our country. The vulgarity and calumny of the press I could put up with, if I could see any tokens of that manly straightforward spirit and manner that once distinguished Virginia. Sincerity and truth are so far out of fashion that nobody now-a-days seems to expect them in the intercourse of life. But I am becoming censorious—and how can I help it, in this canting and speaking age, where the very children are made to cry or laugh as a well-drilled recruit shoulders or grounds his fire-lock.

And on another occasion: "I see that Peyton R. advertises his land on ——— River. This was the last of my name and race whom I would go and see. The ruin is no doubt complete."[40]

For Randolph the England of his travels offered some rest and a change of air, a more complete relaxation into the lost world than America could afford him. But even in England, he could not escape the bitter facts of the loss of that world. Indeed, his visits helped him to see all the more clearly, from a distance and a special perspective, how great had been his own and his country's loss. Randolph's numerous trips abroad in the 1820's were like homecomings for him. It was as if he had a double *patria*—England and Virginia; he talked about sending his protégés to Eton, called London his city, and so on. He spoke of England, finally, as if the Revolution had never occurred: it was the only place where he might encounter the kind of men he understood himself to have been brought up to associate with.

But I should do the greatest injustice were I not to say that the higher ranks—a few despicable and despised fashionables excepted—are as unpretending and plain as our old-fashioned Virginian gentlemen, whom they greatly resemble. This class of men is now nearly extinct, to my great grief, and the shame and loss of our country. They are as distinct from the present race in their manners, dress and principles, and everything but anatomical structure, as an eagle is from a pig, or a wild turkey is from a turkey-buzzard. The English gentleman is not graceful, not affable but plain, sincere, kind, without one particle of pretension in dress, manner or anything else.

Gulliver has met his Houyhnhnms and can no longer bear the sight of the rest of us Yahoos.[41]

At home, Randolph faced the engines of change with unceasing bitterness and eloquence. The full if scattered force of his personality bore down on the conditions and men he deplored. His famous speech on retrenchment and reform, delivered in the House on February 1, 1828, caught his mood. It was a rambling and intermittently brilliant speech, a defense of his conduct and a statement of his dissent. In it were suspended all the elements of "Randolph of Roanoke." The organization was entirely self-willed, the only connections and logic supplied by the speaker's self. It represented political Shandeism of the highest order. Beginning with an almost absurd defense of the queen of France from the aspersions cast upon her reputation by Mr. Everett of Massachusetts, a premise truly plucked from the air of his fancies, Randolph launched into a defense of his truculent mood. His tone was angry because he was defending a lady's honor. He discoursed for a bit on the proper place of women:

I heard him, with horror, introduce the case of the Queen of France—and in answer to what? To a handbill—a placard—an electioneering firebrand; and in the presence of whom? Of those who ought never to be present in a theatre where men contend for victory and empire. Sir, they have no more business there than they have in a field of battle of another sort. Women, indeed, are wanted in the camp; but women of a very different description. What maiden, sir—nay, what matron—could hear the gentleman, without covering her face with her hands, and rushing out of the House? But for some of the remarks of the gentleman from Massachusetts, in relation to newspaper publication, I should have begun in at least as low a key and as temperate a mood as he did.

Thus did Randolph lay down the gauntlet, in the name of honor, of the ladies. It was a truly wild reassertion of his old stance, and its calculated excess is astonishing.[42]

And so the speech proceeded, brimming with learning, allusion, insight, and vituperation, but lacking any structure beyond that provided by the electric if vague trackings of Randolph's own cerebration. Randolph liberated himself from all external restraint, offering the stream of consciousness of his cluttered and embittered mind. The speech defies explication, and yet it had a point. Randolph's very freedom with the language and culture, his extravagant individualism, contrasted with the dull corruption of the society he attacked. His willingness to obtrude himself upon the public business was comment enough on it. Along the way, he struck out at John Quincy Adams, at newspapers, at opponents and policies of every description. He placed Andrew Jackson, who could fight, above Adams, who could write, denigrating the influence of book learning and metaphysical systems on the running of affairs. He attacked lawyers, preferring the ordinary wisdom of ordinary folk as an antidote to the poison of tyrants and philosopher kings: "So even a poor peasant of sense may instruct the philosopher, as the shepherd did, in that beautiful introduction, the finest of Mr. Gay's fables but one, who drew all his notions of men and things from Nature." The people, he reminded Congress "are always unsophisticated—and though they may occasionally be misled, are always right in their feelings."[43]

Finally, Randolph arrived at that self-defense which had prompted his remarks. It is worth excerpting because set in the baroque madness of his extravagance and self-assertion, it exhibits a stance not unfamiliar to the student of his upbringing and education. Indeed it was the learned response of a younger Randolph, cut off from the world that expected it and flung in the teeth of the world that dismissed it:

I do not pretend that my own motives do not partake of their full share of the infirmity of our common nature—but, of those infirmities, neither avarice nor ambition form one iota in the composition of my present motives. Sir, what can the country do for me? Poor as I am—for I am much poorer than I have been—impoverished by unwise legislation—I still have nearly as much as I know how to use—more, certainly than I have at times made a good use of—and, as for power, what charms can it have for one like me. Sir, if power had been my object, I must have been less sagacious than my worst enemies have represented me to be, (unless, indeed, those who would have kindly locked me up in bedlam,) if I had not obtained it. . . . Sir, what can the country give me that I did not possess in the confidence of such constituents as no man ever had before? Sir, I could retire to my old patrimonial trees, where I might see the sun rise and set in peace. Sir, as I was returning, the other evening, from the Capitol, I saw—what has been a rare sight this Winter—the Sun dipping his broad disk among the trees behind those Virginia hills, not allaying his glowing axle in the steep Atlantic stream—and I asked myself if, with this book of nature unrolled before me, I was not the most foolish of men to be struggling and scuffling here, in this heated and impure atmosphere, where the play is not worth the candle; but then the truth rushed upon my mind that I was vainly, perhaps, but honestly, striving to uphold the liberties of the people who sent me here—yes, sir, for can those liberties co-exist with corruption? At the very worst, the question recurs, which will the more effectually destroy them, collusion, bargain, and corruption here, or a military despotism? When can that be established over us? Never, till the Congress has become odious and contemptible in the eyes of the people—Sir, I have learned from the highest of all authority, that the first step towards putting on incorruption is the putting off corruption. That recollection nerves me in the present contest; for I know that, if we succeed, I shall hold over the head of those who succeed the present incumbent, a rod, which they will not dare, even if they had the inclination, to disobey. They will tremble at the punishment of their predecessors. Sir, if we succeed, we shall restore the Constitution—we shall redress the injury done to the people—we shall regenerate the country. . . . But, sir, if we perish under the spasmodic efforts of those now in power to reinstate themselves on the throne, our fate will be a sacred one—and who would wish to survive it?— there will be nothing left in the country, worth any man's possession. If, after such an appeal as has been made to the people, and a majority has been brought into this and the other House of Congress, this Administration shall be able to triumph, it will prove there is a rottenness in our institutions, which ought to render them unworthy of any man's regard.

Through the central theme, the expression of the situation of the country in terms of Randolph's personal drama, the old warrior and his young self merge here in an eloquent kaleidoscopic statement of the concerns of his politics; self and society are joined, informed by the lessons of his education. Randolph's authority in this passage cannot be divorced from the rambling, self-willed discourse that preceded it; that elaboration of personal themes set the stage and warmed up the audience for this wonderfully expressed statement of the old and dignified themes of his first politics. This was "Randolph of Roanoke" still, speaking in his noblest and most moving accents of duty and crisis, of corruption and virtue, of regeneration and reform. Masquerading as the wise yet gallant statesman, grown old and tired in the service of his *patria,* was the disappointed naïf, embittered yet capable of lofty sentiments still. For Randolph's ideals—however misleading and inappropriate and alienating they had proven to be—were high, and his expression of them honest.[44]

We can see what this might mean when we recall Randolph's estranged feelings toward the country he wished to reform and regenerate, to save. There are many indications of his alienation from the development of the United States, but the most telling and dramatic lie in the following assessments of Jefferson and Hamilton from the pen of John Randolph of Roanoke.

I cannot live in this miserable undone country where as the Turks follow their sacred standard, which is a pair of Mahomet's green breeches, we are governed by the old red breeches of that Prince of Projectors, St. Thomas of Cantingbury, and surely Becket himself never had more pilgrims at his shrine than the saint of Monticello.

I have a fellow feeling with H. He was a victim of rancorous enemies, who always prevail over lukewarm friends. He died because he preferred death to the slightest strain of imputation or disgrace. He was not suited to the country, or the times; and if he lived now, he might be admired by a few but would be thrust aside to make room for any fat-headed demagogue, or dextrous intriguer.

As Randolph said of one of his own remarks: "I do not draw my pictures in such a way as to render it necessary to write under them, 'this is a man, this is a horse.' "[45]

CONCLUSION

John Randolph was ill prepared by the education of his youth as well as by temper and circumstance for the America he encountered as an adult. Although he seemed destined to play a major role in national politics, his lasting importance has turned out to lie rather in his trenchant and eloquent perception of what in America's heritage was sacrificed to the demands of democracy and nationhood. By virtue of his outsider's position in politics, near to and yet removed from the centers of power, Randolph was able, earlier than many others, to anticipate certain of the consequences of the American Revolution. Because of his prophetic and wonderfully expressed opposition to American modernity, Randolph has been an attractive figure for students of the past, who have used him, in the main, metaphorically. I have concentrated instead on the sources and reasons for his ill-fittedness to his times and on the consequences in his career and style. It now remains to offer some conclusions about this still-perplexing figure. Specifically, if Randolph was as idiosyncratic as has been argued, wherein lies his interest for the serious student of history? There are two answers. First, Randolph's history, his miseducation, offers some insight into the nature of the cultural changes that followed from the Revolution but were not always consistent with its heritage. Second, Randolph's particular solutions to his personal dilemma may suggest some structural insights into what became in time for many other Americans a cultural dilemma.

Randolph's miseducation had two sources. As has been shown, he was a literal-minded adherent of the lessons of his upbringing, unwilling to change his lights to meet changing circumstances. The personal aspect of this unwillingness, the character that caused Randolph to stick so obstinately to his guns, is of no great consequence for American history. It is interesting, however, that we can see Randolph's lights so starkly; cultural values did not change in him, and these were the values that informed America's Founding. The English provincial country tenets that he kept to were preserved, not altered, in this human vessel. In Randolph's confrontations with democratic America, therefore, we can see something like the drama of America's confrontation with some of her own traditions.

The fact that Randolph's literal espousal of the country stance of principle and the old English values it represented proved so inappropriate may indicate that what began in America in terms of country ideology was transformed by independence into something different. The radical unsuitedness of the cultural baggage of the provincial Englishman to the situation of the nineteenth-century American underscores the really important changes that came about as the result of the colonial revolt. The Virginian stress on character and independence, the Virginian esteem for the landed aristocracy, apparently had increasingly little validity as guides to American national politics, however doggedly Randolph and his constituents continued to adhere to them. Randolph's unsusceptibility to compromise, to democracy, to the commercial spirit, to nationalism, and his consequent isolation illustrate by contrast that these were increasingly the values of American society.

Conclusion

Recent scholarship has emphasized the English ideological origins of American independence and politics. Randolph's career both supports and limits that understanding. What was conventional wisdom in 1775 was no longer especially useful by 1800. What precipitated the birth of the United States of America by no means necessarily characterized it thereafter. The role of English cultural values in an independent America must be re-examined so that we may take into account how little they supported anything but discontent, disenchantment, and disillusionment. This book does not provide conclusions on this subject, but perhaps it does highlight the transformation at the cultural level in the early national period; the contradiction between the exalted ideals of 1776 and the coarser facts of independence isolated the man like Randolph, who would not or could not agree to the new rules; such a man could only decry the loss and breach of the old ways of doing things. Randolph's example, then, may deepen one's sense of what American nationhood might have been about at the same time that it describes the limits of the old wisdom in the new America. Randolph remains the symbol of what America may have lost, what it had lost. Randolph is a historical figure of loss and regret; his strangeness only makes his inappropriateness more comprehensible.[1]

To get at the most interesting aspect of Randolph's relevance to American history, we must take up his most compelling biographer, Henry Adams. For in Adams's concern with Randolph, beyond sectional and family revenge, lies the clue to his most important, if unknowing, lesson: theirs was a common exploration of opposition to the consensus of American culture. In writing his almost-autobiography, *The Education of Henry Adams*, Adams spent considerable energy grappling with what he called "eccentricity." In a central chapter on his life in England during the American Civil War, he offered some observations on national character and eccentricity. He began by describing the English mind as different from others: "The English mind was one-sided, eccentric, systematically unsystematic, and logically illogical." The American mind, in contrast, "was not thought at all, it was a convention, superficial, narrow, and ignorant; a mere cutting instrument, practical, economical, sharp and direct." There was no time for eccentricity: "Americans needed and used their whole energy and applied it with close economy; but English society was eccentric by law and for the sake of eccentricity itself." To a Bostonian, "this eccentricity bore all the marks of strength; perhaps it was actual exuberance of force, a birth mark of genius." But though the representative Bostonian called it national character, Adams concluded that his own experiences had left "the conviction that eccentricity was weakness." Adams's complicated argument identified the dominant strain in American character, and therefore American history, as materialism coupled with energy and an insistence on conformity.[2]

Adams owed this lesson to experience, and blamed his education for not teaching it to him. The confrontation between the cultural values prescribed by tradition and Boston and the rough democratic realities was shattering to Adams's political ambitions and constituted a central theme of his book. He was never able to play in American political life, the conventional role to which he had been bred; he failed to distinguish himself in the compromising arena of force and materialism. The best education his country could afford, as Ernest Samuels exhaustively points out, was not the right kind of preparation for life in America.[3]

Adams did not argue with the European's conception of the American mind as "an economic thinking machine which could work only on a fixed line"; rather, he extended the metaphor, with a dry pride in his country's coarseness, saying that it "exasperated the European as a buzz-saw might exasperate a pine forest." Adams recognized that eccentricity was not to be tolerated in the American forest—Americans lost sight of the trees deliberately. The insistence on conformity, a common level of compromise, and the elevation of the majority to the level of right rendered eccentricity an anti-American weakness and vice. Difference asserted was suspect. The man who would be different would do well in England, which "was much more easy and tolerant" a society.[4]

Adams identified two types of Americans who appeared not to share the dominant national traits of materialism, strength, and a democratic craving for confirming conformity. The first was the Bostonian, obviously and reflexively. The Bostonian might appreciate eccentricity, although fearing it also, because it seemed "a better and nobler thing than the acuteness of the Yankee. . . ." The other American who might find eccentricity viable and even attractive was the southerner. The English sympathized with the Confederacy on this cultural issue of difference:

By natural affinity the social eccentrics commonly sympathized with political eccentricity. The English mind took naturally to rebellion—when foreign—and it felt particular confidence in the Southern Confederacy because of its combined attributes—foreign rebellion of English blood—which came nearer ideal eccentricity than could be reached by Poles, Hungarians, Italians, or Frenchmen. All the English eccentrics rushed into the ranks of rebel sympathizers, leaving few but well-balanced minds to attach themselves to the cause of Union.

The unmistakable irony here does not upset the deeper comparison of rebel and Englishman as eccentric types. The English supporters of the Union were English Yankees like William Forster ("a practical hard-headed Yorkshireman, whose chief ideals in politics took shape as working arrangements on an economical base"). Of course, eccentricity failed diplomatically as it did politically and militarily. The Confederates took a beating all around. The interesting point is Adams's identification of the southerner as an American eccentric. At its deepest, the meaning of eccentricity to Adams had nothing to do with success or even wisdom; he viewed it as a helpless quality, a natural and cultural and circumstantial *inability*. The English Unionist John Bright, "more English than any of his critics", hated "the whole fabric of sham religion, sham loyalty, sham aristocracy, and sham socialism." Fearing no one, dreading no social consequences, he expressed himself freely and publicly. This was the essence of his eccentricity: "He had the British weakness of believing only in himself and his own conventions." This eccentricity was repugnant to his countrymen because it was a reaction to English conditions. He did not live for the sake of eccentricity; it was not a quality prized in itself. He was considered eccentric because he was unable to accept what other Englishmen accepted. This concept of eccentricity as perceived protest was fundamental to Adams's discussion.[5]

Pieced together, Adams's argument on eccentricity went as follows: The eccentric believes only in himself and follows his own lights. This eccentricity is a kind of weakness, especially in politics. It is the refusal by a man to accept the dominant concerns and conventions of his own society. The true eccentric must entertain more than private doubts. The refusal to go along must be public. He must be seen to be believed—seen and heard. Eccentricity is the ordering of one's life in such a way that it becomes a public acknowledgment of a basic disagreement with one's fellows. It is not really adopted as a matter of choice, although it may be consciously realized and refined. Similarly, it reflects not strength but weakness of position. Presumably, eccentricity is a last resort, the most distinctly personal protest available to someone who finds himself alone and unable to have his way with his peers. It is a refuge, a defensive maneuver to preserve one's cherished and helpless way of life—a defensive refuge with a contrastingly aggressive tone. It has the character of an embattled challenge. In America, Adams located this eccentricity in Boston and Virginia, in himself and John Randolph.

Adams explored eccentricity in his books and in his own highly wrought, mannered life. He was disappointed by American society, and although he tried endlessly and wonderfully to understand it, he early gave up on any attempt to reform or even affect it. The descriptions of scientific ventures in his histories indicate how little faith he placed in the efforts of the individual to alter the course of democratic history. He believed that his own education had failed him, deducing that failure from his unsuitedness to the times in which he lived and ought to have led. Underneath the sectional and personal rancor of his book about Randolph, one can sense the identification. Adams understood Randolph's eccentricites and miseducation. Randolph had been born at an unpropitious moment, he had espoused ideas that American history was to make irrelevant, and in this profoundest sense had been miseducated. Randolph's eccentricity would have proved unacceptable to a Yankee constituency, but his southern people loved and appreciated it. His excesses were calculated, and were connected to regional taste and to political disappointment:

He sometimes acted a generous, sometimes a brutal part; the one, perhaps, not less sincere than the other while it lasted, but neither of them in any sense simple expression of emotion. Although he professed vindictiveness as a part of his Powhatan inheritance, and although he proclaimed himself to be one who never forsook a friend or forgave a foe, it is evident that his vindictiveness was often assumed merely to terrify; there was usually a method and a motive in his madness, noble at first in the dawn of young hope, but far from noble at last in the gloom of disappointment and despair.[6]

In Adams's Randolph there was an unmistakable if muted and as yet incomplete aura of identification. In this sense *John Randolph* offered an early version of the *Education*. Putting aside the historical and personal, it told the bare story of a favored American son, disinherited by his inability to meet the changed requirements of a new political world. Randolph's achievement was to see what had changed and to carry on a personal life which contrasted with the new values he despised. He lived in defiance of the norms, in full and insistent view of the people. Randolph's "almost incredible capacity for attitudinizing" did not affect his great achievement: ". . . he discovered and mapped out from beginning to end a chart of the whole course on which the slave power was to sail to its destruction. He did no legislative work, sat on no committees, and was not remotely connected with any useful measure or ideas." Like Henry Adams, he charted political currents; he was the Cassandra who saw what was going wrong and cried out against it. This Randolph was very like Adams's historian, the man who saw the processes of history without being able to change them. It was a story already told and foredoomed in its opening moments. Randolph was born into a condemned world:

This small cheerful world, which was in its way a remarkable phenomenon, and produced the greatest list of great names ever known this side of the ocean, was about to suffer a wreck the more fatal and hopeless because no skill could avert it, and the dissolution was so quiet and subtle that no one could protect himself or secure his children. . . .

As he grew a few years older, and looked about him on the world in which he was to play a part, he saw little but repetition of his own surroundings. When the Revolutionary War closed, in 1783, he was ten years old, and during the next five years he tried to pick up an education. America was then a small, straggling, exhausted country, without a government, a nationality, a capital, or even a town of thirty thousand inhabitants; a country which had not the means of supplying such an education as the young man wanted, however earnestly he tried for it.

The unacknowledged similarity with Adams which was implicit in this version of Randolph he completed in his chronicle of his own miseducation, helplessness, and eccentricity.[7]

Adams and Randolph were not the only Americans who appear to have resorted to eccentricity of one sort of another. The assumption of a style of life anachronistic and hostile to the common ways of democratic America, insisted upon in a public way, is familiar in our history. The connection between disillusion, disappointment in conventional ways of doing things, and a highly personal and nostalgic style of life, all with an edge of self-righteous protest, characterizes such disparate figures in our culture as Leatherstocking, Thoreau, the various literary exiles, and the recent generation of rebellious children of the bourgeoisie. It is tempting to state a law of eccentricity and protest, but that lies far beyond the scope of this discussion. Instead, it will be enough to move from the connection between Adams and Randolph to a consideration of how Randolph's eccentricity may be regarded and how it may illuminate the sources of other protest.

Randolph lived eccentrically. He sought to embody in a public way the values he felt were lacking in American society. He gathered into his personal style the substance of his objections to American realities and forced them back on the public. He was successful in one sense: everyone from Albert Gallatin to Jared Sparks conceded his eccentricity. His style of life, as we have seen, was completely involved with the expression of his political convictions, and his exaggerations resulted from his despair at making his point by other means. He played the role in which he saw himself. His constituents returned him again and again because of what he was. He could not conform to the modes and conventions of American politics and life. He stood up firm and alone throughout his career, accepting support but refusing to tender it in return. His politics required a conception of himself which mirrored a vision of loss. His creation of a public figure to contain and articulate his views was a logical reaction, however unself-conscious, to the changed state of society which he deplored. It was in so many ways the product of his education; and yet in one area it was new. Randolph played to the new American democratic public.[8]

One important reason for Randolph's interest to us remains, of course, the fact that to many Southerners he came to symbolize certain values and positions—a cause. He was the precursor of subsequent southern reaction. Erik Erikson has written of the importance of Luther's personality in his culture: "When he later burst into universality, it was not on the basis of an extensive knowledge of the state of universal questions, but rather because he was able to experience what was immediately about him in new ways." Randolph had this kind of sensitivity to conditions in America, and in a sense interpreted them to the next generation of southerners. His own character, his immediate personal experience, fitted him to be a vehicle or example of the cultural shift he prefigured so eloquently. What was clear to him became in time clear to the rest of the South. It may have been the abnormal workings of his mind that caused him to see what he did so early and so intensely. He was especially attuned (for his own reasons) to the problems the South might feel in the American union. His ventures into politics disappointed him. His education and character made it impossible for him to change his methods and his ideas. What became for future generations a myth of loss was to Randolph the experience of loss. He played the part of the eccentric southerner in protest against American culture, couched directly in the terms of what upset him. Isolated from the raging materialism and democracy of his times, Randolph sought refuge in a conception of himself which made good on his expectations and which he then flung in the face of the nation. His politics of espousal, as opposed to abstract criticism, exemplified the kind of protest that responds not only to the articulation of theory but to the social facts of American society.[9]

Randolph's reactions were clearly more sensitive and extreme and altogether more personal than most; he was driven to action by what was peculiar to him. His eccentricities and opinions were significant only to the degree that they expressed a shared discontent with the development of American society and with the southern position within the Union, and a shared sense of futility about the effectiveness of political protest. The role of the eccentric as protester, or perhaps better, as the expresser of protest is highly interesting. Its implied assumption is that in order to make a point of disagreement outside of politics, one must somehow get people's attention. The weight of mass society and the pressure to conform hide a perverse craving for the raving individual. Living so much alike, we cultivate the life that is different; it mesmerizes us. The exception fascinates the upholders of the rule. Randolph's habitual exaggerations, his insistent dissent from America in his manners, the way of life which he successfully identified with his politics, these illustrate the kind of protest to which many others, in varied situations, have had recourse. Randolph did not influence these others directly, but his example shows how Americans feeling the pressure of majority culture and the inaccessibility of conventional institutional alternatives may assume a distinctive way of life undertaken in order to oppose themselves to standard and restrictive norms. This may include so frivolous a motto as Gerald Murphy's "living well is the best revenge," or so serious a living proof as Thoreau's retreat to Walden, so high-toned an ascent as Bernard Berenson's or so vulgar a retreat as that of Mailer's "White Negro." What they have in common and what was first seen in John Randolph, is the sense that in order to be different in America one must seek the visible privacy of a way of life that compels and intrigues as well as contrasts with the views of the many, that strikes some kind of chord, a resonance of loss or ambition or dream in a people who tolerate exaggeration and dislocation more easily than straight disagreement. It is finally, as Randolph understood, a question of fighting fire with fire.

ACKNOWLEDGMENTS

Leonard Levy has *told* me that the publication of this, my first book, will not change the world, but since we both know that it will, I want to acknowledge my debts to those many people who have helped me in the writing of it.

I remember encountering John Randolph in my brother's copy of Roger Butterfield's *The American Past* when I was a little boy; I owe my brother Donald this, as I do so many of my tastes and ambitions. At Cornell, James Morton Smith first encouraged me to work out my interest in Randolph in an essay. David Brion Davis, who had first given me the heart to abandon myself to Randolph and notions of his eccentricity, made his inspiring and roomy judgment that since I wanted to write about Randolph, why didn't I just. Michael Kammen took me over as a student, kept a watchful and shrewd and a tolerant eye on me, and time after time intervened to help me keep to my work, to help me get a paying job, to brace me with some advice and attention, to send me a printed version of some favorite Randolph speech, in short to help me on my way to becoming a historian. He never got much in the way of pleasantry out of it before, and I am happy to thank him here. Many others of my teachers, associates, and friends at Cornell contributed to this study, and I am mindful and

Acknowledgments

grateful; I would like to mention especially Jim O'Connor, Neil Hertz, Fred Somkin, Isaac Kramnick, and Mary Beth Norton. The folks at Tweitman's gave moral and material support of a very special kind, and I hope they know how grateful "Bobby" is. Dan McCall read my book and my mind and demanded that I take them both seriously.

At the University of Virginia, I had the rare luck of teaching in a fine history department while writing a dissertation based on original sources in the wonderful Alderman Library, whose rare-manuscripts staff I salute and thank. Best of all was the talented and generous company of colleagues and friends whose interest in me extended without intrusion to those subjects which turned into this book; I thank them all. I want to mention W. W. Abbot and Merrill Peterson and Willie Lee Rose, whose very different examples expanded the scope of my aspirations and whose company gave me so much in the way of help and so little in the way of constraint. It was an enviable privilege to spend time talking about Randolph and other subjects with Dumas Malone, whose gracious ways helped me bear up under his judgment that I was perhaps fitted to write about such a pointless rascal as Jack Randolph.

Since coming to the Claremont Graduate School, I have known generosity and support from my colleagues, especially John Niven and Leonard Levy, whose patience and impatience respectively have served me very well indeed. Through the aegis of the Claremont Graduate School, I received a timely grant from the John Randolph and Dora Haynes Foundation, which enabled me to finish this manuscript. Toni Tosch typed this and that, over and over, for years and years, and by the way taught me how to live in California. A corps of volunteers from the staff of the Claremont Graduate School, galvanized by the energy and good offices of Lois Ingram and Alison Mathews, came to my aid by typing large parts of this manuscript. I am grateful for the help of several work-study assistants over the years; they saved me from trouble.

James L. Mairs of W. W. Norton has been a model editor, treating me like a swell and my book like a book. Esther Jacobson paid me more serious attention as a writer than anyone has; her copy-editing of my book contributed decisively to its clarity and to my education.

It comes down, I think, to friends who bear with you and help you bear up. Alex Gold made me an especially luminous suggestion. Barry Weller read my dissertation with gentle care. Erik and Corelyn Midelfort kept a sharp and a tending eye on my conscience. Eddie Strickler showed me Randolph's country, and he and Kate McGee helped me understand something about living there. Eleanor Abbot gave me Lucia. Toni and Nestor Carrion gave me wings and tequila. I don't know how to thank Charles Young. Paula May Cohen helped me discover what I wanted this book concretely to be; she has been my every wish in a reader.

The dedication expresses only the bare fact of my greatest and happiest debt. My sister Judy must own up to a part of everything I do, I am so much hers still.

"Every fool has a rainbow," Merle tells us, and Leslie *must* know by now how glad I am that she was mine.

NOTES

In presenting Randolph's words, I have favored sense over exactness of transcription, especially with printed speeches. Randolph did not care much for his printed words. He spoke, as he said, from impulse and feeling; his were *"verba ardentia."* He usually had nothing to do with printed versions of his words. He was not a writer whose texts have any claim to being sacred. We want his thoughts and his intentions. I know he would haunt me if I littered this book with "[*sic*]," so I have occasionally corrected mistakes of spelling and errors of that sort, not to alter the sense but to give his writings and the transcriptions of his talking the force and clarity they customarily had; he was persnickety about such things, and I have tried to render him in as clear an English as he seems to have been capable of, not encumbered with the encrusted errors of his times or the years since. Since I don't subscribe to most of his opinions, and since I did not write an advocating book, I thought I owed Randolph at least that.

• • • •

The collection of Randolph materials at the Alderman Library in the University of Virginia has originals or copies of all of Randolph's surviving papers. I went through that collection. Where possible, I have cited a printed version—preferably the most easily available—of the letters and other materials to which reference is made. That is one reason for the frequent presence in these notes of certain works, notably the studies of Randolph by Hugh A. Garland, Henry Adams, William Cabell Bruce, and Russell Kirk. There is more to it than that, however. More than most scholars, I suspect, I have benefited from the work of past writers—going, as it were, largely over their forest with my own ground axe. In more than one instance, I have reproduced their arrangement of quotations and the like, preferring my obligation to be known. I have of course noted such debts throughout, but I wanted here to mention in a general way how good I think the biographical work on Randolph is, how many good scholars, not just the above four, have written about him, and how much this interpretive book relies on their labors.

CHAPTER 1

1. To Dr. John Brockenbrough, August 8, 1826, quoted in Hugh A. Garland, *The Life of John Randolph of Roanoke*, vol. 2 (New York, 1856), p. 273; to Dr. John Brockenbrough, December 16, 1832, quoted in Garland, vol. 2, p. 359.

2. *Annals of Congress* (14th Congress, 1st Session, 1815–16), 686, 1339. In some instances, I have changed the third person to the first for clearer reading.

3. Quoted in Russell Kirk, *John Randolph of Roanoke: A Study in American Politics* (Chicago, 1964), p. 106; quoted in Garland, vol. 1, p. 28; *Annals of Congress* (10th Congress, 1st Session, 1807–8), I, 1345; *Annals of Congress* (18th Congress, 1st Session, 1823–24), I, 1299.

4. *Annals of Congress* (14th Congress, 1st Session, 1815–16), 1132; to Edward Booker, February 9, 1816, quoted in William Cabell Bruce, *The Life of John Randolph of Roanoke*, vol. 2 (New York, 1922), pp. 239–40.

5. Quoted in Roger Butterfield, *The American Past* (New York, 1947), p. 37; John Greenleaf Whittier, "Randolph of Roanoke," in *The Writings of John Greenleaf Whittier*, vol. 2 (Boston, 1892), pp. 25–32.

6. This account of Southside Virginia is especially dependent on materials in Bruce, vol. 2, ch. 5.
To Elizabeth T. Coalter, August 9, 1823, Alderman Library, University of Virginia; to F. W. Gilmer, July 30, 1825, Alderman Library; to F. W. Gilmer, July 2, 1825, Alderman Library; quoted in Bruce, vol. 2, p. 111. The descriptions of Roanoke are found in Bruce, vol. 2, pp. 351ff. Bruce is also the source for the estimate of Randolph's holdings.

7. To Elizabeth T. Coalter, November 28, 1828, Alderman Library; Henry Adams, *John Randolph* (Boston and New York, 1882), pp. 255–56; quoted in Bruce, vol. 2, p. 38.

8. Theodore Dudley, ed., *Letters of John Randolph to a Young Relative* (Philadelphia, 1834), p. 208; quoted in Bruce, vol. 2, p. 344; to Elizabeth T. Coalter, October 10, 1828, Alderman Library.

9. Quoted in Kirk, pp. 44–45; Bruce, vol. 2, p. 128.

10. "Virginiana" quoted in Bruce, vol. 2, p. 128.

11. Richard Randolph's will, *Will Book for 1797*, clerk's office, Prince Edward County, Virginia, quoted in Bruce, vol. 1, pp. 104–5.

12. The best collection of material about Randolph the master is in Bruce, vol. 2, pp. 690ff. The information concerning Johnny comes from Randolph's letter to Elizabeth Bryan, January 19, 1828, Alderman Library. The other quotes are from Bruce, vol. 2, pp. 690ff.

13. This discussion of Randolph's political views follows and owes its skeleton of reference to Kirk, especially pp. 170–71. Kirk's assembly of Randolph's views remains standard; I do not subscribe to all his interpretations with a whole heart, but even when differing from Kirk, one wants to do his Randolph scholarship the homage of borrowing and acknowledgment.
Adams, pp. 169–70; *Annals of Congress* (9th Congress, 1st Session, 1805–6), 928; *Annals of Congress* (17th Congress, 1st Session, 1821–22), I, 943; to Josiah Quincy, October 18, 1813, in Edmund Quincy, *Life of Josiah*

Quincy of Massachusetts (Boston, 1867), p. 337; resolution on waves quoted in Kirk, p. 171.

14. *Annals of Congress* (17th Congress, 1st Session, 1821–22), I, 819–22; quoted in Powhatan Bouldin, *Home Reminiscences of John Randolph of Roanoke* (Danville, Va., 1878), pp. 276–78.

15. Quoted in Adams, pp. 278–79; *Annals of Congress* (18th Congress, 1st Session, 1823–24), I, 1296–1311.

16. Quoted in Adams, pp. 277, 280–81.

17. Quoted in Adams, p. 279.

18. Examples of Randolph wit, real and supposed are collected in Bruce, vol. 2, pp. 202ff.; William I. Paulding, *The Literary Life of James K. Paulding* (New York, 1867), p. 238; and Bouldin, p. 310.

Chapter 2

1. To Josiah Quincy, March 22, 1814, quoted in Edmund Quincy, *Life of Josiah Quincy of Massachusetts* (Boston, 1867), pp. 350–53.

2. Henry Adams, *John Randolph* (Boston and New York, 1882), p. 5.

3. Quoted in William Cabell Bruce, *The Life of John Randolph of Roanoke*, vol. 1 (New York, 1922), p. 11. For accounts of the Randolph family see Bruce, vol. 1, pp. 3–34; Jonathan Daniels, *The Randolphs of Virginia, "America's Foremost Family"* (Garden City, N.Y., 1972); William Ewart Stokes, Jr., "Randolph of Roanoke: A Virginia Patriot. The Early Career of John Randolph of Roanoke, 1773–1805" (Ph.D. dissertation, University of Virginia, 1955). J. R. Pole, *Political Representation in England and the Origins of the American Republic* (London, 1966), p. 152; Carl Bridenbaugh, *Myths and Realities: Societies of the Colonial South* (New York, 1965), pp. 16, 10. See also Pole, *passim*, and Charles Sydnor, *Gentlemen Freeholders: Political Practices in Washington's Virginia* (Chapel Hill, N.C., 1952).

4. The influence of the English model on Virginia is indicated, for example, by J. G. A. Pocock's classification of that state as a subculture "within a single Anglophone world," in "Virtue and Commerce in the Eighteenth Century," *Journal of Interdisciplinary History,* III (Summer 1972), p. 122. Bridenbaugh, p. 5. See also my discussion of Revolutionary historiography in chapter 4. Pocock, p. 122.

5. Jack P. Greene, *Landon Carter: An Inquiry into the Personal Values and Social Imperatives of the Eighteenth-Century Virginia Gentry* (Charlottesville, Va., 1967), pp. 90–91.

6. Greene, pp. 18–19, 21–23, 25–26, 40, 46.

7. Jay Hubbell, *Virginia Life in Fiction* (Dallas, 1922), p. 12.

8. On decline in Virginia, Greene, pp. 55ff.; Greene, p. 87.

9. Quoted in Bruce, vol. 1, p. 21; see also pp. 18–21.

10. For the episode of Randolph's unconsciousness, see Hugh A. Garland, *The Life of John Randolph of Roanoke*, vol. 1 (New York, 1856), p. 11; and Bruce, vol. 1, p. 37.

The best source for Randolph's early life consists of the two unpublished works of William Ewart Stokes, Jr.—his Ph.D. dissertation, referred to in note 3, and his M.A. thesis, "The Early Life of John Randolph of Roanoke, 1773–1794" (University of Virginia, 1950). Stokes's research is very sound, and I generally follow and accept his conclusions about the facts of Randolph's life. I have used his work primarily to check Bruce and other sources, and am very indebted to his scholarship. I have not been much influenced by his more impressionistic views about the kind of man Randolph was or the importance of his career. I was disappointed that so keen and knowledgeable a Randolph scholar stuck so closely to the most simple "Virginia" lines of interpretation. I think his research and energy should have resulted in better interpretations than are contained in the theses. I make this point because although I have used his work to check my own facts, I have not followed and do not agree with his more general statements about Randolph. I have found Stokes's most important contribution to be his checklist, compiled with Francis L. Berkeley, Jr., of the Randolph papers in existence. Despite some mistakes and lapses and a need for some revision since its publication over twenty-five years ago, this is a superb and invaluable tool in Randolph research: William Ewart Stokes, Jr., and Francis L. Berkeley, Jr., *The Papers of Randolph of Roanoke, A Preliminary Checklist of His Surviving Texts in Manuscript and in Print* (Charlottesville, Va., 1951), reviewed in *American Archivist,* April 1951.

Garland, vol. 1, pp. 13–14; to Theodore Dudley, February 16, 1817, in Theodore Dudley, ed., *Letters of John Randolph to a Young Relative* (Philadelphia, 1834), reprinted in Bruce, vol. 1, pp. 60–62.

11. On mother's instruction, Randolph to Tudor Randolph, December 13, 1813, typescript in Grinnan MSS, Alderman Library, University of Virginia, quoted extensively in Bruce, vol. 1, p. 31; on mother's expectations and character, Garland, vol. 1, pp. 23, 25; Benjamin Watkins Leigh quoted in Henry A. Wise, *Seven Decades of the Union* (Philadelphia, 1872), pp. 31–32; quoted in Garland, vol. 1, p. 25.

12. Randolph to Elizabeth T. Coalter, dated "Sunday Morn," 1825, copy in Bryan MSS, Alderman Library, partial text in Bruce, vol. 1, p. 30.

13. Adams, p. 6.

14. In a discussion of Charles Dickens' limitation as an artist, Jonathan Bishop remarks on his inability to "imagine how Pip could have come through adulthood," and its corollary, "theatricality" (a return to childhood for themes of resolution and completion): "This skill is the gift of a child who entertains his mother in lieu of facing his father."—Jonathan Bishop, *Something Else* (New York, 1972), p. 185. This may well have been Randolph's situation.

15. In trying to locate Randolph's particular experience in the context of the colonial American family, I have relied on Edmund S. Morgan, *The Puritan Family* (New York, 1966) and *Virginians at Home: Family Life in the Eighteenth Century* (Williamsburg, 1952); Daniel Calhoun, *The Intelligence of a People* (Princeton, 1973); J. William Frost, *The Quaker Family in Colonial America* (New York, 1973); Julia C. Spruill, *Women's Life and Work in the Southern Colonies* (Chapel Hill, N.C., 1935); David Musto, "The Youth of John Quincy Adams," *Proceedings of the American Philosophical Society,* CXIII (August 1969), pp. 269–81; and Robert T. Sidwell, "Writers, Thinkers and Foxhunters—Educational Theory in the Almanacs of

Eighteenth-Century Colonial America," *History of Education Quarterly,* VIII (Fall 1968), pp. 275–88.

Calhoun, pp. 139–44, asserts the practice in the colonies of this new maternally oriented post-Lockean synthesis; see also Calhoun, p. 154; and Frost, esp. pp. 86–88.

Much of this literature is, of course, tentative and dependent on certain daring but inexact precursors, notably Philippe Aries, *Centuries of Childhood* (New York, 1952). A review essay by Lawrence Stone, "The Massacre of the Innocents," *New York Review of Books,* November 14, 1974, deals sensibly if leniently with the cumulative achievements of this recent scholarly exploration of childhood.

My own reservations about this work are considerable. The post-Aries obsession with locating the beginnings of the adult perception and sentimentalization of childhood strikes me as somewhat misleading and anachronistic. Frost's study of the Quakers departs from his usual careful and informative methods of compilation of what we can know, to discourse about the Romantic revolution and modern times in an attempt to explain the new maternally sentimentalized family. One must be careful not to mistake a differing perception for blindness.

My own reading of Randolph's family life brought me separately to the conviction that his was a softer, more maternal family than Morgan's work had led one to expect, that the Virginian family embraced in its informal structure the tension between father and mother as socializing and influential personages that Calhoun too fleetingly alludes to. Indeed, I think it not unlikely that, as in so many other things, Randolph was brought up in the midst of considerable and confusing changes in family structure; for families, like regimes and other aspects of social and economic life, were adjusting to the entrepreneurial, individualistic, democratic America of the nineteenth century. Randolph's family was rooted in the old but used the methods of the new.

16. R. D. Laing and A. Esteron, *Sanity, Madness and the Family* (Baltimore, 1970), p. 130; R. D. Laing, *The Divided Self* (Chicago, 1960), pp. 100ff.; Peter Coveney, *The Image of Childhood: The Individual and Society. A Study of the Theme in English Literature* (Baltimore, 1967), pp. 40–41. See also, Frost, pp. 74–75; Musto; Sidewell; and Calhoun, pp. 134–205.

17. Garland, vol. 1, p. 18. Everyone who has written about Randolph, including Stokes, accepts this anecdote from Garland, who does not offer a source.

18. For particulars on Randolph's land hunger, see Bruce, vol. 2, pp. 668–72.

Letter to an unidentified friend, quoted in Garland, vol. 1, p. 19.

19. See especially Eugene Genovese, *The Political Economy of Slavery* (New York, 1965); Robert McColley, *Slavery in Jeffersonian Virginia* (Urbana, Ill., 1964); and Gerald Mullin, *Flight and Rebellion: Slave Resistance in Eighteenth-Century Virginia* (New York, 1972).

20. Gerald O'Hara to his daughter Scarlett: "Land is the only thing in the world that amounts to anything . . . for 'tis the only thing in this world that lasts."—Margaret Mitchell, *Gone with the Wind* (New York, 1936), p. 35.

21. For the old story of John Randolph and Possum John Randolph see Gerald W. Johnson, *Randolph of Roanoke, A Political Fantastic* (New York, 1929), pp. 13–14. Stokes, in his M.A. thesis, gives the fullest and most recent account of the addition of "of Roanoke" to Randolph's name; see also a communication from George Tucker, then a professor at the University of Virginia, to the *New York American*, January 10, 1837, discussing among other things the English-style name of that "eccentric individual" John Randolph, in which he defends the gentry's use of place names to denominate themselves. For the record, it might be added here that "Possum John" was no Snopes with a Compson name, being the brother of Thomas Mann and Judith and Nancy Randolph and hence the brother-in-law of Richard Randolph and of Thomas Jefferson's daughter Martha.

On John Randolph of Williamsburg see Mary Beth Norton, "John Randolph's Plan of Accommodation," *William and Mary Quarterly,* January 1971, pp. 103–20. The copied-out transcriptions are in the Grinnan MSS, Alderman Library. On family myths see Musto, esp. p. 271. Musto's conceptual statement is suggestive, and in terms of John Randolph's perception of family life, very helpful; Randolph did indeed believe in and live within the outlines of his family myth, although we cannot be too precise about how and when and by whom it was first conveyed to him; the best guess remains that his mother made the point and his whole early social and family life confirmed it. Musto's own use of the idea is complicated by his picture of the young John Quincy Adams sailing alone at a tender age to far-off Europe with only the stern counsel and high expectations of his family myth to sustain him; the fact is that his father and brother were with him constantly. One also wonders if the child of a still-young colonial lawyer and rebel like John Adams would necessarily be the victim of a family myth—a reading of Abigail Adams's letters to her eldest boy suggests the less elaborate but equally demanding stuff of high parental expectations in a family both principled and on the make. In any case, in the instance of John Randolph, this concept is appropriate and descriptive. Randolph learned the story of his family very early and spent a lifetime trying to make it come true, whether that meant his own success and the consequent success of the family or the equally well founded (in the myth) saga of loss, tragedy, and decline.

22. Quoted in Garland, vol. 1, p. 65 (italics inserted); to a friend, January 31, 1826, quoted in Garland, vol. 1, p. 11.

23. To Tudor Randolph, December 13, 1813, typescript in Grinnan MSS, Alderman Library; quoted in Garland, vol. 1, p. 12.

24. For St. George Tucker see Mary Haldane Coleman, *St. George Tucker: A Citizen of No Mean City* (Richmond, 1938).

To St. George Tucker, July 10, 1781, microfilm in Alderman Library, original in Colonial Williamsburg; to St. George Tucker, January 15, 1788, Alderman Library; to St. George Tucker, December 25, 1788, microfilm in Alderman Library, original in Brock Collection, Henry E. Huntington Library, reprinted in Powhatan Bouldin, *Home Reminiscences of John Randolph of Roanoke* (Danville, Va., 1878), pp. 219–20, and in Bruce, vol. 1, pp. 82–83.

25. Randolph to Tudor Randolph, December 13, 1813, quoted in Bruce, vol. 1, p. 74.

26. To Tudor Randolph, December 13, 1813, quoted in Bruce, vol. 1, pp. 74–75; to Henry Middleton Rutledge, February 24, 1791, microfilm in Alderman Library, original at Pennsylvania Historical Society, quoted in Bruce, vol. 1, p. 93.

27. To Tudor Randolph, December 13, 1813, quoted in Bruce, vol. 1, p. 75.

Stokes, in his Ph.D. dissertation, discusses the most recent investigation into Randolph's alleged impotence. I must confess that I do not take especially seriously even Randolph's early engagement to Maria Ward, and certainly believe that after his illness, whatever it was, at nineteen he did not entertain serious hopes of marriage and issue of his own. At best his romantic claims after that date are anxious tales of friendship to his boon companions. Stokes traces his difficulties to a sordid affair that occurred at some time during his dissipated New York and Philadelphia sojourns.

To a friend, January 31, 1826, quoted in Garland, vol. 1, p. 11.

28. For information on Richard Randolph's trial, see Bruce, vol. 1, pp. 106–23; Stokes, Ph.D. dissertation; and for a lurid account, Jay Walz and Audrey Walz, *The Bizarre Sisters* (New York, 1950). Thomas Jefferson wrote to his daughter Martha Jefferson Randolph, Nancy Randolph's sister-in-law, the following advice on how to treat the unfortunate girl: "Everyone at present stands on the merit or demerit of their own conduct. I am in hopes therefore that neither of you feel any uneasiness but for the pitiable victim, whether it be of error or slander. In either case I see guilt in one person and not in her. . . . Never throw off the best affections of nature in the moment when they become most precious to their object, nor fear to extend yourself to save another, lest you should sink yourself."—quoted in Bruce, vol. 1, p. 121.

Diary entries quoted in Bruce, vol. 1, p. 118.

The wounding and vituperative exchange of letters between Nancy Randolph Morris and John Randolph is printed in Bruce, vol. 2, pp. 272–95 (copies are in the New York Public Library and at the Virginia Historical Society). It is a searing and shocking exchange, and I find no discernible pattern of truth and motive except, as indicated, the powerful and lasting impact of Richard's fall. Randolph identified his assumption of Richard's duties with his failure to achieve things in his life that might have made him more happy and steady. In 1824 he wrote: "His [Richard's] sudden and ultimely death threw upon my care, helpless as I was, family, whom I tenderly and passionately loved; and with whom I might be now living at Bizarre if the reunion of his widow with the ——— of her husband had not driven me to Roanoke; where, but for my brother's entreaty and forlorn and friendless condition, I should have remained; and where I should have obtained a release from my bondage more than 20 years ago. Then I might have enjoyed my present opportunities; but time misspent and faculties misemployed and senses, jaded by labor or impaired by excess, cannot be recalled any more than that freshness of the heart before it has become aware of the deceits of others and of its own."—quoted in Garland, vol. 2, pp. 224.

To St. George Tucker, July 24, 1824, in Garland, vol. 1, p. 68.

29. Randolph to Tucker Randolph, December 13, 1813, quoted in Bruce, vol. 1, p. 127; for the duel, Bruce, vol. 1, pp. 124–25.

30. Randolph to St. George Tucker, January 26, 1794, microfilm in Alderman Library, original in Brock Collection, Henry E. Huntington Library, reprinted in Bouldin, pp. 220–21, and in Bruce, vol. 1, pp. 128–29.

For Randolph's travels, Garland, vol. 1, pp. 63–64; and Bruce, vol. 1, p. 130.

31. Nathaniel Beverley Tucker, "Garland's Life of Randolph," *Southern Quarterly Review,* new series, IV (July 1851); to Tudor Randolph, December 13, 1813, quoted in Bruce, vol. 1, pp. 127–8.

32. For Randolph's conduct at night, Garland, vol. 1, p. 70, reporting the testimony of a Mrs. Dudley.

33. To St. George Tucker, July 18, 1796, partial text in Bruce, vol. 1, pp. 132–33.

34. Randolph to Elizabeth T. Coalter, March 22, 1824, quoted in Bruce, vol. 1, p. 101. (Stokes seems to confuse this letter with a letter of March 21, 1824, included in the Bryan MSS, Alderman Library. It is not the same one, nor have I found one of March 22 at the University of Virginia.)

35. Bishop, p. 162.

36. Garland, vol. 1, pp. 72–73, 166–77, 209–10.

37. To William Thompson, December 31, 1800, quoted in Garland, vol. 1, p. 167; to William Thompson, undated, quoted in Garland, vol. 1, p. 176; to Joseph Bryan, February 1800, quoted in Garland, vol. 1, p. 179 (Stokes dates this letter February 20, from internal evidence; I disagree with his reading and would place it before February 20); to William Thompson, undated, quoted in Garland, vol. 1, p. 208.

38. All in Dudley: to "my dear boys," November 2, 1808, pp. 53–54; to Theodore Dudley, December 19, 1807, p. 43; to Theodore Dudley, October 13, 1811, p. 109; to Theodore Dudley, October 6, 1811, p. 106; to Theodore Dudley, September 3, 1811, p. 101; to Theodore Dudley, January 8, 1807, pp. 25–26.

CHAPTER 3

1. Carl Bridenbaugh, *Myths and Realities: Societies of the Colonial South* (New York, 1965), p. 40. See also Richard Beale Davis, *Intellectual Life in Jefferson's Virginia* (Knoxville, 1964). Davis stoutly insists upon the cultivated tone of eighteenth-century Virginia culture. His book is a valuable and comprehensive survey and a necessary antidote to the New England–centered study of early American intellectual history. A more recent work by Davis, *Literature and Society in Early Virginia, 1608–1840* (Baton Rouge, 1973), goes even further along the same lines. Davis's strongest point, and the most relevant to this study, is that the upper-class Virginian might well be a cultivated and even discriminating receiver of cultural goods. I am most impressed with this context for the young John Randolph. Indeed, it

may be that as a provincial audience for culture, Virginia had her last and most exotic flowering with John Randolph. Where I am unable to accept Davis's claim for Virginia, or for Randolph, is in attributing originality and distinction to their literary or cultural efforts. In *The Colonial Virginia Satirist, Mid Eighteenth-Century Commentaries on Politics, Religion and Society,* in *Transactions of the American Philosophical Society,* new series, LVII (March 1967), which he edited, Davis connects Randolph's father, John Randolph, to the group of satirists, the Dinwiddie group; John senior did not write satire but was an intimate and a fellow of the Tuesday Club that did. Here, surely, is another link in John junior's education to satirical poses, something that, along with his reading and his ultimate disillusionment with American politics, would drive him to the stance of the eighteenth-century satirist.

On Randolph's furniture and effects, Powhatan Bouldin, *Home Reminiscences of John Randolph of Roanoke* (Danville, Va., 1878), pp. 20ff., 35. Hugh A. Garland, *The Life of John Randolph of Roanoke,* vol. 2 (New York, 1856), pp. 172–73, quotes Jacob Harvey on Randolph's preference for John Bull over Brother Jonathan: "Never, sir, never; I will neither wear what they make nor eat what they raise, so long as my tobacco crop will enable me to get supplies from *old* England; and I shall employ John Bull to bind my books until the time arrives when they can be properly done, *South of Mason and Dixon's line!*"

To Dr. John Brockenbrough, September 25, 1818, quoted in Garland, vol. 2, pp. 100–103.

2. Randolph to F. W. Gilmer, July 2, 1825 (the first of two letters on this date, the original not extant), quoted in William Cabell Bruce, *The Life of John Randolph of Roanoke,* vol. 1 (New York, 1922), pp. 55–56. William Ewart Stokes, Jr., makes the necessary point that Randolph's recollections of his schooling were pretty unreliable. My interest, however, is not really to establish the facts of his schooling so much as to establish the character of his mind and education. Thus, although I do not accept Randolph's dismal accounts of his schooling literally, I do not feel it necessary to go into his educational sojourns in detail; Stokes does this carefully enough in both "The Early Life of John Randolph of Roanoke, 1773–1794" (M.A. thesis, University of Virginia, 1950) and "Randolph of Roanoke: A Virginia Patriot. The Early Career of John Randolph of Roanoke, 1773–1805" (Ph.D. dissertation, Univeristy of Virginia, 1955). Randolph's views of his schoolmaster pretty much fit the eighteenth-century model of the tyrannical or foolish pedagogue; see Edna L. Furness, "Portrait of the Pedagogue in Eighteenth Century England," *History of Education Quarterly,* II, pp. 62–70.

3. For Randolph's schooling, see Bruce, vol. 1, ch. 3; and Stokes, Ph.D. dissertation.

To St. George Tucker, September 13, 1787, quoted in Bruce, vol. 1, p. 81; to St. George Tucker, August 20, 1789, microfilm in Alderman Library, University of Virginia, original in Library of Congress; to an unidentified person, quoted in Garland, vol. 1, p. 23; to Theodore Dudley, February 15, 1806, in Theodore Dudley, ed., *Letters of John Randolph to a Young Relative* (Philadelphia, 1834).

4. To Henry Middleton Rutledge, February 24, 1791; to Henry Middleton Rutledge, April 29, 1797; to Henry Middleton Rutledge, December 28, 1795. All on microfilm in Alderman Library, originals at Pennsylvania Historical Society.

5. To Theodore Dudley, February 16, 1817, in Dudley, pp. 190–91; to Tudor Randolph, December 13, 1813, typescript in Grinnan MSS, Alderman Library.

6. To Harmanus Bleeker, October 10, 1818, holograph in Alderman Library, reprinted in Russell Kirk, *John Randolph of Roanoke: A Study in American Politics* (Chicago, 1964), pp. 227–30; to Theodore Dudley, February 16, 1817, in Dudley, pp. 190–91; Hugh Blair Grigsby, "The Library of John Randolph," *Southern Literary Messenger,* XX (February 1854), pp. 79–82. Compare Randolph's lasting attachment to fiction with Jefferson's dire dictum: "A great obstacle to good education is the inordinate passion prevalent for novels, and the time lost in that reading which should be instructively employed. When this position infects the mind, . . . reason and fact, plain and unadorned, are rejected. . . . the result is a bloated imagination, sickly judgment, and disgust towards all the real businesses of life."—Jefferson to Nathaniel Burwell, March 14, 1818, quoted in Charles B. Sanford, *Thomas Jefferson and His Library* (Hamden, Conn., 1977), p. 85.

7. Quoted in Garland, vol. 1, p. 15.

8. To Elizabeth Bryan, undated, quoted in Garland, vol. 1, p. 72; Jane Austen, *Persuasion,* ch. 11.

9. Quoted in Garland, vol. 1, p. 65; quoted in Bouldin, pp. 78–79 (compare *Measure for Measure,* act 3, sc. 1, lines 76–79: "The sense of death is most in apprehension,/And the poor beetle, that we tread upon,/In corporal sufferance, finds a pang as great/As when a giant dies"); to Harmanus Bleeker, October 10, 1818, holograph in Alderman Library, reprinted in Kirk, pp. 227–30.

10. W. B. C. Watkins, *The Perilous Balance* (Cambridge, Mass., 1960), p. 165; Charles Dickens, *David Copperfield,* ch. 4; Randolph to Elizabeth T. Coalter, dated "Sunday Morn," 1825, copy in Bryan MSS, Alderman Library, partial text in Bruce, vol. 1, p. 30; Randolph to Harmanus Bleeker, November 16, 1818, holograph in Alderman Library, reprinted in Kirk, pp. 231–32.

11. Garland, vol. 1, p. 15; to Elizabeth Bryan, undated, quoted in Garland, vol. 1, pp. 71–72. Again, one thinks of Jane Austen's characters, especially of Lady Catherine de Bourgh in *Pride and Prejudice,* whose "dignified impertinence" cannot supply her want of taste: "It [music] is of all subjects my delight. I must have my share in the conversation, if you are speaking of music. There are few people in England, I suppose, who have more true enjoyment of music than myself, or a better natural taste. If I had ever learnt, I should have been a great proficient."—*Pride and Prejudice,* vol. 2, ch. 6, 8. Jefferson too provides an interesting comparison. He worried about the dangers of poetry: ". . . much poetry should not be indulged. Some is useful for forming style and taste." "Pleasure and improvement" are the objects of reading poetry. "Of all men living," Jefferson wrote, "I am the last who should undertake to decide as to the merits of poetry. In earlier life I was fond of it, and easily pleased. But as

age and cares advanced the powers of fancy have declined."—quoted in Sanford, p. 87. Randolph never put away childish things.

In his self-lacerations Randolph may have voiced his pride in his lack of discipline; they must be read carefully for these boasts. "But I tell you as a truth unquestionable, that you will hereafter look back with exultation, or remorse, on the conduct that you shall now pursue—on time improved & talents cultivated; or on time misspent & faculties misemployed."—to John Randolph Bryan, January 20, 1824, Alderman Library.

12. To Theodore Dudley, all in Dudley: February 15, 1806, p. 14; August 30, 1806, p. 34; November 2, 1808, p. 54.

13. See Dudley, *passim.* An example of Randolph's niceness, at the end of a letter to Dudley, July 18, 1811, pp. 91–92:

> *Query*—what is a "full new-moon?"
>
> "Inexpressible"
>
> "Torpour"—This word has not, like *honour,* & c., been derived to us through the French. Indeed, it is yet Latin.
>
> "From *there*"—from thence.

14. Although Randolph read fiction most happily, he was also thoroughly versed in other subjects, including philosophy, religion, history, law, and geography. My emphasis on imaginative literature follows his own account and the evidence of his letters and speeches, and is meant to suggest not an exclusive interest, but a dominant one. Randolph's surviving letters and speeches give good evidence of the range and taste of his reading; in addition there is an essay by Hugh Blair Grigsby, written in 1854, recollecting something of the contents of Randolph's library. According to Richard Beale Davis, this varied evidence, including surviving volumes bearing Randolph's bookplates, allows us to "know more of the character of the collection than of any other" of his generation "except the few for which complete catalogues were made." Pope, Swift, Thomson, Burke, Scott, Byron, Shakespeare, Sterne, all the authors discussed in the present analysis, can be located in Randolph's reading and library either by direct testimony or by indirect deduction such as the following with Pope. Grigsby makes a special point of the contents of Randolph's poetry shelves: "He loved poetry, and was well supplied with all the works that bore the stamp of age; for, while you saw no modern writers, or very few, the great English poets from Elizabeth to the early part of George the Third's reign were all there." Were this statement insufficient to establish his familiarity with Pope, there is the ample circumstantial evidence of his interest in and familiarity with all things Augustan and English, including *Sporting Magazine,* Stud Book and Peerage, the writings of Bolingbroke, and "not only the great historical works of the language, but the tracts and essays which the contest about Whig and Tory for a century had called forth." In the face of all this, it would be remarkable if he had *not* read Pope. In addition, there is direct evidence, if quotation be evidence, of his having done so; for example, in a letter of December 15, 1814, to Senator James Lloyd, touching on the political issues of the day, especially the threat of New England secession, Randolph is reminded "of that passage from Pope where Jove 'weighs the beau's wits against the lady's hair.' " —reprinted in Garland, vol. 2, pp. 51–62.

I think there is, however, a much more important issue involved here, with respect to Randolph's reading of any works. Some books are more serious and powerful than others. Randolph's excited perusal of Maria Edgeworth appears to have been a confirming and diverting part of his reading life but not to be of great moment to his historian. His reading of Pope, however, seems to me a significant clue to his habitual expression of political and cultural discontent, having provided both a position to take in opposition to American democracy and a good method of satire, including the persona of the satiric speaker. It is from the evidence of Randolph's mature career that I concluded the likelihood of the connection to Pope, although I already knew that it was certain Randolph had read Pope, and I feel no embarrassment or hesitation in proceeding to explore this connection without a clear record from Randolph of his familiarity with particular works. Indeed, I don't think that kind of evidence tells us much at all. We know for sure that Randolph read Pope. The only reliable testimony about how he read certain authors and what they came to mean for him is where I have sought it, in the facts of his own use of Pope (and Swift, and others) as unacknowledged and perhaps unconscious masters to his opposition.

For Randolph's library, see Hugh Blair Grigsby, "The Library of John Randolph," *Southern Literary Messenger*, XX (February 1854), pp. 79–82; for Alexander Pope's familiarity and importance to Virginians of Randolph's time and class, see Richard Beale Davis, *Intellectual Life in Jefferson's Virginia* (Knoxville, 1964), esp. pp. 108–12 and pp. 12, 80, 82, 96, 319, 327.

15. Even the relatively positive work of Defoe might confirm a critical view of England in the overwhelmingly Tory context which dominated the literary genius of the times. This discussion is especially dependent on and follows Isaac Kramnick, *Bolingbroke and His Circle: The Politics of Nostalgia in the Age of Walpole* (Cambridge, Mass., 1968); and J. H. Plumb, *Sir Robert Walpole*, 2 vols. (London, 1956).

Kramnick, pp. 4–5, 6.

16. See Kramnick, pp. 32, 37, 63, 72–73, 81, 16off.

17. Maynard Mack, for example, takes Pope at his word in *The Garden and the City: Retirement and Politics in the Later Poetry of Pope, 1731–1743* (Toronto, 1969), p. 72: "Yet the conviction that the pursuits of every day should be shot through with the idealism and detachment of poetry, the arts of government lit by the imagination, intuition, and grace of heaven which we represent in the poet's Muse: there is nothing absurd in that. If we have come to think so, it is because we have lost the confidence that widely disparate areas of experience and instruments of knowing may interpenetrate to their mutual advantage."

18. Samuel Holt Monk, "The Pride of Lemuel Gulliver," *Sewanee Review*, Winter 1955, pp. 58–71, reprinted in James L. Clifford, *Eighteenth Century Literature* (New York, 1959), pp. 112–29 (quote is from this reprinting, p. 123).

Quoted in Kramnick, *Bolingbroke and His Circle*, p. 22.

"Even their ridicule of pedantry, dullness and bad taste now assumed a large social significance, as related to their general attack on moral and political corruption."—Louis Bredvold, "The Gloom of the Tory Satirists," in James L. Clifford and Louis A. Landa, eds., *Pope and His Contemporaries: Essays Presented to George Sherburn* (New York, 1959), pp. 1–19, reprinted in Clifford, *Eighteenth Century Literature*, pp. 3–20 (quote is from this reprinting, p. 9). Jonathan Swift, "Some Free Thoughts upon the Present State of Affairs, May, 1714," in Jonathan Swift, *Political Tracts, 1713–1719* (Oxford, 1964).

19. Maynard Mack, "The Muse of Satire," *Yale Review*, Autumn 1951, p. 86; Martin Price, *To the Palace of Wisdom: Studies in Order and Energy from Dryden to Blake* (Garden City, N.Y., 1964), p. 16.

20. See Price, pp. 11–17.

21. Alexander Pope, "An Epistle from Mr. Pope, to Dr. Arbuthnot," lines 392–95, 404–5.

22. "The optimistic view might be restated simply as the claim that man's existence need not be an outrage if his expectations are trimmed to the recognition that he is not a favorite child of an indulgent parent. Optimism reminds us that since we must live in large part through others, we find our real identity (whether we wish it or not) as much in membership as in uniqueness."—Price, p. 39. Needless to say, this was a recognition and a point of view Randolph never consistently perceived or believed. It was the less happy moments of satire that appear to have remained with him. See also, Mack, *The Garden and the City*, pp. 4–5, 8, 9, 100, 188–89.

Samuel Johnson, "Life of Swift," in G. B. Hill, ed., *Lives of the English Poets* (Oxford, 1905), p. 61; Alexander Pope, "Epilogue to the Satires: Dialogue II," lines 90–93; Pope, "The First Satire of the Second Book of Horace Imitated," line 121; Pope, "Epilogue to the Satires: Dialogue II," lines 197–200 (see Price, p. 177).

23. On the role of name calling, see Mack, *The Garden and the City*, p. 163.

Price, p. 205; Pope, "Imitations of Horace: The First Epistle of the Second Book of Horace to Augustus," lines 161–68; Pope, "Epilogue to the Satires: Dialogue II," lines 208–9; Pope, "The First Satire of the Second Book of Horace Imitated," lines 77–78.

24. "Swift's melancholia is the melancholia of Hamlet, and its root is very much the same—a dichotomy of personality, expressing itself in an abnormal sensitivity to the disparity between the world as it should be and the world as one sees it."—Watkins, p. 1.

Watkins, pp. , 5; Monk, in Clifford, *Eighteenth Century Literature*, p. 116.

25. Thomas R. Edwards, *Imagination and Power: A Study of Poetry on Public Themes* (New York, 1971), p. 117.

26. On melancholia, see Watkins, p. 66.

Edwards, p. 136. Compare Randolph's observations in a letter to Josiah Quincy, March 22, 1814: "The sight of the broad bay, formed by the junction of the two rivers, gave a new impulse to my being; but when the boat struck the beach, all was sad and desolate. The fires of ancient hospitality were long since extinguished, and the hearth-stone cold. Here was my mother given in marriage, and here I was born; once the seat of plenty and cheerfulness, associated with my earliest and the dearest recollections, now mute and deserted. One old grey-headed domestic seemed to

render the solitude more sensible."—quoted in Edmund Quincy, *Life of Josiah Quincy of Massachusetts* (Boston, 1867), pp. 350–53.
Monk, in Clifford, *Eighteenth Century Literature*, pp. 118, 129.
27. Davis, *Intellectual Life in Jefferson's Virginia*, ch. 3, 8.

CHAPTER 4

1. Henry Adams, *John Randolph (Boston and New York,* 1882), p. 5.

2. There is again no question that Randolph read and was familiar with the "country party" doctrines of the English opposition; his library included the standard works and also the classics of political writing, such as Machiavelli, Guicciardini, Sidney, and Locke, on which they were founded. The argument, here, however, is again circumstantial, and its conclusiveness does depend on the subsequent attitudes I find in Randolph's congressional career. We know that Randolph was familiar with the ins and outs of English politics. We know that he was raised in the midst of the Revolution and identified that cause with "right politics," judging America's political performance by the standards of virtue and principle he derived from that struggle, something he perceived as a boy and a youth, with a young person's enthusiasm and idealism and his own literalism. Recent scholarship has shown the inherent country-party thrust of much of American (and Virginian) Revolutionary thinking. It is on that basis and the evidence of Randolph's subsequent attitudes that I have examined certain themes of English opposition. When they came to the fore in his opposition to Jefferson, when these old ideas came increasingly to describe the content of his politics or perhaps more accurately his attitude toward the right conduct of public business, this was clearly because of a resurfacing of learned attitudes, not the invention of the attentive student of the early nineteenth century. Randolph was self-consciously old-fashioned in his opinions by the end of the War of 1812. It is perhaps circumstantial to locate his learning of these attitudes in his youth, but the evidence of his reading, his upbringing in a culture oriented to their country-party stance, and his own predilection for the old and the English, as well as the uncanny degree to which these political opinions and attitudes suited his feelings of political isolation and his irritable and honorable character, these seem conclusive to me in the absence of even more particular evidence and of any evidence to the contrary. The most important help that I have had that previous historians of Randolph have not is the recent investigation of the ideological sources of American Revolutionary thought which has stressed the importance of particular English country sources. That, added to what has long been known about Randolph, has made it reasonable for me to proceed with the analysis of the source of his opinions as I have, relying on circumstance and perhaps coincidence of opinion. I have tried to keep my language scaled down to the modest limits of facts. I have avoided words like "influenced" and "absorbed," preferring to say that Randolph's thinking was "remarkably like" certain other kinds of thinking and then to show the several ways in which this coincidence likely came about. But if my

prudence dictates modest juxtaposition, my study of the subject leaves me with no other conclusion but that the connection is real and significant.

See J. G. A. Pocock, *Politics, Language and Time: Essays on Political Thought and History* (New York, 1971), esp. ch. 1, 3, 4; J. G. A. Pocock, "Virtue and Commerce in the Eighteenth Century," *Journal of Interdisciplinary History*, III (Summer 1972), pp. 119–34; Caroline Robbins, *The Eighteenth Century Commonwealthman: Studies in the Transmission, Development and Circumstances of English Liberal Thought from the Restoration of Charles II until the War with the Thirteen Colonies* (Cambridge, Mass., 1959); Gordon Wood, *The Creation of the American Republic, 1776–1787* (Chapel Hill, N.C., 1969); Bernard Bailyn, *The Ideological Origins of the American Revolution* (Boston, 1967); H. Trevor Colbourn, *The Lamp of Experience: Whig History and the Intellectual Origins of the American Revolution* (Chapel Hill, N.C., 1965); J. R. Pole, *Political Representation in England and the Origins of the American Republic* (London, 1966); J. H. Plumb, *Sir Robert Walpole*, 2 vols. (London, 1956); Isaac Kramnick, *Bolingbroke and His Circle: The Politics of Nostalgia in the Age of Walpole* (Cambridge, Mass., 1968); Robert Weir, "The Harmony We Were Famous For, An Interpretation of Pre-Revolutionary South Carolina Politics," *William and Mary Quarterly*, October 1961, pp. 473–501.

Hugh Blair Grigsby, "The Library of John Randolph," *Southern Literary Messenger*, XX (February 1854), pp. 79–82; Pocock, "Virtue and Commerce in the Eighteenth Century," pp. 119–20.

3. Plumb, vol. 1, p. 20. In this passage, Plumb also claims that the existence of this party "forced politicians to clothe their actions in the respectable garb of party principles and to justify themselves in the same terms."

4. Pocock, "Virtue and the Commerce in the Eighteenth Century," pp. 92, 139–40. See also Kramnick, pp. 165–66, 245, and *passim*.

5. On Augustan political concerns, see Plumb, vol. 1, esp. p. 20. Kramnick, p. 32.

6. Pole, p. 288. See also Richard Beale Davis, *Intellectual Life in Jefferson's Virginia* (Knoxville, 1964), pp. 104, 110, 128, 236, 330, 392, for the prominence of Bolingbroke and other country writers in Virginian reading habits. And see also Lance Banning, who observes, for example: "In the colonies the situation was far different. There, for a variety of reasons, the eighteenth-century critics found a more receptive audience among the great and small alike. There, as crisis came upon the empire, the opposition writers would acquire an influence that could not be matched by any other authors, affecting thought on levels that could shape perceptions of the world and alter practical affairs. The influence of an opposition understanding of events led the Americans to revolution. Opposition ideology, as much as any other force, gave purpose and direction to the revolutionary movement. It helped define America. It created a perspective and a vision that would guide the revolutionaries' conduct through the remainder of their lives."—*The Jeffersonian Persuasion: Evolution of a Party Ideology* (Ithaca, N.Y., 1978), p. 72.

Pocock, *Politics, Language and Time*, p. 97.

7. Littleton Waller Tazewell to Hugh A. Garland, January 1, 1844, in

Alderman Library, University of Virginia; quoted in Hugh A. Garland, *The Life of John Randolph of Roanoke,* vol. 1 (New York, 1856), p. 16. Randolph's stepfather was known personally to Washington and Lafayette and was considered a war hero by the boy.

8. On age when he first saw a map other than Virginia's, see Randolph to Theodore Dudley, February 15, 1806, in Theodore Dudley, ed., *Letters of John Randolph to a Young Relative* (Philadelphia, 1834), pp. 13–16.

John Alden, *The First South* (Gloucester, Mass., 1968), pp. 20–21; *Annals of Congress* (17th Congress, 1st Session, 1821–22), I, 903; William Cabell Bruce, *The Life of John Randolph of Roanoke,* vol. 1 (New York, 1922), p. 219; *Annals of Congress* (14th Congress, 1st Session, 1815–16), 534.

9. Bruce, vol. 1, p. 99; to Josiah Quincy, October 18, 1813, quoted in Edmund Quincy, *Life of Josiah Quincy of Massachusetts* (Boston, 1867), p. 337.

10. Quoted in Garland, vol. 1, p. 28; to Francis Scott Key, September 7, 1818, quoted in Garland, vol. 2, p. 103. And again: "Yet as regards the interests of my country—of the State of Virginia . . ."—*Register of Debates in Congress,* vol. 4, part 1, 966. I think the particularism of this generation of Americans has been underemphasized of late, or seen too completely in terms of other issues.

11. Jack P. Greene, *Landon Carter: An Inquiry into the Personal Values and Social Imperatives of the Eighteenth-Century Virginia Gentry* (Charlottesville, Va., 1967), p. 70; Wood, p. 109. See also Wood, ch. 3–4; and Perry Miller, "From the Covenant to the Revival," in James Ward Smith and A. Leland Jamison, ed., *Religion in American Life,* vol. 1 (Princeton, 1961), esp. pp. 363ff.

12. Norman Risjord, *The Old Republicans: Southern Conservatism in the Age of Jefferson* (New York, 1966), p. 35; Alden, p. 4.

13. On Revolutionary Virginia, see Pole, pp. 304ff.; Jefferson quoted in Pole, p. 301; Wood, p. 76. See also Pole, p. 382.

14. Randolph, "Letter to a New England Senator," December 15, 1815, quoted in Garland, vol. 2, pp. 51–63. Randolph's special attachment to the Revolutionary generation is everywhere eivdent in his speeches.

15. Randolph to Tudor Randolph, December 13, 1813, Alderman Library. See description by Littleton Waller Tazewell of Randolph's letters about Washington's Inauguration: Tazewell to Hugh A. Garland, January 1, 1844, Alderman Library; see also Randolph to St. George Tucker, July 30, 1788, on microfilm in Alderman Library, original in New York Public Library.

To St. George Tucker, January 26, 1794, on microfilm in Alderman Library, original in Brock Collection, Henry E. Huntington Library, quoted in Powhatan Bouldin, *Home Reminiscences of John Randolph of Roanoke* (Danville, Va., 1878), pp. 220–21; to Creed Taylor, September 16, 1798, Alderman Library.

See Constance Rourke, *Trumpets of Jubilee* (New York, 1927), pp. 9ff., for a wonderful description of this mood in which Randolph, like so many young folk at the time, was caught. The "new dates" actually emphasize the importance to Randolph of the American Revolution he dated from 1776. Randolph naturally wanted to join the army of the French Republic at one point. Randolph's change from a partisan to an enemy of the French Revolution and of all revolution, due in large measure to his distaste for the hegemony of Napoleon and the change in his own politics, will be examined subsequently, in conjunction with the discussion of his reading of Burke.

16. Merrill D. Peterson, *Thomas Jefferson and the New Nation* (New York, 1970), p. 57.

17. See Bruce, vol. 1, pp. 140ff.

Randolph to Creed Taylor, September 16, 1798, Creed Taylor MSS, Alderman Library.

18. Bruce, vol. 1, p. 143. Stokes of all the biographers reconstructs the episode most convincingly, in William Ewart Stokes, Jr., "Randolph of Roanoke: A Virginian Patriot. The Early Career of John Randolph of Roanoke, 1773–1805" (Ph.D. dissertation, University of Virginia, 1955), pp. 148–53.

19. On Patrick Henry, see William Wirt, *Sketches of the Life and Character of Patrick Henry* (Philadelphia, 1817).

Adams, p. 30; Garland, vol. 1, p. 135; Stokes apparently accepts this exchange, Ph.D. dissertation, p. 156.

CHAPTER 5

1. *Annals of Congress* (6th Congress, 1st and 2nd Sessions, 1799–1801), 300; *Annals of Congress* (6th Congress, 1st and 2nd Sessions, 1799–1801), 298; quoted in William Cabell Bruce, *The Life of John Randolph of Roanoke,* vol. 1 (New York, 1922), p. 161.

2. Henry Adams, *John Randolph* (New York and Boston, 1882), pp. 42, 46–47.

3. See Norman Risjord, *The Old Republicans: Southern Conservatism in the Age of Jefferson* (New York, 1965); Noble E. Cunningham, Jr., *The Jeffersonian Republicans in Power* (Chapel Hill, N.C., 1963); David Hackett Fischer, *The Revolution of American Conservatism* (New York, 1965). Lance Banning, *The Jeffersonian Persuasion: Evolution of a Party Ideology* (Ithaca, N.Y., 1978), makes a strong argument about the traditional English roots of Jeffersonian politics. He does not find in John Randolph a suitable exemplar of that connection.

Richard E. Ellis, *The Jeffersonian Crisis: Courts and Politics in the Young Republic* (New York, 1971), p. 20; to J. H. Nicholson, July 18, 1801, original in Library of Congress, quoted in Adams, p. 51; to J. H. Nicholson, December 17, 1800, on microfilm in Alderman Library, University of Virginia, original in Library of Congress, quoted in Adams, p. 49.

4. Adams, p. 51; Risjord, p. 163.

5. To William Thompson, May 13, 1804, quoted in Hugh A. Garland, *The Life of John Randolph of Roanoke,* vol. 1 (New York, 1856), pp. 209–10.

6. William Plumer, Jr., *The Life of William Plumer* (Boston, 1857), p. 256.

7. Quoted in Adams, p. 55.

8. Quoted in Risjord, p. 46.

9. For the Chase trial, see Ellis. Adams, p. 130. For Madison's reaction,

see John Quincy Adams, *The Memoirs of John Quincy Adams* (Philadelphia, 1874–77), vol. 6, p. 349.

10. Quoted in Powhatan Bouldin, *Home Reminiscences of John Randolph of Roanoke* (Danville, Va., 1878), p. 303; *Register of Debates in Congress,* vol. 4, part 1, 1166; Merrill D. Peterson, *Thomas Jefferson and the New Nation* (New York, 1970), p. 29; Risjord, p. 36.

11. For the Yazoo business, see Adams, ch. 5–6; C. Peter Magrath, *Yazoo: Law and Politics in the New Republic* (Providence, 1966); and Charles H. Haskins, "The Yazoo Land Companies," in *Papers of the American Historical Association* (Washington, D.C., 1891).

12. Adams, pp. 109–10; to Britt Randolph, Jr., April 8, 1802, Alderman Library.

13. *Annals of Congress* (8th Congress, 2nd Session, 1804–5), 1024–26.

14. Martin Price, *To the Palace of Wisdom: Studies in Order and Energy from Dryden to Blake* (Garden City, N.Y., 1964), p. 175. See also Gordon Wood, *The Creation of the American Republic, 1776–1787* (Chapel Hill, N.C., 1969), p. 78.

15. Colonel Benjamin Tallmadge to Reverend Manasseh Cutler, February 19, 1806, in William Perkins Cutler and Julia Perkins Cutler, *Life, Journals and Correspondence of Reverend Manasseh Cutler, L.L.D.,* vol. 1 (Cincinnati, 1888), pp. 326–27.

16. *Annals of Congress* (8th Congress, 2nd Session, 1804–5), 1106–7.

17. Quoted in Garland, vol. 1, pp. 246–47, 244.

18. *Annals of Congress* (9th Congress, 1st Session, 1805–6), 909–13; Bouldin, p. 197.

19. Randolph to Joseph H. Nicholson, April 30, 1805, on microfilm in Alderman Library, original in Library of Congress; Jonathan Swift, "Some Free Thoughts upon the Present State of Affairs, May 1714," in Jonathan Swift, *Political Tracts, 1713–1719* (Oxford, 1964), pp. 82–83.

20. Quoted in Garland, vol. 1, pp. 222–23.

21. Colonel Benjamin Tallmadge to Reverend Manasseh Cutler, April 2, 1806 in Cutler, vol. 1, p. 327.

22. *Annals of Congress* (9th Congress, 1st Session, 1805–6), 985; Adams, p. 124; quoted in Bruce, vol. 1, pp. 268–69.

23. To George Hay, January 3, 1806, Alderman Library; to Joseph Clay, March 23, 1810, Alderman Library; to George Hay, October 4, 1804, Alderman Library; to Edward Lloyd, November 24, 1810, Alderman Library; Garland, vol. 1 p. 217.

24. Adams, p. 172; *Annals of Congress* (9th Congress, 1st Session, 1805–6), 557; Garland, vol. 1, p. 227.

25. Bruce, vol. 1, pp. 245–47.

26. *Annals of Congress,* (9th Congress, 1st Session, 1805–6), 559, 563, 564.

27. Price, p. 165; to Theodore Dudley, January 9, 1812, in Theodore Dudley, ed., *Letters of John Randolph to a Young Relative* (Philadelphia, 1834), p. 116; *Annals of Congress* (9th Congress, 1st Session, 1805–6), 562; quoted in Richard Heath Dabney, *John Randolph: A Character Sketch* (Chicago, 1898), p. 83.

28. Quoted in Dabney, p. 47; Price, p. 125.

29. Edmund Quincy, *Life of Josiah Quincy of Massachusetts* (Boston, 1867), p. 234; Risjord, pp. 56–57, 17. See also Risjord pp. 27ff., esp 29–33, and p. 77.

30. To Caesar Rodney, March 30, 1805, Alderman Library; *Annals of Congress* (18th Congress, 1st Session, 1823–24), II, 2360; speech, February 3, 1809, quoted in Dabney, p. 25; *Annals of Congress* (9th Congress, 1st Session, 1805–6) 567.

CHAPTER 6

1. See Norman Risjord, *The Old Republicans: Southern Conservatism in the Age of Jefferson* (New York, 1965), esp. pp. 96–145; and Henry Adams, *John Randolph* (Boston and New York, 1882), pp. 153–88.

To Francis Scott Key, May 10, 1813, quoted in Hugh A. Garland, *The Life of John Randolph of Roanoke*, vol. 2 (New York, 1856), pp. 11–12 (see also Randolph to Charles Goldsborough, August 7, 1813, Alderman Library, University of Virginia); to James Monroe, March 2, 1811, original in library of Congress, quoted in Adams, p. 245; to Francis Scott Key, May 22, 1813, quoted in Garland, vol. 2, pp. 12–14 (see also Randolph to Key, May 10 and May 23, 1813, quoted in Garland, vol. 2, pp. 11–12, 14); to Henry Middleton Rutledge, July 24, 1815, Alderman Library; to Theodore Dudley, May 11, 1812, in Theodore Dudley, ed., *Letters of John Randolph to a Young Relative* (Philadelphia, 1834), p. 123; Randolph to Francis Scott Key, July 17, 1813, quoted in Garland, vol. 2, p. 17.

2. To Josiah Quincy, May 23, 1813, quoted in Edmund Quincy, *Life of Josiah Quincy of Massachusetts* (Boston, 1867), p. 331.

3. To Dr. John Brockenbrough, June 2, 1813, quoted in Garland, vol. 2, pp. 14–16; to Francis Scott Key, September 12, 1813, quoted in Garland, vol. 2, pp. 19–22; to Francis Scott Key, October 17, 1813, quoted in Garland, vol. 2, pp. 26–27 (see also Randolph to James M. Garnett, October 17, 1813, Alderman Library).

4. The letters of this period, especially to Key and other intimates, make almost unbearably depressing reading. To Francis Scott Key, July 17, 1813, quoted in Garland, vol. 2, pp. 17–18; to Josiah Quincy, June 20, 1813, quoted in Quincy, p. 322; to Francis Scott Key, July 17, 1813, quoted in Garland, vol. 2, pp. 17–18.

5. To Francis Scott Key, March 2, 1814, quoted in Garland, vol. 2, pp. 32–33.

6. To Francis Scott Key, undated, 1814, quoted in Garland, vol. 2, p. 34.

7. To Francis Scott Key, May 7, 1814, quoted in Garland, vol. 2, pp. 35–36.

8. Quoted in Garland, vol. 2, pp. 37–38. For the quarrel, see also William Cabell Bruce, *The Life of John Randolph of Roanoke*, vol. 2 (New York, 1922), pp. 267–72; and four letters from Randolph to St. George Tucker, April 11, 13, 14, 15 (all 1814), on microfilm, Alderman Library, originals in Colonial Williamsburg.

On Randolph's sensitivity to the question of inheritance, it may be noted that soon after his return to Congress he used this analogy in a speech: "The children of the second marriage should not sweep away the

325

whole estate."—*Annals of Congress* (14th Congress, 2nd Session, 1816–17), 467.

9. To Francis Scott Key, June 3, 1814, quoted in Garland, vol. 2, p. 39; to Dr. John Brockenbrough, July 15, 1814, quoted in Garland, vol. 2, pp. 41–42; to Francis Scott Key, July 31, 1814, quoted in Garland, vol. 2, p. 43. See also Randolph to David Parish, July 28, 1814, Alderman Library, for Randolph's comments to Tudor Randolph.

10. To Dr. John Brockenbrough, August 1, 1814, quoted in Garland, vol. 2, pp. 43–44; to Theodore Dudley, September 2, 1814, in Dudley, p. 159; to Theodore Dudley, October 23, 1814, in Dudley, p. 103.

The heated and, it must be said, scandalous correspondence between Nancy Randolph Morris and John Randolph concerning the events at Glenlyvar and their sequel at Bizarre is fully treated, and the letters are reprinted, in Bruce, vol. 2, pp. 272ff.

11. To Josiah Quincy, March 22, 1814, quoted in Quincy, pp. 350, 352.

12. To Josiah Quincy, July 1, 1814, quoted in Quincy, pp. 353–55.

13. *Annals of Congress* (12th Congress, 1st Session, 1811–12), I, 452.

14. To Theodore Dudley, October 23, 1814, in Dudley, p. 103. There is something like a Calvinist disposition in this thinking; what it points up, however, is not that Randolph was a proto-Calvinist but that seventeenth- and eighteenth-century Virginia and Massachusetts thinking were essentially similar on certain central moral issues. The comparison that suggests itself is between Randolph and such descendants of the Puritans as Emerson and the Beechers—how did the nineteenth-century heirs of the old style of American culture deal with their inheritance in changing times?

Randolph letter, February 1, 1819, Alderman Library.

15. To David Parish, June 18, 1812, quoted in Bruce, vol. 2, p. 488; to Joseph H. Nicholson, October 24, 1806, quoted in Bruce, vol. 2, p. 488; to Dr. John Brockenbrough, undated, 1815, quoted in Garland, vol. 2, pp. 69–70; to Richard Stanford, October 13, 1814, Alderman Library.

16. Randolph's religious frenzy has been taken for evidence of his insanity, perhaps because his was surely an extreme conversion. It is tempting to connect it to the religious revivals of the time, but I have not been able to do so to my own satisfaction. What I have tried to do here is to render this enthusiasm intelligible in terms of Randolph's concerns, and the stress and crisis in his life.

To Henry St. George Tucker, 1826, in *Southern Collegian,* March 23, 1872, reprinted in Bruce, vol. 2, pp. 515–18; quoted in Garland, vol. 1, p. 12; to Dr. John Brockenbrough, July 4, 1815, quoted in Garland, vol. 2, pp. 68–69.

17. To Dr. John Brockenbrough, July 4, 1815, quoted in Garland, vol. 2, pp. 68–69.

18. To Francis Scott Key, undated, quoted in Garland, vol. 2, p. 48; to Dr. John Brockenbrough, May 29, 1815, quoted in Garland, vol. 2, p. 65.

19. Randolph to Francis Scott Key, May 31, 1815, quoted in Garland, vol. 2, pp. 65–67. Randolph's attitude reminds one of Walker Percy's character Sister Val, a southern Protestant who converted to Catholicism and entered her novitiate: "What they didn't know was that I am mean as hell too. . . . That's what I don't understand, you know: that I believe the

whole business: God, the Jews, Christ, the Church, grace, and the forgiveness of sins—and that I'm meaner than ever. Christ is my lord and I love him but I'm a good hater and you know what he said about that. I still hope my enemies fry in hell. What to do about that? Will God forgive me?"—Walker Percy, *The Last Gentleman* (New York, 1964), p. 301.

20. To Dr. John Brockenbrough, July 4, 1815, quoted in Garland, vol. 2, pp. 68–69; to Francis Scott Key, February 9, 1818, quoted in Garland, vol. 2, pp. 96–97.

21. To Dr. John Brockenbrough, September 25, 1818, quoted in Garland, vol. 2, pp. 100–102.

22. Russell Kirk offers the most elaborate and convinced comparison of Randolph and Burke. I have indicated that I am not persuaded by his arguments to treat Randolph as a complete or even an accurate Burkean. There is no question, however, that Kirk has documented the connection between Burke and Randolph accurately and in depth. It is a continuing theme of his book. Russell Kirk, *John Randolph of Roanoke: A Study in American Politics* (Chicago, 1864), *passim*.

Nathaniel Beverley Tucker, "Garland's Life of Randolph," *Southern Quarterly Review*, new series, IV (July 1851), p. 43; to Harmanus Bleeker, July 26, 1814, Alderman Library (Randolph's reading of Lord Byron will be discussed in ch. 7); to Harmanus Bleeker, April 14, 1813, Alderman Library; to Francis Scott Key, May 22, 1813, quoted in Garland, vol. 2, pp. 12–14; to Henry Middleton Rutledge, July 11, 1818, in "Pickings from a Portfolio of Autobiography: Two MS. Letters of John Randolph," *Southern Literary Messenger*, XXIII (November 1836), pp. 380–82; quoted in Bruce, vol. 2, p. 78.

23. On Randolph's attitude toward the French Revolution, see Bruce, vol. 1, pp. 141–42.

Annals of Congress (9th Congress, 1st Session, 1805–6), 562; *Annals of Congress* (14th Congress, 1st Session, 1815–16), 586 (this is Randolph's justifiably famous speech on treaty-making powers, delivered January 10, 1816); quoted in Kirk, pp. 36–37.

24. For references to Napoleon by Randolph see, for example, Randolph to Francis Scott Key, February 17, 1814, quoted in Garland, vol. 2, p. 31; and Randolph to Dr. John Brockenbrough, July 15, 1814, quoted in Garland, vol. 2, p. 41.

Randolph's letter to his constituents, dated January 7, 1815, and published in the *Richmond Enquirer* on April 1, 1815; the letter is discussed extensively later in this chapter.

25. *Annals of Congress* (12th Congress, 1st Session, 1811–12), I, 449; Kirk, pp. 26, 19, 26.

26. Speech delivered in Congress, December 10, 1811, reprinted in Garland, vol. 1, pp. 295–97.

27. *Annals of Congress* (18th Congress, 1st Session, 1823–24), I, 1303.

28. J. G. A. Pocock, *Politics, Language and Time: Essays on Political Thought and History* (New York, 1971), p. 230.

29. *Proceedings and Debates of the Virginia State Convention of 1829–30* (Richmond, 1830), 313–21.

30. Pocock, pp. 210–11.

31. *Proceedings and Debates of the Virginia State Convention,* 532–33. See also Kirk, p. 57.

32. There are numerous instances of Randolph's questioning of his own sanity, among which are the following. Thomas Hart Benton has Randolph saying, "I have lived in dread of insanity."—*Thirty Years' View,* vol. 1 (New York, 1856), p. 473. Bruce quotes Dr. Thomas Robinson as testifying that Randolph told him that he had been "stark mad, as well entitled to a cell in Swift's Hospital as anyone who had ever occupied one," and that "he felt conscious that he had not entirely recovered as yet, but confident of ultimate and perfect recovery."—Bruce, vol. 2, p. 338. And in his letters: "My good friend, I am sick in body and mind."—to Dr. John Brockenbrough, October 28, 1828, quoted in Garland, vol. 2, p. 311; "I am unable to enter into the conceptions and view of those around me. They talk to me of grave matters, and I see children blowing bubbles."— to Dr. John Brockenbrough, February 25, 1827, quoted in Garland, vol. 2, p. 288; "My excellent friend, Mr. William Leigh, who lay here last night, left me this morning. Even his presence seemed hardly to exercise any power over the foul fiend that annoys me."—to Elizabeth T. Coalter, October 27, 1828, Bryan MSS, Alderman Library; "Your letters constitute my almost only resource against the dark spirit that persecutes me."—to Elizabeth T. Coalter, February 26, 1823, Alderman Library.

To Theodore Dudley, September 1813, in Dudley, p. 142; to Francis Scott Key, June 16, 1816, quoted in Garland, vol. 2, p. 88 (italics inserted).

33. To Francis Scott Key, February 17, 1814, quoted in Garland, vol. 2, pp. 30–32.

34. To Theodore Dudley, February 11, 1813, in Dudley, pp. 136–37; to Francis Scott Key, April 25, 1815, quoted in Garland, vol. 2, pp. 47–48.

35. *Annals of Congress* (14th Congress, 1st Session, 1815–16), 1110–13; *Annals of Congress* (14th Congress, 1st Session, 1815–16), 1339.

36. *Annals of Congress* (18th Congress, 1st Session, 1823–24), I, 1301; to Theodore Dudley, February 23, 1817, in Dudley, pp. 194–97.

CHAPTER 7

1. For Randolph as a landholder, see William Cabell Bruce, *The Life of John Randolph of Roanoke,* vol. 2 (New York, 1922), pp. 687ff.

Powhatan Bouldin, *Home Reminiscences of John Randolph of Roanoke* (Danville, Va., 1878), p. 168; Hugh A. Garland, *The Life of John Randolph of Roanoke,* vol. 2 (New York, 1856), p. 157.

2. Martin Van Buren, *Autobiography,* ed. John C. Fitzpatrick, in *Annual Report of the American Historical Association for 1918,* vol. 2, (Washington, D.C., 1920), pp. 430–31; Constance Rourke, *American Humor* (New York, 1931), pp. 91–92; quoted in Bruce, vol. 2, p. 436.

3. Norman Risjord, *The Old Republicans: Southern Conservatism in the Age of Jefferson* (New York, 1965), pp. 175, 226. See also Henry Adams, *John Randolph* (New York and Boston, 1882), ch. 11; and Richard E. Ellis, *The Jeffersonian Crisis: Courts and Politics in the Young Republic* (New York, 1971).

4. *Annals of Congress* (18th Congress, 1st Session, 1823–24), I, 1296–1311.

5. See Bruce, vol. 2, ch. 5.

6. Bruce, vol. 2, pp. 99, 216. See Bouldin, pp. 124ff.; Garland, vol. 2, p. 326.

Grigsby quoted in Bruce, vol. 2, p. 95; Carrington quoted in Bouldin, p. 128; Bouldin, pp. 243–44.

Randolph's singularity as a speaker attracted the notice of his political contemporaries as well. John Quincy Adams had no use for Randolph as an orator or a politician and has left this stinging characterization of one of the Virginian's early speeches: "Without order, connection, or argument; consisting of the most hackneyed commonplaces of popular declamation, mingled up with panegyrics and invectives upon persons, with a few well expressed ideas, a few striking figures, much distortion of face and contortion of body, tears, groans, and sobs, with occasional pauses for recollection and continual complaints of having lost his notes." This description is of an early version of what Randolph's speeches were to be and reflects the Harvard rhetorician's disdain for "*verba ardentia*," but substantially confirms one's impressions of the dramatic components of the Randolph performance.

7. Bouldin, p. 64.

8. Bruce, vol. 2, p. 99; John M. Niles to Gideon Welles, November 14, 1829, Welles Papers, Library of Congress. I am indebted to John Niven for bringing this letter to my attention. For Niles, see John Niven, *Gideon Welles* (New York, 1973), esp. pp. 30ff., 91.

9. Bruce, vol. 2, p. 196; quoted in Bruce, vol. 2, pp. 193–94, 188. See also Adams, p. 259.

10. Quoted in Garland, vol. 2, p. 155; *Register of Debates in Congress*, vol. 1, part 2, 117–18.

11. To Dr. John Brockenbrough, November 26, 1820, quoted in Garland, vol. 2, pp. 138–39; to Dr. John Brockenbrough, February 7, 1822, quoted in Garland, vol. 2, pp. 160–61 (see also Randolph to Brockenbrough, January 13, 1822, quoted in Garland, vol. 2, pp. 157–59); to Elizabeth T. Coalter, August 18, 1828, Bryan MSS, Alderman Library, University of Virginia; Bouldin, p. 178.

12. To Dr. John Brockenbrough, February 7, 1822, quoted in Garland, vol. 2, pp. 160–61; to Dr. John Brockenbrough, January 15, 1822, quoted in Garland, vol. 2, pp. 158–59; to Elizabeth T. Coalter, November 28, 1828, Bryan MSS, Alderman Library; Bouldin, p. 11.

13. To Dr. John Brockenbrough, February 23, 1820, quoted in Garland, vol. 2, pp. 131–33; *Register of Debates in Congress*, vol. 2, part 1, 401. See also Risjord, esp. pp. 175–227; Thomas Hart Benton, *Thirty Years' View*, vol. 1 (New York, 1856), pp. 70–77; and Bruce, vol. 2, pp. 512ff.

14. Adams, pp. 258–59; Benton, vol. 1, p. 77; Martin Price, *To the Palace of Wisdom: Studies in Order and Energy from Dryden to Blake* (Garden City, N.Y., 1964), p. 293.

15. Bruce, vol. 2, p. 38.

16. See especially the stimulating discussion of these themes of the

"Yankee" in William R. Taylor, *Cavalier and Yankee* (New York, 1961), from which I have borrowed liberally. On Randolph and Webster, see Bruce, vol. 2, pp. 442–43.

17. "If I were a poet in fact as well as in temperament, I would embody in verse feelings that lie too deep for tears. As I am not, I must refer you to the Lake School whose productions I never have read and probably never shall."—Randolph to F. W. Gilmer, July 22, 1821, Bryan MSS, Alderman Library.

To Elizabeth T. Coalter, November 1, 1828, Bryan MSS, Alderman Library; to Dr. John Brockenbrough, July 25, 1822, quoted in Garland, vol. 2, p. 193. Geoffrey H. Hartman, "Wordsworth, Inscription, and Romantic Nature Poetry," in Frederick W. Hilles and Harold Bloom, eds., *From Sensibility to Romanticism, Essays Presented to Frederick A. Pottle* (New York, 1965), p. 398.

18. To Francis Scott Key, December 15, 1813, quoted in Garland, vol. 2, pp. 28–29; to Francis Scott Key, March 1814, quoted in Garland, vol. 2, pp. 34–35; to Dr. John Brockenbrough, July 24, 1824, quoted in Garland, vol. 2, pp. 223–26; to Josiah Quincy, February 20, 1820, quoted in Edmund Quincy, *Life of Josiah Quincy of Massachusetts* (Boston, 1867), pp. 421–22. See also Randolph to Dr. John Brockenbrough, June 3, 1828, and May 27, 1828, Alderman Library, University of Virginia.

19. E. D. Hirsch, Jr., "Byron and the Terrestrial Paradise," in Hilles and Bloom, p. 468; George M. Ridenour, "Byron in 1816: Four Poems in Diodati," in Hilles and Bloom, pp. 464, 461; Edmund Wilson, "Byron in the 20's," in *To the Shores of Light: A Literary Chronicle of the 1820's and 1830's* (New York, 1952), pp. 50, 57–58.

20. References to Byron in Randolph's letter to Harmanus Bleeker, October 10, 1818, Alderman Library; Nathaniel Beverley Tucker, "Garland's Life of Randolph," *Southern Quarterly Review,* new series, IV (July 1851), p. 44; quoted in Garland, vol. 1, p. 15.

21. To Dr. John Brockenbrough, February 7, 1822, quoted in Garland, vol. 2, pp. 160–61; Louis Bredvold, "The Gloom of the Tory Satirist," in James L. Clifford and Louis A. Landa, eds., *Pope and His Contemporaries: Essays Presented to George Sherburn* (New York, 1959), p. 11.

22. Isaac Kramnick, *Bolingbroke and His Circle: The Politics of Nostalgia in the Age of Walpole* (Cambridge, Mass., 1968), p. 264.

23. To Dr. John Brockenbrough, July 24, 1824, quoted in Garland, vol. 2, pp. 223–26 ("Poor Old Virginia! To what a condition has she reduced herself."—Randolph to Brockenbrough, January 10, 1828, Alderman Library); George Gordon, Lord Byron, "The Dream," II, lines 1, 172–82; to Dr. John Brockenbrough, February 9, 1829, Alderman Library.

24. See Bruce, vol. 2, pp. 338ff.

To Dr. John Brockenbrough, undated letter (1819?), quoted in Garland, vol. 2, pp. 111; Bruce, vol. 2, p. 338; to Theodore Dudley, February 23, 1817, in Theodore Dudley, ed., *Letters of John Randolph to a Young Relative* (Philadelphia, 1834), pp. 194–97.

25. To Francis Scott Key, August 8, 1819, quoted in Garland, vol. 2, pp. 107–8.

26. See Bruce, vol. 2, pp. 338ff., 49ff. The record of the litigation is a

fascinating document—there is a copy in the Alderman Library. Calhoun quoted in Bruce, vol. 2, p. 339.

27. To Henry A. Watkins, quoted in Bruce, vol. 2, p. 9; to Andrew Jackson, March 18, 1832, quoted in Bruce, vol. 2, p. 13; to Andrew Jackson, March 1, 1832, quoted in Bruce, vol. 2, p. 15.

28. To Francis Scott Key, undated, 1819, quoted in Garland, vol. 2, p. 107; Benton, vol. 1, p. 474.

29. Jane Austen, *Mansfield Park*, vol. 3, ch. 3; quoted in Garland, vol. 2, p. 91; *Annals of Congress* (14th Congress, 1st Session, 1815–16), 728; *King Lear*, act 3, scene 6, lines 61–62; to Dr. John Brockenbrough, quoted in Garland, vol. 2, p. 261; *Annals of Congress* (18th Congress, 1st Session, 1823–24), II, 2379; *King Lear*, act 2, scene 4, line 126.

30. See Samuel Holt Monk, "The Pride of Lemuel Gulliver," *Sewanee Review*, Winter 1955, pp. 58–71, reprinted in James L. Clifford, *Eighteenth Century Literature* (New York, 1959), pp. 112–29.

31. *Proceedings and Debates of the Virginia State Convention of 1829–30* (Richmond, 1830), speech quoted in Russell Kirk, *John Randolph of Roanoke: A Study in American Politics* (Chicago, 1964), pp. 456–57; *King Lear*, act 5, scene 3, lines 20–25.

32. To Theodore Dudley, February 8, 1817, in Dudley, p. 189.

33. *Timon of Athens*, act 4, scene 3, lines 303–4, 502–5; Randolph to Dr. John Brockenbrough, August 1831, quoted in Garland, vol. 2, p. 349.

34. William Empson, *Some Versions of Pastoral* (New York, 1960), p. 199.

35. Garland, vol. 2, pp. 92–93.

36. Randolph had little use for Sterne, identifying him with "morbid sensibility" in a letter to Theodore Dudley: "In stead of yielding to a morbid sensibility, we must nerve ourselves up to do and suffer all that duty calls for. . . . What, then, are we to expect from a generation that has been taught to cherish this not 'fair defect' of our perverted nature; to nourish and cultivate, as 'amiable and attractive,' what at the bottom, is neither more or less than the grossest selfishness a little disguised under the romantic epithet of 'sensibility'; This cant . . . has been fashionable since the days of Sterne, a hard-hearted, unprincipled man; a cassocked libertine and 'free thinker' . . . and in a little time, we may consider it, I hope, as entirely passé."—February 22, 1822, in Dudley, p. 245. Speaking in the accents of his conscience, Randolph perhaps protests too much.

Quoted in Bouldin, p. 27; W. B. C. Watkins, *The Perilous Balance* (Cambridge, Mass., 1960), p. 109; Price, pp. 322, 388–89, 324.

37. All quoted in Garland: vol. 2, pp. 346, 344–35; vol. 1, p. 29; vol. 2, p. 171.

38. For the dates of Randolph's visits to Europe, see Bruce, vol. 2, p. 436.

Bruce, vol. 1, p. 530, vol. 2, pp. 438–39; Lord John Russell, ed., *Memoirs . . . of Thomas Moore*, vol. 1 (New York, 1853), p. 415; Washington Irving to Henry Brevoort, June 11, 1822, quoted in Bruce, vol. 2, p. 422; other incidents of Randolph's stays abroad are in Bruce, vol. 2, pp. 440ff.

39. Quoted in Bruce, vol. 2, p. 449; Garland, vol. 2, pp. 192, 223.

40. To Dr. John Brockenbrough, October 13, 1826, quoted in Garland, vol. 2, p. 275; to Dr. John Brockenbrough, September 22, 1826, quoted in

Garland, vol. 2, p. 274; to Dr. John Brockenbrough, October 13, 1826, quoted in Garland, vol. 2, p. 275.

41. On Randolph's visits to England, see Bruce, vol. 2, pp. 412ff.; and Garland, vol. 2, ch. 21.

To Elizabeth Bryan, May 27, 1822, quoted in Garland, vol. 2, p. 184.

42. *Speech of the Honorable John Randolph of Virginia on the Retrenchment Resolutions, Delivered in the House of Representatives of the United States, February 1, 1828* (Boston, 1828), p. 3.

43. *Speech on the Retrenchment Resolutions,* pp. 25, 25–26.

44. *Speech on the Retrenchment Resolutions,* pp. 29–30.

45. To Dr. John Brockenbrough, December 22, 1827, quoted in Garland, vol. 2, p. 296; quoted in Garland, vol. 2, p. 346; *Register of Debates in Congress,* vol. 2, part 2, 401.

CONCLUSION

1. Randolph was not the only American so isolated; such intellectuals as Cooper in their vehement objections to American democratic materialism shared much of Randolph's discomfort with America.

2. The Chapter on eccentricity is ch. 12 of *The Education of Henry Adams* (New York, 1931), pp. 180–93.

Adams, *The Education of Henry Adams,* pp. 180, 181, 193.

3. Ernest Samuels, *The Young Henry Adams* (Cambridge, Mass., 1948), explores the theme of Henry Adams's education measured against his complaints about it in *The Education.*

4. Adams, *The Education of Henry Adams,* pp. 180–81, 182.

5. Adams, *The Education of Henry Adams,* pp. 183, 190.

6. Henry Adams, *John Randolph* (New York and Boston, 1882), pp. 4–5, 256.

7. Adams, *John Randolph,* pp. 299, 4–5, 10–11.

8. Daniel Calhoun, *The Intelligence of a People* (Princeton, 1973), offers suggestions about the nature of the intelligence of the American audience of the nineteenth century that make Randolph's behavior even more plausibly understood in terms of a perceptive and receptive if disagreeing public. See especially pp. 29ff., 33 (top), 41, 60, 81, 326.

9. Erik Erikson, *Young Man Luther* (New York, 1962), p. 87. See also William R. Taylor, *Cavalier and Yankee* (New York, 1961) esp. ch. 7.

BIBLIOGRAPHY

PERSONAL PAPERS,
INCLUDING MANUSCRIPTS AND LETTERS

All Randolph papers cited were seen in the Randolph Collection at the Alderman Library, University of Virginia. That collection is complete, consisting of original documents and copies or microfilms of all items in other collections. See William Ewart Stokes, Jr., and Francis L. Berkeley, Jr., eds. *The Papers of Randolph of Roanoke, A Preliminary Checklist of His Surviving Texts in Manuscript and in Print.* Charlottesville, Va., 1951.
Brock Collection, Henry E. Huntington Library, San Marino, California.
Joseph Bryan MSS, Alderman Library, University of Virginia.
Dudley, Theodore, ed. *Letters of John Randolph to a Young Relative: Embracing a Series of Years from Early Youth to Mature Manhood.* Philadelphia, 1834.
Grinnan MSS, Alderman Library, University of Virginia.
Randolph Papers, Alderman Library.
Speech of the Honorable John Randolph of Virginia on the Retrenchment Resolutions, Delivered in the House of Representatives of the United States, February 1, 1828. Boston, 1828.
Creed Taylor MSS, Alderman Library.

GOVERNMENT PAPERS AND PUBLICATIONS

Annals of Congress.
Proceedings and Debates of the Virginia State Convention of 1829–30. Richmond, 1830.
Register of Debates in Congress, 1824–37. Washington, D.C., 1825–37.

JOURNALS, NEWSPAPERS, PERIODICALS

Historical Magazine.
New York American.

Bibliography

Richmond Enquirer.
Southern Literary Messenger.
Southern Quarterly Review.

BIOGRAPHIES, MEMOIRS, RECOLLECTIONS

Adams, Henry. *The Education of Henry Adams.* New York, 1931.
———. *John Randolph.* Boston and New York, 1882.
Adams, John Quincy. *The Memoirs of John Quincy Adams.* Edited by Charles Francis Adams. 12 vols. Philadelphia, 1874–77.
Benton, Thomas Hart. *Thirty Years' View; or, A History of the Working of the American Government for Thirty Years, from 1820 to 1850.* 2 vols. New York, 1856.
Bouldin, Powhatan. *Home Reminiscences of John Randolph of Roanoke.* Danville, Va., 1878.
Bruce, William Cabell. *The Life of John Randolph of Roanoke.* 2 vols. New York, 1922.
Coleman, Mary Haldane. *St. George Tucker: A Citizen of No Mean City.* Richmond, 1938.
Cutler, William Perkins, and Cutler, Julia Perkins. *Life, Journals and Correspondence of Reverend Manasseh Cutler, L.L.D.* Cincinnati, 1888.
Dabney, Richard Heath. *John Randolph: A Character Sketch.* Chicago, 1898.
Daniels, Jonathan. *The Randolphs of Virginia, "America's Foremost Family."* Garden City, N.Y., 1972.
Erikson, Erik. *Young Man Luther.* New York, 1962.
Garland, Hugh A. *The Life of John Randolph of Roanoke.* 2 vols. New York, 1856.
Johnson, Gerald W. *Randolph of Roanoke, A Political Fantastic.* New York, 1929.
Kirk, Russell. *John Randolph of Roanoke: A Study in American Politics.* Chicago, 1964.
Kramnick, Isaac. *Bolingbroke and His Circle: The Politics of Nostalgia in the Age of Walpole.* Cambridge, Mass., 1968.
McLean, Robert Collin. *George Tucker, Moral Philosopher and Man of Letters.* Chapel Hill, N.C., 1961.
Malone, Dumas. *Thomas Jefferson.* 5 vols. Boston, 1948–74.
Niven, John. *Gideon Welles.* New York, 1973.
Parton, James. *Famous Americans of Recent Times.* Boston, 1867.
Paulding, William I. *The Literary Life of James K. Paulding.* New York, 1867.
Peterson, Merrill D. *Thomas Jefferson and the New Nation.* New York, 1970.
Pickard, Samuel T. *The Life and Letters of John Greenleaf Whittier.* 2 vols. Boston, 1894.
Plumb, J. H. *Sir Robert Walpole.* 2 vols. London, 1956.
Plumer, William, Jr. *The Life of William Plumer.* Boston, 1857.
Quincy, Edmund. *Life of Josiah Quincy of Massachusettes.* Boston, 1867.
Russell, Lord John, ed. *Memoirs . . . of Thomas Moore.* 8 vols. New York, 1853–56.
Samuels, Ernest. *Henry Adams, The Middle Years.* Cambridge, Mass., 1958.
———. *The Young Henry Adams.* Cambridge, Mass., 1948.

Bibliography

Thomas, F. W. *John Randolph of Roanoke, and Other Sketches of Characters, Including William Wirt.* Philadelphia, 1848.

Tucker, George. *The Valley of the Shenandoah, or Memoirs of the Graysons.* Chapel Hill, N.C., 1970.

Tucker, Nathaniel Beverley. *The Partisan Leader: A Tale of the Future.* Introduction by C. Hugh Holman. Chapel Hill, N.C., 1971.

Walz, Jay, and Walz, Audrey. *The Bizarre Sisters.* New York, 1950.

Wirt, William. *Sketches of the Life and Character of Patrick Henry.* Philadelphia, 1817.

Whittier, John Greenleaf. *The Writings of John Greenleaf Whittier.* Vol. 5. Boston, 1892.

SECONDARY WORKS, MONOGRAPHS

Alden, John. *The First South.* Gloucester, Mass., 1968.

Aries, Philippe. *Centuries of Childhood.* New York, 1952.

Bailyn, Bernard. *The Ideological Origins of the American Revolution.* Boston, 1967.

Banning, Lance. *The Jeffersonian Persuasion: Evolution of a Party Ideology.* Ithaca, N.Y., 1978.

Bishop, Jonathan. *Something Else.* New York, 1972.

Bradford, Gamaliel. *Damaged Souls.* New York, 1922.

Bridenbaugh, Carl. *Myths and Realities: Societies of the Colonial South.* New York, 1965.

Calhoun, Daniel. *The Intelligence of a People.* Princeton, 1973.

Clifford, James L. *Eighteenth Century Literature.* New York, 1959.

————, and Landa, Louis A., eds. *Pope and His Contemporaries: Essays Presented to George Sherburn.* New York, 1959.

Colburn, H. Trevor. *The Lamp of Experience: Whig History and the Intellectual Origins of the American Revolution.* Chapel Hill, N.C., 1965.

Coveney, Peter. *The Image of Childhood: The Individual and Society. A Study of the Theme in English Literature.* Baltimore, 1967.

Cunningham, Noble E., Jr. *The Jeffersonian Republicans in Power.* Chapel Hill, N.C., 1963.

Davis, Richard Beale. *Intellectual Life in Jefferson's Virginia.* Knoxville, 1964.

————. *Literature and Society in Early Virginia, 1608–1840.* Baton Rouge, 1973.

————, ed. *The Colonial Virginia Satirist, Mid Eighteenth-Century Commentaries on Politics, Religion and Society, in Transactions of the American Philosophical Society,* new series, LVII (March 1967).

Edwards, Thomas R. *Imagination and Power: A Study of Poetry on Public Themes.* New York, 1971.

Ellis, Richard E. *The Jeffersonian Crisis: Courts and Politics in the Young Republic.* New York, 1971.

Empson, William. *Some Versions of Pastoral.* New York, 1960.

Fischer, David Hackett. *The Revolution of American Conservatism.* New York, 1965.

Frost, J. William. *The Quaker Family in Colonial America.* New York, 1973.

Bibliography

Genovese, Eugene. *The Political Economy of Slavery.* New York, 1965.

Greene, Jack P. *Landon Carter: An Inquiry into the Personal Values and Social Imperatives of the Eighteenth-Century Virginia Gentry.* Charlottesville, Va., 1967.

Hareven, Tamara, ed. *Anonymous Americans: Explorations in Nineteenth Century Social History.* Englewood Cliffs, N.J., 1971.

Hilles, Frederick W., and Bloom, Harold, eds. *From Sensibility to Romanticism, Essays Presented to Frederick A. Pottle.* New York, 1965.

Hubbell, Jay. *Virginia Life in Fiction.* Dallas, 1922.

Laing, R. D. *The Divided Self.* Chicago, 1960.

———, and Esteron, A. *Sanity, Madness and the Family.* Baltimore, 1970.

McColley, Robert. *Slavery in Jeffersonian Virginia.* Urbana, Ill., 1964.

Mack, Maynard. *The Garden and the City: Retirement and Politics in the Later Poetry of Pope, 1731–1743.* Toronto, 1969.

Magrath, C. Peter. *Yazoo: Law and Politics in the New Republic.* Providence, 1966.

Morgan, Edmund S. *The Puritan Family.* New York, 1966.

———. *Virginians at Home: Family Life in the Eighteenth Century.* Williamsburg, 1952.

Mullin, Gerald. *Flight and Rebellion: Slave Resistance in Eighteenth-Century Virginia.* New York, 1972.

Peterson, Merrill D. *The Jeffersonian Image in the American Mind.* New York, 1962.

———. *Thomas Jefferson and the New Nation.* New York, 1970.

Pocock, J. G. A. *Politics, Language and Time: Essays on Political Thought and History.* New York, 1971.

Pole, J. R. *Political Representation in England and the Origins of the American Republic.* London, 1966.

Price, Martin. *To the Palace of Wisdom: Studies in Order and Energy from Dryden to Blake.* Garden City, N.Y., 1964.

Risjord, Norman. *The Old Republicans: Southern Conservatism in the Age of Jefferson.* New York, 1965.

Robbins, Caroline. *The Eighteenth Century Commonwealthman: Studies in the Transmission, Development and Circumstances of English Liberal Thought from the Restoration of Charles II until the War with the Thirteen Colonies.* Cambridge, Mass., 1959.

Rourke, Constance. *American Humor.* New York, 1931.

Sanford, Charles B. *Thomas Jefferson and His Library.* Hamden, Conn., 1977.

Smith, James Ward, and Jamison, A. Leland, eds. *Religion in American Life.* Vol. 1. Princeton, 1961.

Spruill, Julia C. *Women's Life and Work in the Southern Colonies.* Chapel Hill, N.C., 1935.

Stokes, William Ewart, Jr., and Berkeley, Francis L., Jr., eds. *The Papers of Randolph of Roanoke, A Preliminary Checklist of His Surviving Texts in Manuscript and in Print.* Charlottesville, Va., 1951.

Sydnor, Charles. *Gentlemen Freeholders: Political Parties in Washington's Virginia.* Chapel Hill, N.C., 1952.

Taylor, William R. *Cavalier and Yankee.* New York, 1961.

Bibliography

Trent, William P. *Southern Statesmen of the Old Regime.* New York, 1897.
Watkins, W. B. C. *The Perilous Balance.* Cambridge, Mass., 1960.
Wilson, Edmund. *To the Shores of Light: A Literary Chronicle of the 1920's and 1930's.* New York, 1952.
Wise, Henry A. *Seven Decades of the Union.* Philadelphia, 1872.
Wood, Gordon. *The Creation of the American Republic, 1776–1787.* Chapel Hill, N.C., 1969.

ARTICLES, REVIEWS, THESES

Furness, Edna L. "Portrait of the Pedagogue in Eighteenth Century England." *History of Education Quarterly,* II, pp. 62–70.
Grigsby, Hugh Blair. "The Library of John Randolph." *Southern Literary Messenger,* XX (February 1824), pp. 79–82.
Haskins, Charles H. "The Yazoo Land Companies," in *Papers of the American Historical Association.* Washington, D.C., 1891.
Kilpatrick, James. "Mr. Buckley and Tax Equality." *Charlottesville* (Virginia) *Progress,* January 13, 1974.
Mack, Maynard. "The Muse of Satire." *Yale Review,* Autumn 1951, pp. 80–92.
Musto, David. "The Youth of John Quincy Adams." *Proceedings of the American Philosophical Society,* CXIII (August 1969), pp. 269–81.
Norton, Mary Beth. "John Randolph's Plan of Accommodation." *William and Mary Quarterly,* January 1971, pp. 103–72.
Pocock, J. G. A. "Virtue and Commerce in the Eighteenth Century." *Journal of Interdisciplinary History,* III (Summer 1972), pp. 119–34.
Sidwell, Robert T. "Writers, Thinkers and Foxhunters—Educational Theory in the Almanacs of Eighteenth-Century Colonial America." *History of Education Quarterly,* VIII (Fall 1968), pp. 275–88.
Stokes, William Ewart, Jr. "The Early Life of John Randolph of Roanoke, 1773–1794." M.A. thesis, University of Virginia, 1950.
———. "Randolph of Roanoke: A Virginia Patriot. The Early Career of John Randolph of Roanoke, 1773–1805." Ph.D. dissertation, University of Virginia, 1955.
Stone, Lawrence. "The Massacre of the Innocents." *New York Review of Books,* November 14, 1974.
Tucker, Nathaniel Beverley. "Garland's Life of Randolph." *Southern Quarterly Review,* new series, IV (July 1851), pp. 41–46.
———. "Sketches of John Randolph." *History Magazine,* 1838.
Weir, Robert. "The Harmony We Were Famous For, An Interpretation of Pre-Revolutionary South Carolina Politics." *William and Mary Quarterly,* October 1961, pp. 473–501.

INDEX